HOUSE&
GARDEN

A YEAR IN
THE KITCHEN

Seasonal recipes for everyday pleasure

BLANCHE VAUGHAN

MITCHELL BEAZLEY

CONTENTS

....

INTRODUCTION

These are the recipes I love to cook at home, dishes that I turn to throughout the year because they answer a craving for a particular thing to eat at a particular time. The recipes evolved from ideas for what to cook and what I chose to include in the food pages of *House & Garden* each month; a reflection of our appetites, the food growing then, the weather and how we are living and eating each season.

When I think about what to cook, the first question I ask is: how will we eat this? Is it a simple weekday supper in the kitchen for two? A group of friends for a relaxed lunch in the garden? Or a celebratory family dinner where time and a little more effort is required? Sometimes I'm using up things I have in the refrigerator, or I may start with an idea or a recipe and shop for those particular ingredients; but mostly I am led by what's growing in the garden, what tempts me at the market or the contents of my weekly veg box. When I see baskets of ripe tomatoes and piles of green beans at the farmers' market, I might make a salad with slow-cooked tomato sauce and beans with fresh oregano for a casual kitchen-table lunch. In February, I may be lured by a bright pink bunch of early rhubarb to make a tart when friends come for supper; in July, when the peas and broad beans are growing in the garden, I'll braise them with mint and serve them among other vegetable dishes and salads to eat outside. These ingredients become the inspiration and the framework for what I make. This is a collection of recipes I've written with a scattering of recipes from some of my favourite cooks and chefs who have contributed to the magazine. This isn't a vegetarian cookbook, but the emphasis is on seasonality, with vegetables and fruit as the building blocks for most of the recipes.

This is more than just coming up with ideas, though; it's an opportunity to love the process the whole way through, culminating in the pleasure of eating the food and sharing that experience with others. As American writer Laurie Colwin writes in her book *Home Cooking,* 'I love to eat out, but even more, I love to eat in.'

The story of the meal begins with gathering the ingredients, followed by their careful preparation and finally enjoying the effort you've put in. So when we're sitting down around the wooden table in the garden with the sun on our backs, great bowls of courgette and lemon pasta and leafy green salads laid out in front of us, glasses of wine and easy conversation, any effort it takes to cook is rewarded by a shared experience, a moment together and an appreciation of good things.

Day-to-day cooking, making something to eat to satisfy our appetites, is where one's instincts and creativity can be set free. I spend time thinking about flavours before I even enter the kitchen. Walking back from the farmers' market with my bags of vegetables, I picture them roasting in the oven, undergoing the transformation of cooking. And every time I think of what to eat, it's an opportunity for pleasure.

In answer to the question 'What will we eat tonight?', I'm always looking for inspiration. I might flick through a pile of cookbooks because I have an ingredient in the refrigerator I want to use – some peppers from our farm share (see page 13) that I stew with onions and tomatoes, paprika and oregano. There may be some dish I've seen on Instagram, or I look at old issues of *House & Garden*. I'm never organized enough to make a scrapbook and I don't like tearing the pages out, but I do jot down things I've cooked and really enjoyed in a notebook, then I turn to it to remind myself of what I was eating at that time or place. Often I see something in the shops that takes my fancy and I build a dish around that. On weeknights, I tend to make things that I can have ready in an hour, the time between putting my daughter to bed and guests arriving, and we will eat at the round table in

Cooking may take place in the kitchen, but the pleasure of food enhances our daily life

the kitchen, informal and cosy. Dinner is usually just one course, then maybe a bit of Clarke's nougat or some chocolate-covered oranges with a cup of verbena tea. If I do make dessert, I always do it in advance, a hangover from chef days, usually a tart or galette. Most nights my husband would eat soup in front of the TV if he could, but I like the ritual of supper; a joyful end to the day. If I haven't had time to shop, I always manage to make something from what's in the refrigerator or the cupboards.

Sometimes these incidental dishes have been the best things I've made and they take their place in a repertoire of things I cook again and again. A trip to London to browse a new shop, where a shelf displaying mirin, soy and ponzu sauces leads my mind down a different culinary path. Spinach takes on a new life dressed with a sesame sauce, and cubes of turnip and sweet potato are transformed by the sweet, earthy flavours of miso. I enjoy choosing different bowls and plates from the cupboard to serve these things.

Laying the table, albeit simply, sets the scene for the enjoyment of the food. Thinking about which plate or bowl to eat from or the cutlery to use can elevate the simplest of meals into something worth sitting down for and spending time over. In these days when sitting down and eating together is becoming the exception, not the rule, even just choosing colourful glassware, lighting some candles, using ironed linen napkins or putting a few stems of flowers in a small vase on the table can transform a day-to-day activity, elevating the experience into something more special. I'm always looking out for pretty serving dishes, little vases etc. Luckily it's part of my job: I often feature new discoveries of tableware in my Taste Notes pages.

When I put flowers on the table, I keep them low so that you can see over the top. I'll put small terracotta pots with herbs or ferns, or pots of auriculas in spring, in a cluster in the middle of the table. We spend much of the year eating indoors, so this feels like bringing the outside in. Light is so important too. I love those little alabaster candleholders with tea lights inside; they make a gentle glow and the light shows the delicate veins of the material. Or I buy tall, brightly coloured dining candles and vary the heights, arranged in a line down the middle of the table. It's about the atmosphere of the experience, not just the food.

On a winter's evening, I want to arrange flowers and candles and set each place, tidier and simpler, letting guests help themselves from the sideboard. However we eat, I want to be able to sit down among my friends and family, to take my apron off and partake as though I have been cooked for myself. What I want to cook is what I enjoy eating myself, never to impress. I prefer not to make complicated dishes, especially when cooking for friends. Tried and tested is what I go for. Keep the experimenting for other nights.

Even in a small space, changing the position of the table can completely alter your experience. For larger numbers, I've set up a trestle in the sitting room or moved a small round table to a spot close to the fire when it's really cold. Or I've laid a table in a bedroom for my father when he was ill so that we could all sit and eat together.

From just a small cast of tableware, the scene can be rearranged and things swapped in and out to change the look and style. Napkins are essential and placemats anchor the layout. I like the informality of food in the middle of the table, although sometimes when space is tight I put it on a sideboard, letting the guests see it all laid out before them to help themselves. Rarely do I plate things individually; I'll leave that to restaurants. I like the spectacle of serving too. A whole pumpkin with bubbling soup inside, a pillowy soufflé on the sideboard or a cake on a pretty stand or under a glass dome. Food is elevated by being nicely presented.

Cooking may take place in the kitchen, but the pleasure of food enhances our daily life. My experience from cooking at the River Café and Chez Panisse taught me to find the best ingredients and treat them simply. For me, the joy starts with the sourcing. The seasonal arrival of ingredients reminds me of recipes I've cooked at that time the year before. When the Crown Prince squash appear in our weekly vegetable share, it makes me want to cook Sally Clarke's luxurious soup with Gruyère and cream baked in the hollowed-out gourd (see page 161). From the joy sparked by picking a ripe plum and eating it under the tree, to the last mouthful of a decadent chocolate cake (see page 266), these experiences and the people we share them with are what living and eating are all about: making the best of life.

Spring

In spring, we crave lighter food that makes the break from heavy winter dishes yet is still sustaining and comforting

Spring doesn't happen all at once: the icy fingers of winter stretch into the early months, before there is increasing warmth in the sun, then the birds begin to sing and colour and life gradually returns. The first place I look for spring is in the woods, where the ferns slowly unfurl and wild flowers search for the sun before the soft green new leaves create cover.

Spring is the most extreme of the transitional seasons. The weather can range from snow-covered fields to bright sun and scatterings of celandine and primroses, then later in the season, shady damp woodlands are carpeted in bluebells and wild garlic, and if you're lucky you'll see wild orchids in the fields. Farmers call this time of year the 'Hungry Gap', an empty period between the last of winter's harvest and before the new season's crops start to grow – it's a time to be inventive with what we have.

Much of what we think of as spring vegetables – peas, artichokes and broad beans – are really imports from hotter countries; ours in the UK don't come until much later. However, this scarcity makes me appreciate any new vegetable arrivals even more: the beauty of forced bright pink rhubarb for puddings, papery-skinned early potatoes, the abundance of nettles and the lush leaves of wild garlic to forage and, later in the season, the first sprue asparagus from Norfolk and Herefordshire.

In spring, we crave lighter food that makes the break from heavy winter dishes yet is still sustaining and comforting. It's a time for using up leftovers – a historic tradition in preparation for Lent. Or relying on the convenience of rice and other store-cupboard ingredients, being inventive and some occasional foraging. Eggs are symbolic of new life, not just in chocolate form at Easter – the hens that spend time outdoors will start to lay more with the increased daylight hours.

Beyond the famous Jersey Royals, which are just one variety, other early maturing varieties of potatoes including Rocket, Jazzy and Lady Christl are the first to be harvested, coming from milder parts of the country. Given how ubiquitous the potato is throughout the year, these earlies stand out like the caviar of the potato world. The flavour is nutty and sweet (because they've been freshly dug, they still contain lots of natural sugars), and their pleasing waxy texture holds the shape when cooked. They respond best to the simplest cooking, and their soft skins don't require peeling. Boil them in well-salted water with a sprig of mint and served drenched in melted butter alongside asparagus and a soft-boiled egg; any leftovers make the best potato salads.

Watercress grows wild in freshwater streams and tastes best at this time of year, before the warmer weather causes it to flower and become bitter. (If you are lucky enough to find it growing wild, it's advisable to cook it first, in case of any bacteria.) I like to make a super green soup with watercress and foraged nettles, or I stir it into braised lentils for some structure. It's delicious in a potato salad with chopped cornichons and capers or with beetroot and boiled eggs. Later in the season, if I'm short of watercress, I use nasturtium leaves to bring that spicy, mustard flavour instead.

As the season progresses, tiny crocuses and then drifts of narcissi appear under the trees and in the long grass, or grown in pots to put inside the house. Now there are some flowers to pick for the table – hyacinth-scented bluebells, pretty yellow primroses and boughs of blossom to hang painted Easter eggs from. Then, the cherry, pear and apple trees are covered in a cloud of blossoms and in my tiny greenhouse seeds begin to germinate. It's warm enough to sit outside for lunch or tea, surrounded by the colour of spring.

LEEKS

Ubiquitous and often undervalued, leeks are the gentlest-flavoured members of the onion family. An onion is reliable and stores through winter; a leek is vigorous and fresh, like spring. Although often consigned to stocks and stews, they shine as a vegetable in their own right. Inexpensive and readily available, they can be utilized from top to tail: cook the tightly rolled pearly white base and keep the emerald tail leaves for adding to stock. Boiled, steamed, braised, grilled or roasted, they show off their delicate flavour and protean character in many ways: a key ingredient cooked in salads with new potatoes, or blended into creamy soups, stewed to sweetness and mixed with ham and savoury custard in a tart or mixed with cream and cheese and topped with crunchy breadcrumbs for a gratin. Buy a bunch and sweat them in butter or steam them until tender to keep in the refrigerator and you'll have the beginnings of any number of dishes.

Community Supported Agriculture (CSA), a term coined by US farmers with its roots in biodynamic agriculture ideas formed by Rudolf Steiner, is a sort of precursor to the weekly veg box movement. CSA is simply a partnership between farmers and their consumers, who share the risks and rewards of agriculture. I've been a subscriber to our local CSA for over ten years, receiving a weekly box of their harvest and occasionally volunteering in picking or planting and learning about how they farm. A weekly letter is included with the veg share, and I've learned more about growing and agricultural politics from these than anything else I've ever read. Ed, the farmer, has an ongoing mission to save seeds and cultivate healthier and more resilient crops for the following harvests. The leeks he grows are proof of the success of these endeavours; a humble vegetable taken to another level of taste.

RECIPES

Roast leeks with yogurt, caramelized butter, chilli flakes and dill
Vichyssoise with herbs and cream
Leek and potato vinaigrette with egg mimosa
Leek, potato and Taleggio galette

ROAST LEEKS
WITH YOGURT, CARAMELIZED BUTTER,
CHILLI FLAKES AND DILL

*The combination of sweet caramelized leeks
and soothing yogurt is inspired by the Turkish
leek and yogurt soup I learned to make during
my time cooking at Moro restaurant in London.
Spiked with chilli and dill and finished with nutty
butter, this is a simple yet luxurious dish. You can
serve it as a starter with bread to swirl around the
plate, or as a side dish with white fish. Use baby leeks
or cut large ones into quarters lengthways so that their
leaves fan out to make a tangle of white and green.*

SERVES 4

6 medium leeks
2 tablespoons olive oil
1 garlic clove, peeled
4 tablespoons natural yogurt
1–2 teaspoons Aleppo chilli flakes and/or hot
**   chilli flakes**
small bunch of dill, chopped
25g (1oz) butter
sea salt and freshly ground black pepper

1. Preheat the oven to 200°C (180°C fan), 400°F, Gas
mark 6. Trim the dark green ends of the leeks and any
tassels from the roots. Leaving the root attached, cut
into quarters lengthways. Wash carefully to remove
any grit and shake dry. Lay on a baking tray, pour over
the oil and season well.
2. Roast for 15 minutes, then turn and cook for
another 5–10 minutes, or until completely cooked
and starting to brown and crisp at the ends.
3. Meanwhile, crush the garlic and, in a small bowl,
mix it with the yogurt, chilli flakes and most of the
dill (leave a little for serving). Season to taste and
add 1 tablespoon of water to loosen it slightly.
4. When the leeks are cooked, arrange them on a
plate – they will become a wonderful tangle of leaves.
Spoon over the yogurt dressing. Melt the butter in a
small pan until it bubbles. Continue to cook until it
starts to turn brown and smell nutty, then remove
from the heat and pour over the dressed leeks. Scatter
over the remaining dill and serve.

VICHYSSOISE
WITH HERBS AND CREAM

For over 30 years, Sally Clarke's eponymous restaurant and shop has been a London institution. She is one of the pioneers of well-sourced, seasonal ingredients cooked to the highest standards. Like any good restaurateur or home cook, Sally avoids wastage, in this recipe she uses the entire leek – the base for the soup and ends for the stock. An elegant soup like this never goes out of fashion – chilled or warm in shallow soup dishes scattered with chives.

SERVES 6

4 medium–large leeks
50g (1¾oz) butter
4 tablespoons olive oil
4 bay leaves
1 sprig of rosemary
2 medium–large potatoes, peeled and roughly
    chopped
sea salt and freshly ground black pepper

For the vegetable stock
(or use 850ml/1½ pints light chicken stock or water)
1 small onion, finely chopped
½ fennel bulb, finely chopped
2 celery sticks, finely chopped
a few bay leaves
1 sprig of rosemary
5–6 black peppercorns

To serve
200ml (7fl oz) double cream
2 tablespoons finely chopped chives

1. Wash the leeks well, then trim the very dark tips and root away. Remove the outside leaf, then cut the leeks in half lengthways. Wash again thoroughly under a gently running tap to remove all traces of grit. Drain well, then chop roughly, placing a handful of the darkest pieces in a saucepan and setting the rest aside.
2. Add the stock vegetables, herbs and peppercorns to the pan. Cover with 1 litre (1¾ pints) cold water, bring to the boil, then simmer for 30 minutes until flavourful. Strain and discard the debris.
3. Place the butter and oil in a large, heavy-based pan over a medium heat, add the bay leaves and rosemary and stir until fragrant (1–2 minutes). Add the chopped potatoes and the reserved chopped leeks and continue to stir over the heat until the oils have been absorbed.
4. Pour over 850ml (1½ pints) of the vegetable stock (or chicken stock or water) to barely cover, season with salt and bring to the boil. Immediately turn the heat down, cover and simmer for 20–30 minutes until the vegetables are soft. Remove from the heat and allow to cool a little. Remove the herbs.
5. Transfer the soup, little by little, into a blender or food processor and purée until smooth. Pour through a sieve into a clean saucepan, pressing the debris through as much as possible.
6. Taste for seasoning and reheat gently. Adding the cream and chives at the last minute, pour into warm bowls. Alternatively, serve chilled – after sieving, cool, then refrigerate for up to 5 days, covered. Add the cream and chives just before serving.

LEEK AND POTATO VINAIGRETTE

WITH EGG MIMOSA

This substantial salad celebrates the finest ingredients of spring: young leeks, waxy new potatoes and fresh eggs. Ex-food editor and cookbook author Lucas Hollweg wrote this recipe for a spring issue of the magazine, and like the title of one of his books Good Things to Eat, *this is exactly that. Lucas knows how to make the best of what is around, reminding us that: 'In France, leeks used to be known as "poor man's asparagus". This variation on a classic French first course shows just how luxurious they can be.' It makes a fine first course served from a large platter in the middle of the table for everyone to help themselves.*

....

SERVES 6

For the vinaigrette
3 tablespoons Dijon mustard
1½ tablespoons red wine vinegar
150ml (5fl oz) sunflower oil
50ml (2fl oz) extra virgin olive oil, plus extra
    for drizzling
1½ tablespoons chopped tarragon
1 teaspoon coriander seeds, coarsely ground in
    a pestle and mortar
2 tablespoons chopped chives
sea salt and freshly ground black pepper

For the leeks
6 medium or 12 small leeks
2 bay leaves
10 small waxy salad potatoes
2 eggs, at room temperature

1. Start with the vinaigrette. Put the mustard in a bowl and whisk in the vinegar, some black pepper and ¼ teaspoon of sea salt. Whisk in the oils, drop by drop, to make a thick dressing. Gradually whisk in 1½ tablespoons of cold water, then stir in the tarragon, ground coriander seeds and three-quarters of the chives. Set aside.

2. Wash the leeks and trim off all but 1cm (½in) of the green. Cut in half across the middle. Drop into a large pan of salted boiling water with the bay leaves and simmer for 12 minutes, or until easily pierced with a knife. Remove and slit lengthways. Transfer to a plate and splash 4–5 tablespoons of the dressing over the top.

3. Drop the potatoes into the same pan and simmer for 20 minutes, or until soft. Add the eggs for the final 9 minutes. Scoop the eggs from the pan and plunge into a bowl of cold water. Drain the potatoes and leave to cool. Place in a bowl with 4 tablespoons of the dressing and gently toss.

4. Peel the eggs, separate the yolks and grate them into a small bowl, then chop the whites and add to the bowl.

5. When the leeks and potatoes are at room temperature, arrange on a serving plate. Blob more dressing on and trickle a little extra virgin olive oil around the outside. Scatter with the egg and remaining chives before serving.

LEEK, POTATO AND TALEGGIO GALETTE

I always like to keep some pastry in the freezer, homemade or not. This will inevitably come to your aid when trying to turn odds and ends into a respectable meal. There's an abundance of leeks and potatoes at this time of year and I often cook the leeks as soon as I buy them, whether I have a plan for them or not, then when it comes to cooking from scratch, it gives me a real head start. Leeks become soft and sweet when cooked for a long time in plenty of oil and butter, and add a great depth of flavour to everything from tarts and pies to stews and soups. With the pre-cooked leeks and pastry to hand, this is quick to assemble and you can substitute the Taleggio for another melty cheese. Embrace adaptability and ease will be on your side. I serve this tart on a wooden chopping board so that everyone can cut their own slices, perfect help-yourself food for an informal lunch. All you need is a big bowl of salad to go with it.

....

SERVES 6

For the pastry
140g (5oz) plain flour, plus extra for dusting
140g (5oz) wholemeal flour
170g (6oz) very cold unsalted butter, cut into cubes
large pinch of flaked sea salt
1 egg, beaten for egg wash
4–5 tablespoons iced water

For the filling
5 medium leeks (about 800g/1lb 12oz)
25g (1oz) butter
2 tablespoons olive oil, plus extra for brushing
a few sprigs of thyme, leaves picked
2 tablespoons crème fraîche
400g (14oz) potatoes, cut into 3mm (⅛in) slices
270g (9¾oz) Taleggio cheese, rind removed
sea salt and freshly ground black pepper

To serve
green salad

1. To make the pastry, put the flours and butter in a food processor with the salt and blitz briefly until the butter pieces are about the same size as petits pois. Tip into a bowl and add the iced water, 2 tablespoons at a time, mixing by hand as you go in order to bring the mixture together. Roll the dough into a ball and squash to a thick disc, then wrap with clingfilm and chill in the refrigerator for at least 20 minutes.
2. For the filling, wash the leeks well, then trim the very dark tips and root away. Remove the outside leaf, then cut the leeks in half lengthways. Wash again thoroughly under a gently running tap to remove all traces of grit. Drain well, then chop roughly. Melt the butter and the 2 tablespoons of oil in a large saucepan over a medium heat. Add the leeks and thyme leaves, and season well with salt and pepper. Cook, stirring, for at least 20 minutes until very soft and sweet. Remove from the heat and set aside.
3. Preheat the oven to 180°C (160°C fan), 350°F, Gas mark 4. On a floured surface, roll the pastry into a large circle or oval shape, then lift on to a sheet of baking parchment and lay on a baking sheet.
4. Mix the leeks with the crème fraîche and season well with salt and pepper. Brush the pastry with a little oil and cover with a layer of potato slices, leaving a 3cm (1¼in) border around the edge. Sprinkle with salt and pepper. Cover with a layer of leeks and slices of Taleggio. Repeat with the remaining potato, leeks and cheese. Fold back the edges of the pastry to make a border around the filling. Paint the pastry with the egg wash.
5. Bake for 40 minutes, or until the pastry is golden brown and the filling is soft and melting. Serve with a green salad.

FOOD TO FORAGE

Richard Mabey's *Food for Free* is an aptly titled book to guide any aspiring forager. Now you can find shops selling nettles and wild garlic and restaurants with these ingredients on their menus, but if you have access to pick them yourself, they really are nature's free gifts.

It's exciting to see the ground carpeted with the glossy green leaves of wild garlic, or to discover a stream where a forest of watercress grows on its banks. Picking food in the wild gives you the greatest connection to the natural rhythms of nature, and is domestic economy at its best! People say wild garlic is taking over from bluebells, so that's even more reason to harvest as much as you can find. Greengrocers are now making the most of this. Buy or pick too much and make purées, pestos and herb oils to flavour dressings and green mayonnaise. It's good with chicken and fish and potatoes; or scatter the pretty white star-shaped flowers in salads.

Nettles are nature's superfood; full of nitrogen, they are a natural fertilizer and work wonders on the compost heap. They are also one of the easiest ingredients to forage. Don your rubber gloves and pick basketfuls while they are young and tender in spring. Pinch just the top leaves and avoid cooking the stalks, which are fibrous and tough. Italians often use nettles in cooking: wilted and stirred into plain pasta with lots of butter and Parmesan or boiled, puréed and added to risotto. I also like to use them as I would other greens – try them in a frittata with spring onions and goats' cheese or added to a green soup.

RECIPES

Spaghetti with nettles
Nettle risotto with shrimps
Chicken with wild garlic
Pea and wild garlic risotto with Parmesan

SPAGHETTI
WITH NETTLES

Wandering into the fields for some easy foraging is a good excuse for a walk, and everyone can get involved. Nettles are full of vitamins and minerals. They also grow in abundance in the wild. I love their rich, earthy-green, ferrous flavour, which you can really taste in this dish. This is a good way to introduce nettles into your cooking, as you can supplement them with parsley, lovage or celery leaves if you don't want the full nettle flavour. Everyone loves a plate of pasta and this is a thrifty dish to make.

....

SERVES 6

300g (10½oz) nettles
50g (1¾oz) butter
1 garlic clove, finely chopped
1 red chilli, finely chopped
4 tablespoons crème fraîche
zest and juice of ½ lemon
**40g (1½oz) Parmesan cheese, grated, plus extra
    to serve**
**600g (1lb 5oz) dried spaghetti (or use fresh if you
    can – you will need about 780g/1lb 11oz)**
sea salt and freshly ground black pepper

1. Wearing rubber gloves, remove any tough stalks from the nettles and wash the leaves well.

2. Bring a large pot of water to the boil, add 1 teaspoon of salt and cook the nettles for 3 minutes. Remove the nettles from the water with a slotted spoon – keep the water, as you will use it to cook the pasta. Drain the nettles well, gently squeezing out any excess water, and then chop roughly.

3. Melt 25g (1oz) of the butter in a large saucepan and fry the garlic and chilli until the garlic just begins to colour. Add the nettles with the crème fraîche, lemon zest and juice and the Parmesan. Season well with salt and pepper. If the nettles look a little dry, add a splash of the cooking water.

4. Cook the pasta in the boiling nettle water until just al dente, drain (reserving a cup of the water) and add to the pan of nettles. Return to the heat, add the remaining butter and a splash of cooking water and season to taste. Cook for 1 minute, mixing well, until the sauce is absorbed and the pasta looks luscious and juicy. Serve with a sprinkle of Parmesan.

NETTLE RISOTTO
WITH SHRIMPS

Rowley Leigh is one of the great British chefs and a regular contributor to House & Garden. *With economy in mind, he suggests, 'What you save with the nettles can be spent on the shrimps and even bottarga if you are feeling flush.' He doesn't use stock in the recipe, which makes one less ingredient and keeps 'the risotto lighter and allows the flavour of the nettles and shrimp to shine'.*

....

SERVES 6

big bunch of young nettles
2 onions, finely chopped
100g (3½oz) unsalted butter
400g (14oz) carnaroli, vialone nano or arborio rice
½ teaspoon chilli flakes
zest of ½ orange
375ml (13fl oz) prosecco
140g (5oz) cooked peeled brown shrimps
juice of 1 lemon
sea salt and freshly ground black pepper
30g (1oz) bottarga (if available), to serve

1. Wearing good gloves and long sleeves, pick a basketful of young nettles. Strip the leaves from the stalks, wash in cold water and then drop them into a large saucepan of salted boiling water. Drain almost immediately and refresh in cold water. Squeeze them dry, then chop finely.

2. Soften the onions in a heavy-based casserole with 50g (1¾oz) of the butter for 10 minutes and then pour in the rice, turning it until well coated in butter. Add the nettles and season generously with sea salt, toss in the chilli flakes and orange zest, then pour in the prosecco. Stir gently for a few minutes until the wine has been absorbed.

3. With a kettle standing by, add around 200ml (7fl oz) boiling water, equivalent to half the volume of the rice. Stir the risotto gently and occasionally (continuous stirring breaks up the rice and increases the liquid needed to absorb the starch thus released) until the water has been absorbed, and then repeat the process.

4. Continue cooking for a further 20–25 minutes until the rice is cooked through but still slightly firm. The risotto should still be slightly liquid. Check the seasoning, then add the shrimps, stir in the remaining butter and sharpen with the lemon juice. Serve immediately, grating the bottarga over each plate if you are using it.

CHICKEN
WITH WILD GARLIC

At this time of year, the woods become pungent with the scent of wild garlic. Picking the lush green leaves was one of my first foraging adventures as a child. It's funny to smell what you associate with the kitchen when you're walking in the woods. Think of wild garlic as a softer version of garlic, or a mixture of garlic and spring onion flavours, and use as an alternative in recipes. I love to use their lush green leaves to make this spiced marinade for chicken.

SERVES 4

4 cardamom pods
pinch of saffron strands
1 teaspoon cumin seeds
1 teaspoon ground turmeric
2 large handfuls of wild garlic leaves, washed
100g (3½oz) natural yogurt
4 chicken breasts, skin on
olive oil
sea salt and freshly ground black pepper

1. Lightly crush the cardamom pods to release the little black seeds inside and discard the green husky outer layer. In a dry, hot pan, lightly toast the saffron and cumin seeds, then crush in a pestle and mortar with the cardamom seeds. Add the ground turmeric and mix well.

2. In a food processor, finely chop the wild garlic leaves. Add the spices and yogurt, and blend well. Season with salt and pepper. Place the chicken breasts in one layer in a roasting tin, then smear most of the marinade all over the chicken, saving a little to serve. Cover and leave in the refrigerator to marinate for at least 1 hour.

3. Preheat the oven to 200°C (180°C fan), 400°F, Gas mark 6. Pour a little olive oil over the skin and roast the chicken, skin-side up, for 10–15 minutes until it is just cooked through. Serve sliced with rice or potatoes and the remaining spiced wild garlic yogurt.

PEA AND WILD GARLIC RISOTTO
WITH PARMESAN

Sally Clarke suggests using this recipe 'as a base for many a risotto, using a variety of ingredients – depending on the season'. To get the most from the flavour of the peas, save the pods to add to the vegetable stock, using celery, fennel and leek trimmings too.

SERVES 6

800ml (1⅓ pints) vegetable, light chicken or
    fish stock
350g (12oz) podded peas
50ml (2fl oz) olive oil
100g (3½oz) butter
2 teaspoons chopped thyme, plus extra sprigs to serve
3 small shallots, finely chopped
350g (12oz) arborio or carnaroli rice
1 glass dry white wine or prosecco
large handful of wild garlic leaves, washed, stalks
    removed and each leaf cut into 2 or 3 pieces
90g (3¼oz) Parmesan cheese, freshly grated
sea salt and freshly ground black pepper

1. Bring the stock to a simmer and set aside. Blanch the peas for 1–2 minutes, drain and set aside.

2. Heat the olive oil and 25g (1oz) of the butter in a large, heavy-based pan. Add the thyme and shallots, and cook over a medium heat, without colouring, for a few minutes. Add the rice and stir. Season well with salt and pepper and cook gently for a few minutes, stirring. Add the wine, stirring continually.

3. Start to add the warm stock, little by little, gently shaking the pan to prevent the risotto sticking. As soon as it starts to look dry, a top-up of stock is required.

4. Continue cooking for a further 20–25 minutes until the rice is cooked through but still slightly firm. When it is to your liking, add the peas, wild garlic and remaining stock, if required. As the leaves wilt, remove from the heat, stir in the remaining butter vigorously, then fold in half the Parmesan.

5. Pour into warmed bowls and scatter over the remaining Parmesan and a few extra sprigs of thyme.

FISH

Every Friday, Ross and his fish van stop at our door with a hand-picked selection of fish from the day boats that land at Brixham, a natural harbour on the Devonshire coast. He tells me what's in season, what's best that day and he even knows which boat each fish has come from. Increasingly companies are connecting customers directly with day boats, smaller boats with lower quotas, which fish sustainably and return their catch to the shore while it is fresh. Alternatively, buy scrupulously monitored farmed fish.

In terms of speed and simple preparation, cooking fish is easier and quicker than cooking most vegetables. Many varieties can be interchanged with others to make the same recipe work just as well. Seeing what looks good on the fish counter can liberate you from the disappointment of them not having what you planned to buy. And remember that fishmongers will be happy to tell you about their catch. My fishmonger will scale and gut whole fish or cut large fish into fillets to make portion sizes, and he'll then throw the bones in a bag for me to make stock at home.

Fish prices vary enormously, so substitute turbot for brill or hake. Cook lots of mackerel or sardines 'whole, hot and fast, like a hot dog', as the brilliant food writer Tamar Adler prescribes. When you feel like splashing out on something like red mullet, cook it on a special occasion for two. Leftover cooked fish need not be wasted – mix with mashed potato and herbs and you have a meal of fishcakes.

Fish bones mean an extra, free ingredient to use. Make stock; it's easy. Throw vegetable trimmings, leeks, onions, celery, carrot, fennel tops, celeriac peelings, some herbs, garlic and peppercorns, fennel and coriander seeds, and a bay leaf if you have one, into a pot with the bones of any non-oily fish, cover with water and cook until it tastes delicious, then strain. If you're going to spend money on crab or lobster, use the shells and do the same.

And for the days you can't make it to the fishmonger, keep a few cans of sardines or mackerel, or some smoked mackerel or kippers. Eat the mackerel on toast with chopped parsley and lemon juice, or with the kohlrabi salad opposite, or use canned sardines instead of crab in the spaghetti recipe on page 35.

RECIPES

Mackerel with gremolata and kohlrabi salad
Mediterranean fish stew with saffron mayonnaise
Butterflied sardines stuffed with preserved lemon and rosemary
Plaice with fried capers and brown butter
Turbot roasted over celeriac, fennel and leeks
Crab spaghetti

MACKEREL

WITH GREMOLATA AND KOHLRABI SALAD

When fresh, mackerel is one of the best fish and it makes an easy, healthy meal; iridescent rainbow skin, bright eyes and firm to the touch. If you can't face cooking fresh mackerel, you could serve this as a simple lunch dish with plump canned mackerel fillets or skinned smoked mackerel fillets (you might want to add a dollop of horseradish if you're serving smoked). The pale green or purple UFO-like orbs of kohlrabi have the finesse of a fresh radish with the ballast of a turnip. At London's St John restaurant they make a salad of wafer-thin slices tossed with lemon, oil and feathery chervil leaves. This is the perfect foil for oily fish.

....

SERVES 6

For the salad
1kg (2lb 4oz) or 2 large kohlrabi
200g (7oz/2 large handfuls) radishes
20g (¾oz) curly parsley
4 sprigs of tarragon, leaves picked
1 garlic clove, crushed
2 tablespoons lemon juice
4 tablespoons extra virgin olive oil

For the mackerel and gremolata
1 teaspoon olive oil
6 mackerel, butterflied and gutted (see page 30)
2 tablespoons chopped curly parsley
zest of 1 lemon
1 garlic clove, chopped
sea salt and freshly ground black pepper

To serve
lemon wedges

1. Peel and halve the kohlrabi, then use a mandoline or the large blade on a grater to slice it into wafer-thin sheets. Finely slice the radishes and mix with the kohlrabi in a salad bowl.

2. Roughly chop the parsley and tarragon leaves and add to the bowl. Make a dressing by mixing the crushed garlic with the lemon juice and oil, and some salt and pepper to taste. Pour over the salad and toss well.

3. Preheat the oven to 200°C (180°C fan), 400°F, Gas mark 6. Choose 1 or 2 baking trays large enough to fit the mackerel in a single layer and brush the surface of the tray lightly with the oil. Lay the fish flat, skin-side down, and season with salt and pepper.

4. To make the gremolata, mix the parsley, lemon zest and garlic together on a board and finely chop them.

5. Bake the fish for 8–10 minutes until the flesh is just cooked. Lift on to a serving dish and sprinkle with the gremolata. Serve immediately with the salad and lemon wedges.

MEDITERRANEAN FISH STEW
WITH SAFFRON MAYONNAISE

When it comes to cooking fish stew at home, I usually adapt the recipe to make it suit the ingredients that I can find. The main thing is to achieve a balance of firm, sweet-fleshed fish and shellfish, which imparts maximum flavour to the broth. I serve it in a wide, shallow bowl, with a platter of garlic bread to pass around and bowls of saffron mayonnaise. A dollop stirred in at the end gives the dish another layer of richness and texture. Embrace the messiness of eating – you'll want big napkins and bowls for empty shells.

....

SERVES 6

For the saffron mayonnaise
2 egg yolks
290ml (9¾fl oz) olive oil
pinch of saffron strands, crushed and soaked in
**   1 tablespoon boiling water for 5 minutes**
lemon juice, to taste

For the tomato base
600g (1lb 5oz) fresh tomatoes
2 tablespoons olive oil
2 garlic cloves, finely sliced
pinch of hot chilli flakes
sea salt and freshly ground black pepper

For the shellfish
1 tablespoon olive oil
600g (1lb 5oz) mussels, cleaned (see page 193)
800g (1lb 12oz) clams, rinsed
200ml (7fl oz) light, fruity white wine

For the rest of the stew
12 scallops, removed from the shells and cleaned
1 tablespoon olive oil
600g (1lb 5oz) firm white fish fillets, such as
**   mullet, bream or gurnard, skin on, cut into**
**   finger-sized pieces**
20g (¾oz) flat-leaf parsley, finely chopped

To serve
1 garlic clove, halved
6 large slices of white sourdough, toasted
olive oil, for drizzling

1. For the mayonnaise, put the egg yolks in a bowl and whisk while adding the oil in a thin stream until the mixture thickens and emulsifies. Add the saffron and its soaking water, continue to whisk and add salt and lemon juice, 1 teaspoon at a time, tasting for a balance of richness, acidity and saltiness. Cover and refrigerate until needed.

2. Put the tomatoes in a bowl and cover with boiling water. Leave for 30 seconds, then refresh under cold water and peel. Halve, scoop out the seeds and cut out any white core, then roughly chop the flesh.

3. Heat the oil in a deep frying pan and cook the garlic briefly so that it just starts to colour around the edges. Add the tomatoes and a good pinch of salt and cook for about 10 minutes, mashing with a wooden spoon until you have a relatively smooth sauce. Add some black pepper, the chilli flakes and more salt if necessary.

4. For the shellfish, choose a large pan with a lid and put it over a high heat. Add the oil, mussels, clams and wine, and cover. Cook for a minute or so, giving the pan a gentle shake, until the shells just open. Remove from the heat, transfer the shellfish to a bowl and set aside, covered, but leaving the liquid in the pan.

5. Return the pan to the heat and boil the liquid to reduce it slightly and cook off the alcohol. Add the tomato base and 1.2 litres (2 pints) water, and heat to make a delicately flavoured broth.

6. Pat the scallops dry and season with salt on both sides. Heat a frying pan until very hot and add the oil. Fry the scallops until they are nicely browned but have not become completely firm; a couple of minutes on each side. Remove from the pan and set aside.

7. Bring the broth to the boil, then add the white fish, parsley and some salt and pepper, turning down the heat to allow the fish to cook gently – this will take a minute or so. Add the scallops and shellfish to the broth.

8. Rub the garlic on the toasted bread and drizzle with oil. Serve with the fish stew and saffron mayonnaise.

BUTTERFLIED SARDINES

*STUFFED WITH PRESERVED LEMON
AND ROSEMARY*

This recipe came from a friend who cooked it for me at their home by the sea in Morocco where we sat under the shade of a vine-covered arbour. Plates of silvery skinned sardines marked with charred stripes were served tongue-scorchingly hot from the barbecue with bowls of carrot salad, peppery rocket leaves from the garden and spiced potatoes. Sardines are one of the most prolific fish of the ocean. I always encourage buying fish from a fishmonger where possible and this is especially relevant with sardines, which need to be spanking fresh. If you don't want to butterfly the fish, either keep them whole and stuff the cavity, or ask your fishmonger to butterfly them for you – watch how they do it and you can have a go yourself next time.

....

SERVES 6

24 sardines, scaled

For the stuffing
1 garlic clove, finely chopped
4 tablespoons finely chopped preserved lemon skin
3 sprigs of rosemary, finely chopped
sea salt and freshly ground black pepper

1. Use a sharp knife to cut the heads off the sardines, just below the gills. To butterfly the fish, make a deep incision running the length of the belly from the head end all the way down to the tail. Remove any guts and open out the fish like a book, then turn it over skin-side up. Holding the tail with one hand, slide your other hand along the length of the fish to flatten it on the board. Flip it over and, starting at the head end, gently peel the backbone away from the flesh until you reach the tail. Snip it off with scissors and discard. Brush off any stray bones or pick them out with tweezers. Repeat with the rest of the sardines.
2. Mix together all the ingredients for the stuffing and season well with salt and pepper. Lay a sardine, skin-side down, opened out flat on a board and spread it with 2 teaspoons of the stuffing. Then place a second sardine on top and press down to create a sandwich. Repeat with the rest. Up to this point, everything can be done several hours in advance and the fish kept in the refrigerator until needed.
3. Either preheat the grill to its highest setting, heat a griddle pan or, ideally, light a barbecue. Grill the sardine sandwiches for 2–3 minutes on each side. The skin will become charred and the cooked flesh should flake easily when prodded with a fork.

PLAICE
WITH FRIED CAPERS AND BROWN BUTTER

*Even (or especially) when there's only two of us,
making a bit of effort goes a long way. A few additional
props transform the kitchen table. A couple of stems
of flowers borrowed from another bunch in the house
and some lit candles make the food feel more special
and take the rush out of eating. Simple, classic and
incredibly quick to make, this works well with any
type of white fish; plaice are the flat fish with rust-
coloured top skin, but at other times of year I use whole
lemon sole, or you could use fillets of John Dory, or even
gurnard or skate. If you're using lemon sole, which is
very delicate, you could omit the capers and add wine
instead of lemon juice. And because the fish is cooked
in the oven, not a frying pan, you needn't worry about
flipping it or making the kitchen smell. Serve with
samphire or spinach and potatoes, or chips.*

SERVES 2

1 tablespoon olive oil
4 plaice fillets (ask for skin-on double fillets for ease
   of cooking)
sea salt and freshly ground black pepper

For the sauce
40g (1½oz) unsalted butter
2 tablespoons capers, dried on kitchen paper
juice of ½ lemon
20g (¾oz) flat-leaf or curly parsley, finely chopped

1. Preheat the oven to 190°C (170°C fan), 375°F, Gas
mark 5. Oil the plaice fillets on both sides and place on
a baking tray, skin-side down. Season well. Bake for
10–12 minutes. To test if the fish is cooked through,
insert a skewer through the thickest part of the flesh –
it should meet no resistance.
2. While the fish is cooking, heat a frying pan over a
medium heat and add the butter. When it has melted,
add the capers and fry until the butter starts to foam
and smells nutty, and the capers brown slightly. Stir in
the lemon juice and parsley, then remove from the heat.
Serve the fish with the butter spooned over the top.

TURBOT ROASTED OVER CELERIAC, FENNEL AND LEEKS

My mother always serves fish on Friday and I often find myself maintaining this tradition, not least as a prompt for something to cook. Either presented on the roasting tray or carefully transferred to a great big fish plate, serving a whole fish like this gives the meal a sense of ceremony and a chance to admire a huge, beautiful creature. This is a blueprint recipe for any whole fish roasted over vegetables; throughout the seasons you can vary the fish and the bed of vegetables it cooks on. Celeriac, a vegetable stalwart at this time of year, goes beautifully with the firm, meaty flesh of turbot. You could also use brill or hake if you're cooking for fewer people, or if you don't want to deal with bones, just cook the base and add fillets of fish for a shorter time in the oven. If I'm feeling energetic, I might make a beurre blanc to serve with it, otherwise it's just a big bowl of rainbow chard and extra virgin olive oil to pour over the fish at the table.

SERVES 6

30g (1oz) unsalted butter
100ml (3½fl oz) olive oil
2 leeks, trimmed, washed and finely sliced
2 fennel bulbs, halved and sliced
1 small celeriac, peeled, quartered and sliced
large bunch of thyme
1.5kg (3lb 5oz) turbot, gutted
3 slices of lemon
sea salt and freshly ground black pepper

1. Preheat the oven to 200°C (180°C fan), 400°F, Gas mark 6. Heat a large, heavy-based casserole and melt one-third of the butter with one-third of the oil, then add the leeks and a large pinch of salt. Fry over a medium–high heat until they start to colour, then add a splash of water and continue to cook for 10 minutes or so until they soften but retain a bit of bite. Remove to a large bowl and set aside.

2. Cook the fennel in the same way, and then the celeriac, making sure you scrape up all the caramelized sediment from the casserole at the end to add to the bowl. When all the vegetables are cooked, return the mixture to the casserole along with the sprigs of thyme, and heat, gently folding them together so that they are well mixed, then season with salt and pepper.

3. Choose a roasting tray large enough to fit the whole fish with the braised vegetables underneath. Spread the vegetables in a layer, then lay the fish on top, tucking the lemon slices into the cavity around the head. I don't bother to season the skin of the fish, as I end up removing it to serve anyway and instead offer flaked salt at the table.

4. Roast the fish and vegetables for 25–30 minutes. The length of time will depend on the thickness of the fish, but a good way to check is to insert a skewer just below the head and through the fish. If the flesh is cooked, it will meet no resistance.

5. Remove the fish to a serving plate and put the vegetables in a separate dish. I like to serve the whole fish and fillet it at the table, or allow everyone to serve themselves. A bowl of watercress dressed with lemon and oil or some boiled potatoes are all you will need as accompaniment.

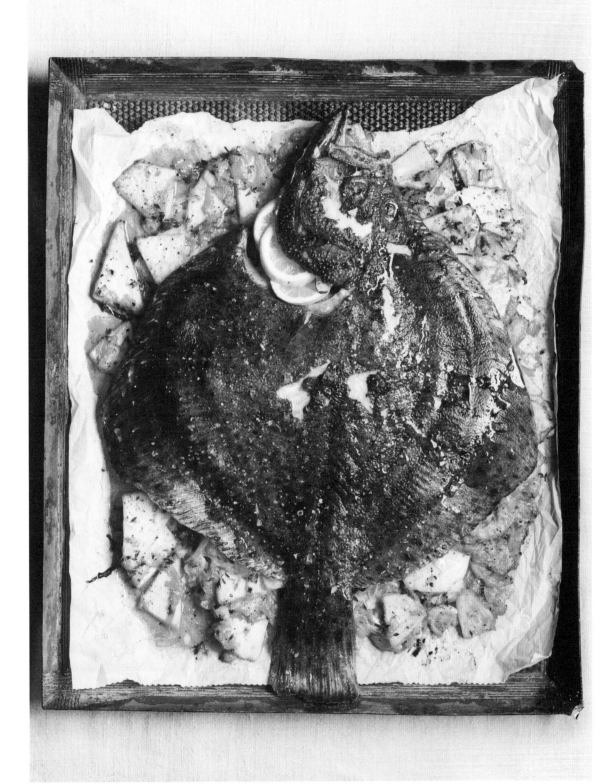

CRAB SPAGHETTI

If I ever see hand-picked white crab meat for sale,
I buy it. It's the gift of an easy meal, and although not
something I cook regularly, it's a treat when I do. To
really taste the sweet, fresh flavour of the meat, serve as
in this recipe. Or if you feel like some embellishment,
you could throw in some thinly sliced fennel to cook
for the last minute with the pasta, or do the same with
a handful of samphire or agretti (monk's beard). We
have a very resilient wild fennel plant that grows
from a crack in the garden and produces beautiful
bright yellow pollen – I might toss some of that in too,
or 1 teaspoon of crushed fennel seeds instead. If you're
brave and like fiddly tasks, you could buy whole
cooked crabs and pick the meat out yourself, then make
a superb stock from the shells to use in any kind of
fish stew, soup or risotto. One of the simplest and most
luxurious risottos I make is with lobster or crab stock
and fresh tomatoes. It's worth searching out unwaxed
Italian lemons, as they have the best-tasting zest.

....

SERVES 4

400g (14oz) dried spaghetti
400g (14oz) crab meat
½ garlic clove, crushed
**4 tablespoons extra virgin olive oil, plus extra
   to serve**
½ teaspoon chilli flakes
**20g (¾oz) flat-leaf parsley, chopped (or fennel
   herb if available)**
zest and juice of 1 lemon
sea salt and freshly ground black pepper

1. Cook the spaghetti according to the packet
instructions in plenty of well-salted boiling water.
2. Mix the crab with all the other ingredients and
season well with salt and pepper. The crab mixture
should be highly flavoured before it is mixed with
the spaghetti.
3. Drain the cooked pasta and mix with the crab
mixture and more seasoning to taste. Dress with
olive oil to serve.

RICE

Rice is comforting, filling, cheap, versatile and digestible. There's no need to be nervous of cooking rice; just do what it says on the packet and you won't go wrong. It provides the perfect store-cupboard ingredient: an indispensable base to which to add flavours and colourful things. It's what one wants to eat when you fancy something lighter than mashed potatoes, yet it's still comforting and starchy. It's also a good way to make smaller amounts of other ingredients into a bigger meal – using them to make a pilaf, in a rice salad or as toppings for a rice bowl.

It's light on the purse and something to fall back on when either there's not much to cook with or you haven't much time; a great way to use up leftovers, turning a plate of cooked vegetables, some pieces of cooked chicken or disparate salad ingredients into a meal. Leftover rice is the beginning of the next meal and can be used in all of these recipes.

There are thousands of different types of rice, and increasingly more varieties available to buy, although I tend to keep just two or three in my cupboard: short-grain (risotto and sushi), brown long-grain and white basmati. These hard grains can be transformed into rich and creamy, light and fluffy, sweet or savoury things to eat.

RECIPES

Jewelled pilaf
Brown rice and salmon bowl
Wild rice salad
Lu rou fan (Taiwanese pork rice)
Egg fried rice

JEWELLED PILAF

I eat this on its own (I like it with a dollop of yogurt)
or serve it as a side dish with grilled lamb chops or
chicken, decanted on to a colourful serving plate.
The other ingredients give the rice a beautiful colour
and texture, it's like finding jewels in each mouthful.
Layering the rice means the flavours are well
distributed, and the butter helps create a gorgeous
caramelized crust on the bottom of the pan.

....

SERVES 6

300g (10½oz) white basmati rice
50g (1¾oz) butter
1 red onion, diced
6 allspice berries, crushed (about 1 teaspoon ground)
50g (1¾oz) dried barberries or a mixture of dried
    cranberries and sour cherries
80g (3oz) pistachios, roughly chopped
20g (¾oz) dill, finely chopped
20g (¾oz) flat-leaf parsley, finely chopped, plus extra
    to garnish
500g (1lb 2oz) podded broad beans
large pinch of saffron strands, soaked in
    4 tablespoons boiling water for 5 minutes
sea salt and freshly ground black pepper
mint leaves, to garnish

1. Rinse the rice well and put in a saucepan with
2 teaspoons of salt. Add enough water to cover the rice
by 1cm (½in). Put on a lid, bring to the boil and cook for
8 minutes. Turn off the heat and leave the lid on while
you prepare the other ingredients.

2. Choose a heavy-based, lidded saucepan or
casserole, large enough to fit the rice and the other
ingredients. Melt half the butter and gently fry the
onion with a large pinch of salt for 5–10 minutes until it
is soft and sweet and just beginning to colour. Remove
to a bowl and set aside. There is no need to wash the
pan, as you will be using it again in a minute.

3. When the rice is cooked, lay out the rest of the
prepared ingredients. You are going to make layers of
these with the rice and the other mixed ingredients.

4. Mix together the allspice, barberries (or cranberries
and sour cherries), pistachios and herbs with some
pepper in a bowl.

5. Melt the remaining butter in the saucepan until
it is foaming, then turn off the heat. Add a shallow
layer of rice, one-quarter of the cooked onions, the
spice and nut mixture, broad beans, 1 tablespoon
of saffron water and a good pinch of salt. Repeat
this until you have used all the ingredients, ending
with a layer of rice.

6. Cover with a piece of baking parchment and the
lid, and cook over a medium heat for 20 minutes.
Then turn off the heat and leave to steam for a further
10 minutes before serving, garnished with flat-leaf
parsley and mint leaves.

BROWN RICE AND SALMON BOWL

Brown rice has shed its image associated with seventies health-food cafés and we have come to appreciate its texture and nutritional benefits. As a rule of thumb, less refined rice (darker-coloured, firmer-textured grains) equals more fibre, protein and nutrients. This is good for informal, comforting eating. I have some old Leach stoneware bowls that I pile the warm rice into and present the rest of the ingredients on various plates for guests to help themselves, mixing everything into the rice to eat with chopsticks or a fork, as they choose. Other toppings I love are leftover chicken and crispy kale or just roasted vegetables and lots of coriander. Add hot sauces at the end for some enlivening fire.

....

SERVES 6

300g (10½oz) brown short-grain rice
400g (14oz) hot-smoked salmon, skin removed
3 avocados, skin and stones removed
200g (7oz) watercress
6 spring onions, chopped
sea salt

For the dressing
4 tablespoons dark soy sauce
2 tablespoons rice vinegar
1 teaspoon grated fresh root ginger
1 garlic clove, crushed
4 tablespoons sesame oil

To serve
4 tablespoons sesame seeds
additional spicy condiments, such as black bean
    rayu or sriracha sauce (optional)

1. Rinse the rice and put it in a saucepan with 1.5 litres (2⅔ pints) water and 2 teaspoons of salt. Cover the pan with a lid and bring to the boil. Reduce the heat and simmer for a further 35 minutes. Then test the rice to make sure it is tender and pour off any excess water. Replace the lid to keep it warm while you prepare the toppings and dressing.

2. On a large serving plate, arrange the hot-smoked salmon (torn into bite-sized pieces), the avocados (evenly sliced), a generous pile of watercress and the chopped spring onions.

3. For the dressing, mix all the ingredients together in a small bowl and whisk well. Pour into a serving jug.

4. To serve, divide the warm rice into 6 bowls and allow everyone to add their own toppings from the sharing plate, along with the dressing and some sesame seeds to sprinkle over the top. Offer chopsticks or forks for guests to mix all the ingredients together themselves in the bowls. If they like spicy flavours, you can offer one of the additional condiments on the side.

250g (9oz) **wild rice or red Camargue rice**

For the dressing
½ tablespoon **cider vinegar**
½ tablespoon **Dijon mustard**
1 tablespoon **dark soy sauce**
½ teaspoon **honey**
½ **garlic clove, crushed**
6 tablespoons **extra virgin olive oil**

For the salad
½ **shallot, finely sliced**
2 **carrots, peeled and grated**
1 **fennel bulb, halved and finely sliced**
50g (1¾oz) **dried barberries or a mixture of dried**
    cranberries and sour cherries
80g (3oz) **blanched almonds**
20g (¾oz) **oregano, leaves picked**
20g (¾oz) **curly or flat-leaf parsley, leaves picked**
20g (¾oz) **basil, leaves picked**
a few sprigs of **mint**
handful of **rocket leaves, to serve**

WILD RICE SALAD

I make this with wild or semi-wild red Camargue rice partly for the pleasing nutty texture and flavour but also for their added health benefits. Wild rice is not actually rice but a semi-aquatic grass that is grown mainly in North America and China. It takes longer to cook because the grains (or seeds) are left intact, unlike other types of rice, which are polished to remove the outer layers. You could use brown or white short-grain rice too. This is good as part of a spread – cold roast chicken, some greens, a platter of salad. I like lots of dishes crammed on the table, everyone picking up plates and passing the food around.

1. Put the rice in a large saucepan with 1.5 litres (2⅔ pints) water. Bring to the boil and cook, covered, for 35 minutes. Once cooked, drain the rice and put it in a large bowl.
2. Put all the ingredients for the dressing together in a separate bowl and whisk well to combine.
3. Add all the salad ingredients to the cooked rice. Then pour in the dressing, mixing well.
4. Stir the rocket leaves through the salad just before serving.
5. Arrange everything in a shallow bowl and allow people to help themselves. (It also works served as a side dish.)

LU ROU FAN

TAIWANESE PORK RICE

This recipe from Erchen Chang, chef-proprietor of Bao London, is as much about the rice as it is the meat. She explains: 'Lu rou fan is a national dish that you can find in most Xiao Chi houses in Taiwan. The fatty nature of the sauce means it coats the steamed rice nicely, making it a perfect rice bowl. Usually it is served in small shallow bowls; this means the lu rou and the braising liquor have a perfect sauce-to-rice ratio, making every mouthful flavoursome.'

....

SERVES 4

For the pickled radish
200g (7oz) red radishes
1 red finger chilli
130ml (4fl oz) Chinese red vinegar
50g (1¾oz) caster sugar
2 teaspoons salt

For the pork
1kg (2lb 4oz) boneless pork belly
40ml (1½fl oz) michiu rice wine or cooking sake
thumb-sized piece of fresh root ginger, left whole,
    plus 1cm (½in) piece, peeled and crushed
3–4 garlic cloves: 2–3 left whole and peeled, 1 crushed
1 red apple, peeled, cored and diced
1 shallot, diced
1 tablespoon rapeseed oil
4 tablespoons light soy sauce
2 dried red chillies
2 star anise
1 small cinnamon stick
2 tablespoons Shaoxing rice wine
1 tablespoon mirin
2 spring onions, halved
1 tablespoon rice vinegar
1–2 teaspoons dark soy sauce

For the rice
300g (10½oz) short-grain rice
300ml (10fl oz) filtered water

1. To make the pickled radish, trim the radish leaves to 5mm (¼in) and halve the radishes. Put in a sterilized jar with the chilli, vinegar, sugar and salt. Leave to pickle overnight in the refrigerator.

2. Place the pork belly, skin-side down, into a deep pot and cover with cold water so that it is submerged. Add the michiu wine or sake, whole ginger and garlic cloves. Poach over a low heat for about 1 hour until the pork feels firm and the skin looks translucent. Leave to cool and rest in the liquid so that the moisture drawn out is reabsorbed.

3. Remove the cooled pork from the pot, reserving the poaching liquid, and cut into 1cm (½in) cubes.

4. In a clay pot or cast-iron pan, gently fry the apple, shallot and pork belly cubes in the oil until soft and fragrant. Add 500ml (18fl oz) of the poaching liquid with the light soy sauce, chillies, spices, Shaoxing wine, mirin, crushed ginger and garlic, spring onions and vinegar. Bring to the boil, then turn the heat to low, cover and braise for 2 hours. Make sure the pork is covered with liquid, adding more poaching liquid if necessary.

5. After 2 hours, remove the lid and increase the heat to medium, add the dark soy sauce and give it a good stir. Let it reduce to a light, sticky consistency. The fat from the belly should melt in the mouth, but the cubes must maintain their shape; the braising liquid should be shiny and golden brown, and not overly sticky. Discard the star anise and cinnamon.

6. Wash the rice over a colander 3 times. Then let it soak in water for 30 minutes–1 hour, before draining well. Bring the filtered water to the boil in a pan, add the rice and bring to the boil again. Then put on the lid and reduce the heat to low; cook for 12 minutes. Turn off the heat and let it rest for 10 minutes.

7. Scoop the rice into 4 small, shallow bowls, ensuring it retains its fluffiness. Ladle over the pork with enough of the braising liquor to cover the meat and flavour the rice. Serve with the pickled radishes – you could put one on the inner rim of each bowl. Any leftovers can be kept in the refrigerator for up to 3 days.

EGG FRIED RICE

This is a meal in itself and is a particularly good way to use up any vegetable or rice leftovers you might have. I often cook extra rice just so that I can make this dish the next day, then supper can be ready quickly and a plate of eggs and rice seems something worth sitting down for. When cooking long-grain basmati rice, it is important to always rinse the grain first. This removes some of the starch to prevent the grains from sticking together when cooking. If you have the time, it also benefits from being soaked in water for up to 30 minutes, which helps to ensure even cooking of the individual grains.

300g (10½oz) white or brown long-grain basmati
    rice, rinsed
4 tablespoons vegetable or groundnut oil
150g (5½oz) streaky bacon or pancetta lardons
6 spring onions, finely chopped
200g (7oz) white cabbage or other leafy greens,
    such as kale, finely shredded
2 carrots, peeled and cut into long thin strips
200g (7oz) peas, defrosted if using frozen
2 tablespoons fish or oyster sauce
2 tablespoons dark soy sauce
6 large eggs, lightly beaten
sea salt and freshly ground black pepper
small bunch of chives, finely chopped, to serve

1. Put the rice in an appropriate-sized saucepan: it should fill at least half of it, leaving room to expand. Add a generous 1 teaspoon of salt, cover with 1cm (½in) water and cook with a lid on. Turn down the heat as soon as it boils and simmer for 10–12 minutes. Taste a few grains and, if tender, remove from the heat and replace the lid. Allow to steam for 5–10 minutes before fluffing with a fork.

2. In a wok or high-sided frying pan, heat 2 tablespoons of the oil and fry the lardons until crispy. Add half the spring onions and all the greens and carrots. Add plenty of salt and stir-fry until the vegetables begin to wilt and soften. This should take a couple of minutes. If the pan gets too hot and singes the vegetables, add a splash of water. Add the peas and cook for 1–2 minutes, then add the sauces.

3. Remove the stir-fried vegetables to a bowl, wipe out the wok and add the remaining 2 tablespoons of oil. When the oil is hot, pour the eggs into the wok and let them cook until they begin to set. Using a wooden spoon, scrape the still-wet egg – as though slicing it – so that it forms large curds. Quickly add the cooked rice and stir together.

4. Return the vegetables to the wok, fold everything together and season to taste with salt and pepper. Serve with the rest of spring onions and the chives sprinkled on top.

EGGS

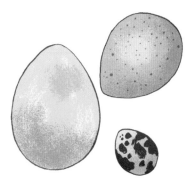

Eggs are synonymous with spring: rebirth, new beginnings, Easter. And hens that live outside all year round start to lay again in spring when there's more light.

Not all eggs are created equal: a good, fresh egg has a pert bright orange yolk and thick, gelatinous white that clings around it. The sensation of plucking a warm egg, fresh from the nest, and cupping it in your hand is one of life's greatest pleasures, but realistically, most of us are taking a box from the supermarket shelf. If you live in the country, it's likely there will be someone nearby who wants to sell you their eggs, which will undoubtedly come from free-range and kindly treated hens. It makes sense, as free-range hens that are fed natural feeds and move about in spacious areas lay healthier, stronger eggs.

These beautiful ovoid forms are one of the greatest gifts nature ever gave to the cook – the cornerstone of cookery. The addition of an egg transforms most things into a meal. It turns the banal into the luxurious – a simple dressing with chopped egg becomes a sauce, some chopped cooked vegetables with an egg becomes lunch and a sauce with added eggs gives it a reason to be.

RECIPES

Vegetables à la Grecque
Soft-boiled eggs with anchovy toast
Chard, spinach and egg gratin
Khatteh ande (Boiled eggs in tamarind sauce)
Asparagus with warm melted cheese and egg yolk sauce
Asparagus carbonara

VEGETABLES À LA GRECQUE

This fanfare of spring vegetables arranged beautifully on your prettiest serving plate is a perfect dish to cook in advance when you're hosting guests. Serve at room temperature or chilled on a large serving plate as a centrepiece on the table from which everyone can help themselves.

....

SERVES 6

For the vegetables and poaching liquid
12 baby leeks, trimmed and well washed
3 carrots, peeled
6 celery sticks
small bunch of asparagus
½ cauliflower
juice of ½ lemon
100ml (3½fl oz) white wine
1 teaspoon coriander seeds
½ teaspoon black peppercorns
1 fresh bay leaf
1 sprig of thyme

For the sauce
2 tablespoons capers, rinsed
1 tablespoon Dijon mustard
½ tablespoon mild red wine vinegar (I use Volpaia)
20g (¾oz) flat-leaf parsley, finely chopped
20g (¾oz) basil, finely chopped
5 tablespoons extra virgin olive oil, plus extra
    to serve
4 hard-boiled eggs, peeled
sea salt and freshly ground black pepper

1. For the vegetables and poaching liquid, prepare the vegetables so that they are roughly the same size: cut the leeks into short lengths, the carrots into sticks and the celery and asparagus into similar lengths; break the cauliflower into small florets.
2. Put the lemon juice, wine, spices, bay leaf and thyme into a large saucepan and add 1 litre (1¾ pints) water and 1 teaspoon of salt. Bring to the boil, then add the leeks. After 1 minute, add the other vegetables and

simmer for 3–4 minutes, or until the vegetables are tender with a little bite. Remove with a slotted spoon and transfer to a serving dish, reserving the poaching liquid. Pour a spoonful of the liquid over the vegetables.
3. For the sauce, roughly chop the capers and put them in a bowl with the mustard, vinegar, herbs and oil. Finely chop the eggs and add to the bowl with a couple of spoonfuls of the poaching liquid. Stir to make a loose sauce. Season with salt and pepper. Serve the vegetables, warm or cold, drizzled with extra virgin olive oil and with the sauce spooned over.

SOFT-BOILED EGGS
WITH ANCHOVY TOAST

A deeply comforting Sunday-night dinner that even the most scantily stocked kitchen could usually stretch to.

....

SERVES 2

4 salted anchovy fillets
20g (¾oz) very soft butter
squeeze of lemon juice
2 slices of sourdough toast
2 soft-boiled eggs
freshly ground black pepper

1. Pound the anchovies with the butter in a mortar with a pestle to make a paste. Alternately, you can finely chop them into the butter. Add the lemon juice and mix well with some black pepper.
2. Spread the anchovy paste all over the toast. Cut into soldiers and dip into the soft-boiled eggs.

CHARD, SPINACH AND EGG GRATIN

Chard and spinach are available all through spring and usually they're the only leaves still growing in my garden at this time of year, so I rely on them regularly. You can omit the eggs and serve this as a side dish, but the eggs make it a meal in itself. If you can find any sorrel, add that too and omit the lemon juice. I always turn the ends of my sourdough loaves into breadcrumbs and keep them in the freezer, then they come in handy for dishes like this.

....

SERVES 6

For the breadcrumb top
2 tablespoons olive oil
100g (3½oz) fresh breadcrumbs

For the gratin
500g (1lb 2oz) chard leaves and stalks
500g (1lb 2oz) large-leaf spinach
25g (1oz) butter
2 tablespoons olive oil
8 garlic cloves, finely chopped
3 teaspoons plain flour
200ml (7fl oz) full-fat milk
a few gratings of nutmeg
juice of ½ lemon
6 eggs
20g (¾oz) Parmesan cheese, grated
sea salt and freshly ground black pepper

1. Heat the oil in a frying pan. Add the breadcrumbs and ½ teaspoon of salt, and stir until the crumbs begin to turn golden. Remove from the heat. Set aside.

2. Preheat the oven to 200°C (180°C fan), 400°F, Gas mark 6. Separate the chard stalks and cut into 2cm (¾in) lengths. Fill a large saucepan with salted water and bring to the boil. Cook the stalks – they should take 3 minutes – then the chard leaves for 1–2 minutes and finally the spinach for a minute. Drain and refresh the cooked leaves in cold water, squeeze dry, then chop them finely.

3. Place a saucepan over a medium heat. Melt the butter with the oil and fry the garlic until starting to colour. Add the chopped leaves and stalks. Season with salt and pepper and stir, cooking for a minute until well combined.

4. Sprinkle over the flour and stir well, then add the milk, stirring and cooking until the leaves and stalks are coated with sauce. Add the nutmeg and squeeze over the lemon juice. Taste for seasoning.

5. Put half the mixture into a blender. Blitz to a purée, then mix with the remaining mixture.

6. Spread the mixture into a rectangular gratin dish, approximately 30 × 18cm (12 × 7in), and create 6 indentations. Crack an egg into each one and cover the surface with the fried breadcrumbs and Parmesan. Bake for 20 minutes, then remove and allow to sit for 5 minutes before serving.

KHATTEH ANDE (BOILED EGGS IN TAMARIND SAUCE)

This recipe comes from Indian-born British chef, restaurateur and cookbook author Asma Khan. Her childhood memories of this dish remind us of the importance of small things: 'Eggs are monsoon food. When the rainy season began in Calcutta, we waited for the days of relentless rain, because what came after that was waterlogged streets. No school. No electricity for days, as the power stations were underwater. Food rationing because the bazaars were closed. But eggs were delivered to us by the anda wallah (the egg man), who would cycle through streets that were knee-deep in water and bring us 24 eggs every other day. At first, everyone got a whole egg, but if the rains continued, we would get only half an egg a day. The eggs were always prepared with great care and mealtimes were something of an occasion, with a lantern at the edge of the table, followed by a long night of storytelling by my father.' These boiled eggs in a tamarind gravy are garnished with chopped coriander; an inexpensive pretty dish that can be made in advance and reheated, and brings something unusual to the table.

....

SERVES 6 AS PART OF A MEAL WITH LENTILS, RICE AND BREADS

6 large hard-boiled eggs

6 tablespoons vegetable oil

2 medium onions, thinly sliced

¾ teaspoon garlic paste (crushed by hand or in a blender)

1 teaspoon ginger paste (crushed in a blender or grated)

¾ teaspoon ground turmeric

½ teaspoon chilli powder

6 tablespoons tamarind extract (3 tablespoons if ready-made)

50g (1¾oz) coriander, chopped, plus a handful to garnish

pinch of sugar (optional)

sea salt

1. Peel the hard-boiled eggs and make 3 shallow slits on the surface of each one. This will help the eggs absorb the tamarind gravy when they are added to the pot. Set aside.

2. Heat the oil in a deep saucepan over a medium–high heat. Add the sliced onions and stir until they start to turn a light caramel colour. Add the garlic and ginger pastes, then the turmeric and chilli powder, and continue to cook, stirring frequently, for a further 4–5 minutes until the raw smell of the garlic and ginger has gone.

3. Add the tamarind extract, 400ml (14fl oz) water and some salt, then reduce the heat to a simmer. Add the chopped coriander and cook until the liquid has reduced by half. Add the hard-boiled eggs and cook, uncovered, for 10 minutes over a low heat. You can add a good pinch of sugar if you would like the dish to have a sweet and sour taste. Garnish with the extra coriander before serving.

ASPARAGUS

*WITH WARM MELTED CHEESE AND EGG
YOLK SAUCE*

*I am blind to asparagus on supermarket shelves most
of the year, until the season starts in late spring and
I see those first bulging bunches of fat stalks of British
asparagus for sale. One of my favourite ways to eat
early asparagus is bathed in a sauce of melted cheese,
thickened with egg yolks. You can also stir the sauce
into cooked tagliatelle, with the asparagus chopped
into bite-sized pieces, sprinkled with extra Parmesan.*

SERVES 4

800g (1lb 12oz) asparagus
½ garlic clove, peeled
2 egg yolks
100g (3½oz) crème fraîche
50g (1¾oz) Parmesan cheese, grated, plus extra
  to serve
sea salt and freshly ground black pepper

1. Boil or steam the asparagus for 2–3 minutes.
2. Rub the inside of a heatproof bowl with the garlic
clove half. Add the egg yolks, crème fraîche and grated
Parmesan, and season with salt and pepper, whisking
well. Place the bowl over a pan of boiling water,
whisking continuously as it heats, until it thickens to
a custard-like consistency.
3. Pour the sauce over the asparagus and sprinkle
with extra Parmesan to serve.

ASPARAGUS CARBONARA

*Once the English asparagus season begins, I make
sure I enjoy it in every possible way, including in a
vegetarian version of this classic pasta sauce. The
pleasure of dishes like this is as much about how you
serve them – on a wide, shallow serving plate taken
to the table while the sauce is still hot and glossy.*

SERVES 4

400g (14oz) fresh egg tagliatelle (or any long dried
  pasta will do)
4 eggs
100g (3½oz) Parmesan cheese, grated, plus extra
  to serve
small bunch of curly or flat-leaf parsley, finely
  chopped
300g (10½oz) asparagus, cut into long, thin strips
sea salt and freshly ground black pepper

1. Boil the spaghetti in a large pan of well-salted water
according to the packet instructions.
2. Meanwhile, whisk the eggs with the Parmesan in a
bowl, season with salt and lots of pepper and add the
parsley, leaving some to sprinkle over before serving.
3. About 3 minutes before the pasta is done, add
the asparagus. Drain, reserving a cup of the cooking
water. Return the pasta and asparagus to the pan.
4. Whisk 2 tablespoons of the cooking water into
the eggs to make a loose sauce and add to the pasta,
stirring all the time. If it starts to look dry, add more
cooking water – you should have a glossy coating on
all the strands of pasta and a slightly liquid sauce.
Serve with the rest of the parsley sprinkled over and
some extra Parmesan.

LEFTOVERS

I like the challenge of leftovers. The waste-not-want-not attitude of our grandparents can be extremely satisfying. I also can't bear throwing away food that I know people have taken great care to grow. We all have leftovers to deal with, whether it's those stray vegetables at the bottom of the refrigerator, the meat from a roast, a loaf of bread that's no longer fresh or the end of the cheeseboard. Although I love to cook more than I need when making soups and stews to have extra, some dishes just don't work if you reheat them and need to be transformed into something else. I hope these recipes can be adapted using whatever ingredients you may have.

Leftover pieces of cheese never need to go to waste: mix them into dishes like the one opposite; melt soft cheese over sliced potatoes and bake; fold grated cheeses into an omelette or blend with crisp breadcrumbs for cheesy gratinated toppings; or put chunks of the ends of cheese into the bottom of a bowl of soup. Blue cheeses can be whisked into salad dressings, and Parmesan rinds added to stock or soup give a great depth of flavour.

I always turn leftover bread into breadcrumbs, which I keep in the freezer to have on hand. Use these for breading goujons, creating a crunchy top on a gratin, for frying in oil and garlic to sprinkle on spaghetti with chilli and parsley or to add a crunchy topping to baked eggs. Stale sliced bread of any sort, including panettone, can be used for bread and butter pudding, eggy bread or a savoury bread pudding.

Roasted vegetables, boiled vegetables, small quantities of odds and ends in the refrigerator – often what's left from a vegetable box that didn't make it into the first round of cooking: these are all leftovers we can cook with. When you're preparing vegetables, it's easy to forget that (with the exception of rhubarb leaves) all parts of the plant are edible. Strip the leaves from chard to use in one dish and keep the stalks to add to a soup or gratin. Peelings go into the stock pot, and when you boil vegetables, keep the water for the base for your next broth. When I receive my veg box, I often cook some of the vegetables to have them ready to use – it speeds up preparation of other recipes and somehow makes the idea of cooking much more effortless and inspiring.

RECIPES

Cheese and greens turnovers
Roast vegetable toad in the hole
Crisp breaded lamb

CHEESE AND GREENS TURNOVERS

Use whatever vegetables you have, cooked or raw, but the leafy element is important here. It's always worth having good all-butter puff pastry in the freezer, but if not, make these with a simple shortcrust pastry and cook for longer at a lower temperature. I've made these for a picnic to eat in our hands, like Cornish miners would eat their pasties.

···

SERVES 6

200g (7oz) uncooked greens, such as kale, spinach, cavolo nero, or 6 handfuls of cooked, chopped greens

2 tablespoons olive or rapeseed oil

3 spring onions or 1 medium onion, finely chopped

100g (3½oz) root vegetables, such as potatoes, celeriac and parsnips, peeled and diced, or leftover cooked vegetables

150g (5½oz) firm goats' cheese or strong-flavoured hard cheese, crumbled or grated

2 tablespoons chopped herbs, such as oregano, parsley, mint or basil

1 tablespoon dill, coriander or fennel seeds, or 1 tablespoon mixture of all of them

2 eggs, beaten

plain flour, for dusting

320g (11½oz) packet ready-rolled all-butter puff pastry

sea salt and freshly ground black pepper

1. Cook the raw greens in plenty of salted boiling water, then refresh and squeeze out the moisture. Chop coarsely.

2. Heat the oil in a frying pan and cook the onion until soft. Add the raw root vegetables. Fry for 1 minute, then add a splash of water and cover. Cook until soft. Add any cooked veg to the onion when soft.

3. Place the greens in a large bowl and mix with all the other ingredients, except for the flour and pastry (saving a little of the egg mix for an egg wash). Season the mixture to taste with salt and pepper.

4. Preheat the oven to 200°C (180°C fan), 400°F, Gas mark 6. Lay out the pastry on a floured surface and cut into 6 squares. Line a baking sheet with baking parchment and lay the pastry pieces on top.

5. Put 4 dessertspoonfuls of the vegetable mix in a strip diagonally from one corner to the other. Fold the other 2 corners together and brush with a little egg wash. Bake for 30 minutes until golden and crisp.

ROAST VEGETABLE
TOAD IN THE HOLE

We often have this for Saturday lunch, made with the week's leftovers, served in its roasting dish so that you can scrape the crispy bits sticking to the edges. All sorts of vegetables work in this, but if you have the opportunity, try to introduce some crunch or crispness, either from roasting them before cooking or, if they're leftover boiled vegetables, coat them in oil and give them 20 minutes in a hot oven before you add them to the batter. Add crisp cooked bacon too if you want some salty smoky background flavour. Any leftover gravy from a roast is delicious poured on top to serve.

....

For the batter
5 eggs
300ml (10fl oz) full-fat milk
300ml (10fl oz) water (fizzy mineral water is best)
1 tablespoon Dijon mustard
250g (9oz) plain flour
2 tablespoons chopped mixed sage, rosemary
    and thyme

For the vegetables
400g (14oz) uncooked or leftover cooked vegetables
4 tablespoons olive oil (if using uncooked vegetables)
120ml (4fl oz) sunflower oil
sea salt and freshly ground black pepper

1. To make the batter, put the eggs, milk, water and mustard in a large bowl and whisk vigorously until foamy. Add the flour, 1½ teaspoons of salt and the herbs. Fold together to make a smooth batter. Set aside for at least 30 minutes.
2. Preheat the oven to 220°C (200°C fan), 425°F, Gas mark 7.
3. If your vegetables are raw, cut them into long batons (the size of chipolatas) or, if they are round, cut into wedges. Place them in a roasting tray with deep sides, about 40 × 30cm (16 × 12in).
4. Cover with the olive oil and plenty of salt and pepper. Roast for 20 minutes until browned and cooked through (the edges should be starting to crisp). Transfer to a bowl and set aside.
5. Add the sunflower oil to the tray and return to the oven to heat for at least 5 minutes. It should be really hot when you add the batter.
6. Remove the tray from the oven and pour in the batter. Add the cooked vegetables, distributing them evenly so that there is space between them.
7. Bake for 20 minutes until the batter has puffed up and started to brown. Reduce the oven temperature to 180°C (160°C fan), 350°F, Gas mark 4 and cook for another 20 minutes. Remove and serve straight away.

CRISP BREADED LAMB

I first ate this at Coombeshead Farm in Cornwall and was immediately seduced by the unctuous texture of meat inside the crisp breadcrumb shell. This is a great way to turn a leftover slow-cooked joint of lamb into a completely different and delicious dish. Excellent served with chutney and salad. When you cook any meat, it's always worth keeping any cooking juices; they can be added to stock or soups and provide valuable flavour and moisture. I've successfully made this with leftover 'pink cooked' leg of lamb too – put the meat on the bone in a pot with water and herbs and cook as you would stock, simmering for about 1 hour until the meat falls from the bone.

SERVES 6

For the lamb
700g (1lb 9oz) leftover slow-cooked lamb
4 tablespoons mixed sage, rosemary and parsley,
    finely chopped
3 tablespoons wine vinegar or cider vinegar

For the breadcrumb shell
300g (10½oz) plain flour
2 eggs, beaten
300g (10½oz) fresh or dried breadcrumbs
    (see page 54)
5 tablespoons olive oil or vegetable oil

To serve
condiments, chutneys or mustard
green salad

1. Remove all the meat from the bone. If it has been slow-cooked, it should fall off easily. Reserve any cooking juices.
2. Chop the meat roughly and place in a bowl with the herbs, vinegar and just enough of the cooking juices to make it wet, without it leaking liquid.
3. Line a square dish, approximately 18 × 25cm (7 × 10in), with clingfilm and press in the meat to a depth of 4cm (1½in). Cover and chill for at least 2 hours.
4. The meat will now have set in its juices. Remove it from the dish and cut it into wide slices.
5. For the breadcrumb shell, line up 3 shallow dishes – one containing the flour, one the beaten eggs and one the breadcrumbs. Dip each piece of meat into the flour – tapping off any excess – then into the egg and then into the breadcrumbs, making sure you completely cover it at each stage.
6. Heat the oil in a frying pan until sizzling hot and fry as many pieces as you can comfortably fit in at once. Brown the crumbs on each side before turning.
7. Serve with any leftover condiments or chutneys you have or with mustard and a green salad.

RHUBARB

The forced rhubarb that brightens the shelves of greengrocers in winter carries on through spring – thankfully, as there are very few other fresh fruits around apart from pineapple, mangoes and other imported tropical fruit and stored apples and pears.

Forced rhubarb is more tender and sweet than summer rhubarb, which grows outdoors. An otherwise overlooked vegetable/fruit, it gets a chance in the limelight and really sings for its supper. Colourful, sweet-sour and adaptable, it can be stewed and kept in the refrigerator to have with yogurt and granola for breakfast; with meringues and cream; as the base of a crumble, or on top of rice pudding or a custard tart. Or use it in savoury dishes, paired with oily fish like mackerel or roast pork. I even make cordial – mix it with sugar syrup and strain into sterilized bottles.

To cook the rhubarb, cut into batons and roast for 20 minutes at 150°C (130°C fan), 300°F, Gas mark 2 with strips of orange zest, a vanilla pod and plenty of sugar or honey. Its otherworldly colour will brighten your table when the sky can still look drab, and it is great in a martini.

RECIPES

Filo pastry with rhubarb, rosewater and cardamom cream
Rhubarb and star anise upside-down cake
Rhubarb pavlova
Rice pudding with cardamom and rhubarb

FILO PASTRY

*WITH RHUBARB, ROSEWATER AND
CARDAMOM CREAM*

*Sam and Sam Clark's recipe for this traditional
British vegetable transforms it into a special yet easy
pudding, the sort that appeals to me. Once you've
bought the filo pastry, you'll find plenty of other recipes
in the book to use up the rest.*

....

SERVES 6

3 tablespoons unsalted butter

6 sheets of filo pastry

500g (1lb 2oz) rhubarb, cut into 4cm (1½in) lengths

250g (9oz) caster sugar (or more if desired)

4 tablespoons rosewater

200g (7oz) cream cheese

200g (7oz) Greek yogurt

150ml (5fl oz) single cream

juice of 2 lemons

**6 cardamom pods, green husks removed and seeds
    crushed to a fine powder**

150g (5½oz) unsalted pistachios, crushed

2 tablespoons icing sugar, for dusting

1. Preheat the oven to 180°C (160°C fan), 350°F, Gas
mark 4. Melt the butter in a small saucepan and set
aside. Place a sheet of pastry on a small baking tray
and brush generously with butter. Place another sheet
on top and brush with more butter. Continue until all
6 sheets are layered on top of each other on the tray.
Score the pastry with a sharp knife into squares or
diamonds. This will allow air to enter so that it can
puff up in the oven. Bake for 15–20 minutes, or until
golden brown. Remove from the oven and set aside.

2. Place the rhubarb in a roasting tray. Sprinkle with
150g (5½oz) of the sugar and the rosewater, and cook
in the oven for 15–20 minutes, or until tender. Remove
from the oven and set aside.

3. Put the cream cheese, yogurt, cream, lemon juice
and the remaining sugar into a bowl. Whisk gently
with a hand-held electric whisk or hand whisk until
smooth and thick. Stir in the ground cardamom, then
refrigerate until you are ready to serve.

4. To serve, place a few pieces of golden pastry on each
plate, reserving 6 pieces. Add a generous tablespoon
of the cream mixture, followed by some of the rhubarb
and the crushed pistachios. Finish by placing a
reserved piece of filo pastry over the top of each
serving and dusting with the icing sugar.

RHUBARB AND STAR ANISE UPSIDE-DOWN CAKE

I was given a pretty glass cake plate on a stand with a glass dome and there's always some sort of cake under it. At this time of year it usually contains rhubarb. This is cakey enough to serve with cream as a pudding or for teatime.

....

SERVES 6–8

For the topping
350g (12oz) rhubarb
80g (3oz) caster sugar
40g (1½oz) unsalted butter, cut into cubes
2 tablespoons double cream (serve the rest of the pot with the cake)
pinch of sea salt
3 star anise

For the base
180g (6oz) caster sugar
200g (7oz) unsalted butter, softened
1 vanilla pod
4 eggs
4 tablespoons natural yogurt
200g (7oz) self-raising flour
1 tablespoon baking powder

1. Preheat the oven to 160°C (140°C fan), 325°F, Gas mark 3 and cut the rhubarb into 3cm (1¼in) strips.
2. Melt the sugar for the topping, without stirring, in a saucepan until it becomes chestnut brown. Remove from the heat and whisk in the butter cubes to make a thick caramel sauce. Whisk in the cream and salt.
3. Pour the caramel into the bottom of a 20cm (8in) round springform cake tin and arrange the star anise on the base, equally spaced apart, then lay the rhubarb pieces in an attractive pattern on top.
4. Beat the sugar and butter for the base together until light and pale. Halve the vanilla pod lengthways and scrape out the seeds, then beat in along with the eggs, one by one, followed by the yogurt.
5. Mix the flour and baking powder together well and fold this into the butter mixture. Pour the batter over the rhubarb and smooth the surface. Put the cake tin on a baking sheet to catch any caramel that may ooze out of the sides.
6. Bake for 40–45 minutes, or until the middle feels firm to the touch and a skewer inserted into the centre comes out clean. Allow to cool before inverting on to a serving plate and removing the tin. Serve warm with the remaining cream.

RHUBARB PAVLOVA

Given how simple this is to make, it's an extravagant-looking dessert and a great way to show off the beautiful pink rhubarb available at this time of year. For a special occasion you could decorate the serving plate with flowers or blossom.

....

SERVES 6

For the rhubarb
500g (1lb 2oz) rhubarb
juice of 2 oranges
150g (5½oz) dark soft brown sugar
1 vanilla pod

For the meringues
about 210g (7½oz) egg whites
¼ teaspoon cider vinegar
420g (15oz) caster sugar

For the filling
100g (3½oz) flaked almonds
500ml (18fl oz) whipping cream

1. To cook the rhubarb, preheat the oven to 160°C (140°C fan), 325°F, Gas mark 3. Remove and discard any leaves. If the stalks are very thick, halve them lengthways, then cut into finger-length sticks. Place in a single layer in a roasting tray (you may need 2 trays for this). Pour over the orange juice and sprinkle with the brown sugar. Halve the vanilla pod lengthways and scrape out the seeds, then add these and the empty pod. Cook in the oven for 30 minutes, or until completely soft. Remove and set aside to cool.

2. To make the meringues, reduce the oven to 150°C (130°C fan), 300°F, Gas mark 2. Whisk the egg whites until they start to foam, then add the vinegar and the caster sugar, a large spoonful at a time, while continuing to whisk. When all the sugar is added, keep whisking until the whites are glossy and form stiff peaks and all the sugar has dissolved. Check this by squeezing a little between your fingers – you should not be able to feel any sugar granules.

3. Line 3 baking sheets with baking parchment, then dot fingernail-sized blobs of meringue at each corner to hold the paper down. Spoon one-third of the meringue on to each sheet, smoothing with a spatula to form equal-sized circles (about 20cm/8in in diameter).

4. Bake for 1 hour, or until set; they should be crisp to the touch, but still a little gooey inside. Remove from the oven and allow to cool completely. Meanwhile, toast the flaked almonds in the oven for 15 minutes until they are starting to colour. Set aside to cool.

5. When you are ready to assemble, whip the cream until it forms soft peaks and spread one-third of it over a meringue disc. Add one-third of the rhubarb and some juice, then a third of the almonds. Repeat until you have a tower of 3 discs, covered in cream, rhubarb and almonds. Pour any remaining rhubarb juice over the top so that it dribbles down the sides.

RICE PUDDING

WITH CARDAMOM AND RHUBARB

I no longer buy pudding rice especially to make this. Instead, I use either risotto or sushi rice I have in the cupboard; their short grains produce the creamy, sticky texture that makes this so good. The rhubarb brings some beautiful bright pink colour and a nice balance of acidity, but the key ingredient here is the cardamom, which gives it a whisper of fragrance.

SERVES 6

For the rice pudding
700ml (1¼ pints) full-fat milk
500ml (18fl oz) double cream
100g (3½oz) caster sugar
6 cardamom pods, lightly crushed
1 vanilla pod, split in half
120g (4¼oz) risotto or sushi rice

For the rhubarb
500g (1lb 2oz) rhubarb (about 5–6 stalks)
50g (1¾oz) caster or light soft brown sugar
1 orange
4cm (1½in) piece of fresh root ginger, peeled

1. Preheat the oven to 160°C (140°C fan), 325°F, Gas mark 3. To make the rice pudding, put the milk, cream, sugar and cardamom in a large saucepan. Scrape the seeds from the vanilla pod and add to the milk, along with the pod. Bring to the boil, then remove from the heat.

2. Choose a baking dish that is large enough to fit all the milk and cream with a bit of extra room so that it doesn't slosh over the sides when you put it in the oven. Scatter the rice over the bottom of the dish and carefully ladle the milk mixture in so that the rice remains evenly distributed.

3. Bake for 1 hour 20 minutes, then check that the skin is not getting too brown. If it is, reduce the temperature to 140°C (120°C fan), 275°F, Gas mark 1 for the final 30 minutes of cooking.

4. Top and tail the rhubarb stalks, then cut into finger-length batons. Lay them in a single layer in a baking tray and sprinkle with the caster or brown sugar.

5. Peel 4 lengths of zest from the orange. Add this to the rhubarb along with the orange juice. Grate the ginger over and toss the rhubarb so that it is well coated.

6. Bake for 20 minutes in the same oven as the rice pudding, preferably on the shelf below, until the rhubarb is tender but not mushy.

7. Remove the rhubarb from the oven and then allow it to cool a little before serving with the rice – it makes a good temperature contrast to the hot rice pudding.

SPRING MENUS

....

SOMETHING QUICK

Asparagus with warm melted cheese and egg yolk sauce page 51

Crab spaghetti page 35

Filo pastry with rhubarb, rosewater and cardamom cream page 61

Quality ingredients need little done to them to make an excellent meal. To speed things up, I use the same pot of water to cook the asparagus and then the pasta. Meanwhile, the rhubarb and filo are baking in the oven while I'm stirring the asparagus sauce and chatting with a glass of wine.

COOKING IN ADVANCE

Vichyssoise with herbs and cream page 15

Mediterranean fish stew with saffron mayonnaise page 29

Rhubarb and star anise upside-down cake page 63

When I'm cooking several courses for a crowd, I enjoy it so much more if I've made most of it in advance. The soup can be done the day before and the rhubarb, if not the day before, then that morning. Then I make the base for the fish stew and the only thing I'll have to do last minute is cook the fish in the sauce.

A SPRING FEAST

Leek and potato vinaigrette with egg mimosa page 16

Chicken with wild garlic and jewelled pilaf pages 24 and 37

Rhubarb pavlova page 64

These dishes sing of spring. A celebration of the season and a reason to go foraging in the woods. They are pretty and colourful yet light, like spring.

COOKING FOR 2 OR 4

Roast leeks with yogurt, caramelized butter, chilli flakes and dill page 14

Plaice with fried capers and brown butter page 31

Rice pudding with cardamom and rhubarb page 67

Cooking for smaller numbers is an opportunity to make things that require a bit more time or use expensive ingredients. I relish these moments in the kitchen with no time or space pressure.

....

FLOWERS AND TABLE DECORATIONS

The flowers that I pick at this time of year tend to be grown from bulbs, wild flowers and blossom. I love branches of blossom in a tall vase, or little glasses filled with bluebells and flowers of wild garlic. If you have primroses, you could dig up a couple and put them in small terracotta pots on the table, then replant them in your garden when they finish flowering. Or fill china bowls and soup tureens with bulbs of pale yellow narcissi and white muscari.

Summer

Eating is more relaxed, it's warm enough to sit in the garden and friends join in with the cooking preparations, popping pearl-like peas from their pods in the sunshine

When summer arrives, the herbs growing outside the kitchen burst into life and I fill vases for the table with purple-flowering chives, bronze fennel and pink salvias that smell of blackcurrants. Eating is more relaxed, it's warm enough to sit in the garden and friends join in with the cooking preparations, popping pearl-like peas from their pods in the sunshine. I lay the table with my candy-coloured glasses and pink and yellow tablecloth; even if they're rather mismatched, this colourful informality suits the season.

Outdoor eating allows me to cook food that can be served at room temperature or cool, rather than piping hot: salads, tarts or simple chicken dishes, fragrant with herbs or poached with all the summer vegetables, can sit on the table outside and still taste good when cooled to pick at for second helpings.

Asparagus, peas, beans, tomatoes and courgettes – food that grows in summer – is quicker to cook or can be eaten raw. A handful of peas or beans boils in minutes, courgettes soften in no time in the frying pan and ripe juicy tomatoes can be plucked and eaten straight from the plant. More recipes can be made last minute – a quick pasta sauce with broad beans and Pecorino or a Moroccan salad of grated raw courgette and preserved lemon. In early summer, asparagus season reaches its peak. I use the green spears for everything I can before they disappear until next year – tarts, risottos or grilled and arranged in salads.

There are now so many interesting and delicious-tasting heritage varieties of vegetables that farmers and gardeners are discovering and growing. I search out courgettes that are yellow, round or stripy; tomatoes that are bulbous and ridged, long and smooth or tiger-striped. I grow and buy as many heritage varieties of tomatoes as I can because they taste better and never go to waste; what I don't eat straight away I preserve for when the season is over – slow-roasted and frozen, or made into passata that I keep in jars.

August is the month for the local agricultural show, which takes place in the fields below our house in the West Country. It reminds me of the strength of the community around us and the number of entries to the vegetable competition is evidence of the enduring love of the home-grown.

As the season runs on, the vegetable patch gets into full swing. There are beautiful violet artichokes, a jungle of courgettes, the bright yellow fennel pollen, honeysuckle, roses and sweet pea flowers and trellises of beans. I try to shuffle the vegetables around into different parts of the growing patch each year so that it keeps the soil healthy, and always planting beans, which fix nitrogen back into the soil as well as producing a great crop to eat.

Soft fruits of summer like apricots, raspberries, peaches and figs need little doing to them to make them into pudding. Their tart flavours can be simply enriched with a spoonful of cream or a jug of custard.

ASPARAGUS

The flavour of freshly picked spears, sweet and juicy and quick to cook, is incomparable to out-of-season imported asparagus. The British asparagus season is fleeting, so I like to make the most of it before it is gone again until next year.

Traditionally, asparagus is boiled or steamed and served with melted butter; I sometimes mash salted anchovies with butter and pepper. But I also love to roast asparagus, brushed with oil and salt. To prepare the spears before cooking, bend the stems and they will naturally snap off at the point where they are no longer tender. Don't throw these away – you can add them to stock, especially good for making asparagus risotto.

The green shoots grow from an underground rhizome or 'crown' and asparagus beds can be productive for many years. Green asparagus (rather than white, which is deliberately grown with no exposure to light) shoots up from the ground and is picked when the tips are still firm and closed.

RECIPES

Asparagus, feta and dill

Asparagus and prosecco risotto

Asparagus soldiers and Parmesan custard

Open puff pastry tart with asparagus, soured cream, smoked salmon and watercress

Grilled asparagus with almond and orange mojo

ASPARAGUS, FETA AND DILL

This is a springtime combination of sweet, juicy asparagus and salty crumbled feta with the soft fronds of aniseed-flavoured dill. But don't feel confined to these ingredients; try this with any salty cheese – Pecorino, Parmesan or firm goats' cheese – and use whatever soft herbs you have – marjoram, basil or even fennel tops. Cooking asparagus without water really intensifies the flavour, so I either put it on the barbecue or roast it in the oven. The fresher the asparagus, the quicker it cooks.

SERVES 4 AS A STARTER

1kg (2lb 4oz) asparagus
2 tablespoons olive oil
150g (5½oz) feta cheese
20g (¾oz) dill, fronds picked
zest of 1 lemon, plus 1 tablespoon juice (optional)
sea salt and freshly ground black pepper

1. Preheat the oven to 200°C (180°C fan), 400°F, Gas mark 6. Snap the woody ends from the asparagus – bend them and allow to break naturally. Lay in a single layer, not touching, in a roasting tray and roll in the oil. Sprinkle with salt and roast for 10–15 minutes until the spears start to brown and feel soft.
2. Arrange on a plate and crumble the feta over them. Chop the dill and sprinkle over, then sprinkle over most of the lemon zest (avoiding the pith, which is bitter).
3. Season with pepper and add the lemon juice if the feta is particularly salty. Serve warm or at room temperature.

ASPARAGUS AND PROSECCO RISOTTO

The creamy texture of risotto depends on two things: short-grain, starchy rice and the gentle coaxing of the cook stirring the grains so that they release their starch. It should be an informal dish to make for friends, stirring and chatting and maybe having a glass of prosecco while you do it. I like the acidity of prosecco paired with fresh asparagus, but you could use white wine instead. Carnaroli rice has short stubby grains that release starch when stirred, making a creamy sauce but retaining a little bite in the centre. Think of the rice as the carrier of the other ingredients; you don't need much asparagus for this, and if you're short, supplement with peas, broad beans or even small pieces of courgette.

....

SERVES 6

700g (1lb 9oz) asparagus
1.2 litres (2 pints) chicken stock
50g (1¾oz) butter
1 red onion, diced
350g (12oz) carnaroli rice
150ml (5fl oz) prosecco
40g (1½oz) Parmesan cheese, grated, plus extra
   to serve
20g (¾oz) basil
20g (¾oz) flat-leaf parsley
sea salt and freshly ground black pepper

1. To prepare the asparagus, bend the stalks until the ends snap off naturally – these ends will be fibrous but full of flavour, so you can add them to the stock. Set aside the rest of the stalks.

2. Put the chicken stock in a saucepan and add the asparagus ends. Bring to the boil, then reduce to a low simmer.

3. In a separate large, heavy-based pan melt half the butter, then add the onion and ½ teaspoon of salt. Sauté gently over a medium heat until soft and translucent.

4. Add the rice and cook, stirring, for 2–3 minutes before adding the prosecco. Stir constantly until all the liquid has been absorbed, then add a ladleful of stock, avoiding the asparagus bobbing around in it.

5. Stir the rice intermittently to agitate the grains so that they release their starch – this makes the sauce creamy and unctuous. When the rice becomes dry rather than soupy, add another ladleful of stock.

6. Between stirring, chop the asparagus stalks into short pea-sized lengths, leaving the very tips of the spears whole. When you have used about half the stock, add the chopped asparagus to the rice and continue to cook, stirring and adding stock as needed.

7. After about 20 minutes, or when the stock is nearly used up, taste a few grains. They should be yielding and soft with a small residual bite. If they seem chalky, keep cooking. Turn off the heat, and vigorously stir in the remaining butter and the Parmesan. Season to taste and add enough stock to ensure the rice is wet enough to fall off a spoon when tilted.

8. While the rice rests, remove any large stalks from the herbs and chop finely. Taste and stir in the herbs before serving, sprinkled with Parmesan.

ASPARAGUS SOLDIERS AND PARMESAN CUSTARD

When Rowley Leigh was chef proprietor of Café Anglais restaurant in London, they used to serve anchovy toasts with Parmesan custard, which I often ordered. I was thrilled when he contributed this recipe, not least so that I could try to emulate a similar and probably simpler variation of the dish at home. The clean vegetal flavour of asparagus is perfectly suited to the savoury cheesy custard. Of course, if you don't have time to make the custard, I'm sure he wouldn't mind if you served the 'soldiers' with boiled eggs topped with cream and Parmesan as an easier version instead.

SERVES 6

20g (¾oz) butter, for greasing
240ml (8½fl oz) full-fat milk
75g (2½oz) Parmesan cheese, grated
240ml (8½fl oz) single cream
2 large egg yolks
1 large egg
pinch of cayenne pepper
1kg (2lb 4oz) asparagus
sea salt
toast, to serve (optional)

1. Preheat the oven to 140°C (120°C fan), 275°F, Gas mark 1, then lightly butter six 125ml (4fl oz) ramekin moulds or cups.

2. In a saucepan, combine the milk and 60g (2¼oz) of the Parmesan, saving a little Parmesan for the topping. Bring gently to a simmer, then remove from the heat and whisk until the cheese has completely melted.

3. In a bowl, whisk together the cream, egg yolks and egg, then whisk in the warm milk. Add ¼ teaspoon of salt and the cayenne, then pour into the moulds.

4. Place the moulds in a deep ovenproof dish and pour boiling water around them up to half their depth. Cover the dish with foil and bake for 30 minutes. Turn the oven off and leave until just before serving, up to 30 minutes.

5. Preheat the grill to high. Sprinkle the reserved Parmesan on the surface of the custards and place under the grill to brown for 30 seconds. Return them to the warm oven while you prepare the asparagus.

6. Snap off the woody ends of the asparagus. Bring a large pot of well-salted water to the boil and cook the asparagus for 2–3 minutes – the spears should still be firm and bright green – then drain.

7. Guests should dip the asparagus in the custard and suck the shoots. Serve with teaspoons or perhaps toast.

OPEN PUFF PASTRY

WITH ASPARAGUS, SOURED CREAM,
SMOKED SALMON AND WATERCRESS

As well as her seminal restaurant, Sally Clarke
also runs two food shops with cafés serving simple
but luxurious plates, like this. The ingredients are
the luxury element, yet the preparation, especially
in the case of this recipe, provides simplicity. You
could pick up all these items in a supermarket
after work and have something impressive on the
table with very little fuss.

....

SERVES 6 AS A STARTER

plain flour, for dusting
200g (7oz) all-butter puff pastry
2 large onions, very finely sliced
2 tablespoons olive oil, plus extra to drizzle
1 teaspoon chopped dill, plus a few sprigs to garnish
100g (3½oz) soured cream
small bunch of green asparagus, tough bases
    removed
100g (3½oz) smoked salmon
large bunch of watercress, thick stalks removed
sea salt and freshly ground black pepper

1. On a floured surface, roll the puff pastry into a rectangle roughly the size of a baking sheet (about 40 × 20cm/16 × 8in) and neaten the edges. Lift it on to the baking sheet and, with a knife, score a 1cm (½in) border around the edge. Using a fork, prick the central area of the dough but not the border. Chill while you prepare the rest of the ingredients.

2. Fry the onions in the olive oil in a large frying pan over a medium–high heat until soft and golden. Add half the chopped dill with salt and pepper, then drain over a sieve.

3. Season the soured cream with salt and pepper, and add the remaining chopped dill.

4. Preheat the oven to 180°C (160°C fan), 350°F, Gas mark 4. Bake the pastry for 12–16 minutes until puffed and pale golden. Remove from the oven and gently spread the drained onion over the centre (not over the border). Continue to bake for a further 6–8 minutes, or until the base of the pastry is firm and the edges are a deep golden colour.

5. Meanwhile, peel the lower two-thirds of each asparagus spear. Cook in salted boiling water for 3 minutes until tender, drain and lay on a plate. Drizzle with oil and season with salt and pepper.

6. Remove the pastry from the oven and cool a little, before cutting into 6 portions using a serrated knife. Lay the asparagus on top, then the smoked salmon in 'curls', followed by the watercress and dollops of the soured cream. Finish with the dill sprigs. Alternatively, leave the pastry whole, add the toppings as above and slice at the table.

GRILLED ASPARAGUS
WITH ALMOND AND ORANGE MOJO

When the phenomenally successful first Moro cookbook by husband and wife Sam and Sam Clark was published over 20 years ago, their tales of discovering the spices and flavours of North African, Spanish and Eastern Mediterranean cooking from their extensive travels began a new wave of cooking. This recipe that they wrote for the magazine was photographed in their beautiful London home, demonstrating how we can easily introduce these flavours to change familiar ingredients into something magical. They explain how mojo sauce 'originates from Moorish Andalusia with its use of almonds, orange and cumin. We first tried it in a restaurant in Antequera near Malaga called Arte de Cozina, which specializes in dishes that are steeped in history. Any leftover sauce is also delicious with chicken or fish. The extra step of grilling the asparagus will achieve a more complex, smoky flavour, which goes so well with the mojo.'

For the mojo
125g (4½oz) blanched almonds
125g (4½oz) roasted almonds
juice of 3 oranges, plus zest of 1
¼ teaspoon ground cumin
1 teaspoon sweet white wine vinegar

For the asparagus
1.5kg (3lb 5oz) firm asparagus
4 tablespoons extra virgin olive oil
juice of ½ lemon
sea salt and freshly ground black pepper

1. Start with the mojo. Place the almonds in a food processor and blitz to a powder. Continue to blitz for several minutes until the mixture begins to resemble butter. If your machine is struggling, add 1 tablespoon of the orange juice and continue until you have a smooth paste. Add the remaining orange juice and blitz again until the mixture has the consistency of double cream. Transfer to a bowl and add the orange zest, cumin and vinegar, and season to taste.
2. Remove the woody and stringy root ends of the asparagus by gently flexing the end of each spear until it snaps at its natural breaking point. Alternatively, peel the ends.
3. Bring a wide saucepan of salted water to the boil. Add the asparagus and cover while it comes back to the boil, then remove the lid and boil for 2–3 minutes until the asparagus is almost tender – or if you are not planning to grill them, cook for a minute longer until tender (you can test them by pricking with a skewer or sharp knife). Drain carefully.
4. Heat a griddle pan until smoking hot and lightly char the asparagus spears on both sides. Remove and place in a bowl, pour over the olive oil and lemon juice, season with salt and pepper and serve immediately, with the mojo poured over the top.

BEANS AND GREENS

I pick broad beans every day at this time of year, to get the beans while they are green inside the pods, before a pale skin forms that toughens them. They are sweet and tender, and it would be wrong to cook them when they're this perfect raw. Within half an hour, we're eating them in the shade of the veranda, on a wooden table, just with some olive oil, salt and Parmesan. A good ingredient has a power of its own and you need little else.

I don't like green beans or French beans served too al dente, when they can be squeaky; a little further cooking brings out more flavour. Serve them with pesto or I also like them stewed in tomato sauce: Greek-style with onions, garlic and a little cumin or Italian-style with olive oil and basil. A favourite salad of mine is cooked beans, ripe tomatoes, salty olives and anchovies, dressed with a mustardy vinaigrette and topped with a soft-boiled egg.

Early summer is the season for spinach, chard, sorrel and other greens – when it's warm enough for them to grow but before they start to go to seed. If you grow your own, they're a great cut-and-come-again crop, so you can keep harvesting throughout the season.

To keep in as many nutrients as possible, I avoid boiling green leaves: I wash them and put them dripping wet into a large pot over a high heat. Cover with a lid and steam in their own moisture for a minute or two before draining. All they need is your best olive oil and a squeeze of lemon, to eat hot or at room temperature. Or toss with raisins, pine nuts and sweated onions.

RECIPES

Broad bean spaghetti with Pecorino

Broad bean bruschetta

Braised summer peas with lettuce

Sea bass ceviche with broad beans, mint and lemon

Potatoes, green beans and pesto

Gratin of greens

Summer greens and soft cheese pie

Green lasagne

BROAD BEAN SPAGHETTI
WITH PECORINO

Rowley Leigh suggests Pecorino here because it combines with the sauce to make more of an emulsion than Parmesan would. In the same way that artisan 'bronze extruded' pasta has rougher edges, so it catches and holds the sauce. It all comes down to chemistry and none of these things should deter cooks from having a go with what they have available. So if you only have Parmesan and factory-made pasta, that's no reason not to make this.

SERVES 6

1kg (2lb 4oz) broad beans (in their pods)
450g (1lb) spaghetti
50g (1¾oz) butter
75g (2½oz) Pecorino cheese, grated
sea salt and freshly ground black pepper

1. Pod the broad beans and then peel off their skins with your thumbnail. Chop the raw beans very roughly. Bring a large saucepan of well-salted water to a rolling boil and drop in the spaghetti.
2. Heat a second large saucepan and melt the butter. Add the chopped beans with a pinch of salt and a ladleful of the pasta cooking water, then simmer very gently.
3. After 8 minutes, with the spaghetti still slightly hard, use tongs to lift the pasta out of the water and into the beans. Add 1 teaspoon of black pepper and stir, adding a little more of the pasta water until the pasta is just cooked.
4. Add two-thirds of the cheese and stir to make a creamy emulsion. Serve straight away, with a little sprinkling of the remaining cheese on each plate.

BROAD BEAN BRUSCHETTA

Picking the beans and then podding them myself is as much a part of the ritual as eating them. This is more about preparation than cooking. If you want to make a pile of freshly picked beans into lunch, just add toast. Call it bruschetta and rub with garlic, douse with good olive oil and smash the beans with grated Parmesan or Pecorino.

SERVES 4 AS A STARTER

700g (1lb 9oz) broad beans (in their pods)
50g (1¾oz) Pecorino cheese, grated
1 tablespoon lemon juice
4 tablespoons olive oil
handful of mint leaves, torn
sea salt and freshly ground black pepper

To serve
4 slices of sourdough bread
1 garlic clove, peeled

1. Pod the beans, keeping aside any that are larger than your thumbnail. Cook the larger beans and half of the smaller ones in a pan of salted boiling water for 2 minutes. Drain and refresh under cold water.
2. Leave the remaining smaller beans raw. Slip the skins off the larger beans if desired (this gives texture and colour variation). Mash all the beans, cooked and raw, in a pestle and mortar (or food processor), together with the grated Pecorino, lemon juice, olive oil and torn mint leaves, and some salt and pepper.
3. Toast the sourdough, then lightly rub with the garlic clove and top with the broad bean mixture.

BRAISED SUMMER PEAS

WITH LETTUCE

Cooked lettuce is silky and luxurious, and this is a good recipe to make with fresh peas that have become a bit mealy textured. You can use chicken or vegetable stock and vary the herbs to suit what you have to hand; mint, parsley or basil all work well.

SERVES 4–6 AS A SIDE DISH

50g (1¾oz) butter
4 shallots, finely chopped
8 Little Gem lettuces, quartered
500g (1lb 2oz) podded peas
300ml (10fl oz) chicken stock
handful of chopped herbs, such as parsley, mint
 or tarragon
sea salt and freshly ground black pepper

1. Melt 40g (1½oz) of the butter in a saucepan and sweat the shallots with a little salt for several minutes until they are soft and sweet.
2. Add the lettuce and the peas, and continue to cook for a minute before adding the chicken stock and seasoning well with salt and pepper. Reduce the heat and simmer gently for about 20 minutes, shaking the contents of the saucepan every now and then to prevent sticking.
3. To finish, stir in the remaining 10g (¼oz) butter and the chopped herbs.

SEA BASS CEVICHE

WITH BROAD BEANS, MINT AND LEMON

Sam and Sam Clark recommend this as an impressive-looking light lunch or starter. You can assemble it before your guests arrive too, so it's one less thing to deal with. Baby broad beans will not only be more tender, to complement the texture of the sea bass, but will look dainty too. If you only have overgrown beans, cook them a bit longer and slip off their outer skins to achieve a similar effect.

SERVES 6

400g (14oz) broad beans, podded (ideally
 thumbnail size)
450g (1lb) very fresh skinless sea bass fillets
juice of 2½ lemons, plus zest of 1½
2 teaspoons sweet white wine vinegar
2 tablespoons finely shredded mint leaves
1 small spring onion, very thinly sliced
1 tablespoon extra virgin olive oil
sea salt

1. Bring a saucepan of unsalted water to the boil and blanch the broad beans for about 2–3 minutes until tender. Drain in a colander and then cool under running water. If the broad beans are large, peel off their pale outer skins. Set aside.
2. With a very sharp knife, slice the sea bass paper thin, either directly down or slightly at an angle. Cover 6 individual serving plates with a single layer of the fish. This can be done up to 3 hours in advance – cover in clingfilm and chill in the refrigerator.
3. Ten minutes before you are ready to eat, mix together the lemon juice, vinegar and a good pinch of salt. Spoon evenly over the fish, lifting it up so that the underside gets a bit of the marinade as well as the top. Leave to cure for 3–5 minutes – 3 minutes will be medium rare, 5 minutes will be well done.
4. Now the finishing touches: grate the lemon zest directly on to the fish as evenly as possible. Sprinkle over the mint, spring onion and broad beans, drizzle with the olive oil and serve straight away.

POTATOES, GREEN BEANS AND PESTO

This mixture of beans, potatoes and pesto is a classic Ligurian dish, although it is usually served with pasta too. I like to use a variety of long beans that grow at this time of year for added colour and varied shapes – yellow, green, purple and even runner beans. Pesto is such an easy sauce to make and keeps well under a layer of oil in the refrigerator, so make extra to use throughout the next couple of weeks.

SERVES 6

2 garlic cloves, crushed
60g (2¼oz) pine nuts
100g (3½oz) basil
25g (1oz) Parmesan cheese, grated
2 tablespoons extra virgin olive oil
1.5kg (3lb 5oz) small waxy potatoes, halved
600g (1lb 5oz) mixed green and runner beans
large handful of rocket
sea salt and freshly ground black pepper

1. To make the pesto, put the garlic, pine nuts and a large pinch of salt in a pestle and mortar, and pound until almost smooth. Strip the basil leaves from the stalks and roughly chop. Add the leaves to the mortar in stages, pounding and grinding around the sides of the bowl. When the texture is fairly smooth, add the Parmesan and olive oil, and stir to combine. Taste for salt and add more if necessary.

2. Put the potatoes in a pan, cover with cold, well-salted water and bring to the boil. Cook for 10–15 minutes, or until tender. Top the beans and cut any large ones into smaller pieces. Steam the beans for 3–4 minutes (either over the potatoes as they cook, or separately) until they are soft but still al dente.

3. Drain the potatoes and put them into a large salad bowl. Add the beans and pesto, and mix while warm. Season with salt and pepper to taste. Just before serving, stir in the rocket leaves.

GRATIN OF GREENS

This is a household favourite and a great way to use the abundance of green leaves that appear in my vegetable box. It works well with all sorts of greens; I sometimes use beetroot tops, spinach or chard instead. It freezes well too and makes the perfect side dish to roast chicken, or served on its own with a salad.

SERVES 6

500g (1lb 2oz) cavolo nero, kale or a mixture
   of greens
500g (1lb 2oz) broccoli
25g (1oz) butter
2 tablespoons olive oil
8 garlic cloves, finely chopped
3 teaspoons plain flour
200ml (7fl oz) full-fat milk
a few gratings of nutmeg
½ teaspoon cayenne pepper
juice of ½ lemon
100g (3½oz) fresh or dried breadcrumbs
20g (¾oz) Cheddar cheese, grated
sea salt and freshly ground black pepper

1. Preheat the oven to 200°C (180°C fan), 400°F, Gas mark 6. Fill a large pot or saucepan with well-salted water and bring to the boil. Add the leaves and cook for 2–3 minutes, or until wilted and soft. Remove and refresh under cold water, squeeze dry, then chop finely. Cook the broccoli in the same water for 5 minutes, then drain and roughly chop.

2. In a large pot, heat the butter and oil over a medium heat, add the garlic and fry until starting to colour. Add the chopped leaves and broccoli. Season with salt and pepper and stir well, cooking for a minute so that the greens and garlic are well combined and heated through.

3. Sprinkle over the flour and stir well, then add the milk a little at a time, stirring and cooking until the greens are coated in a smooth sauce. Add the nutmeg, cayenne pepper and lemon juice, and season to taste.

4. Blitz half the mixture to a purée in a food processor, then mix with the remaining greens mixture. Transfer to a 30cm (12in) round gratin dish and cover the surface with the breadcrumbs and cheese.

5. Bake for 20 minutes. Remove and allow to sit (it continues cooking) for 5 minutes before serving.

SUMMER GREENS
AND SOFT CHEESE PIE

*Served with the tomato salad, this green-filled pie
makes a satisfying vegetarian meal. I use any leafy
greens I may have a glut of – sorrel, dandelion, turnip
tops and beetroot leaves. It's also a good opportunity
to try some British cheeses made in a Mediterranean
style, such as Westcombe ricotta and Medita, a feta-
style organic sheep's milk cheese made in Sussex.*

SERVES 6

600g (1lb 5oz) **large-leaf spinach**
400g (14oz) **chard (leaves and stalks)**
100ml (3½fl oz) **olive oil**
2 **red onions, roughly chopped**
20g (¾oz) **curly or flat-leaf parsley leaves,**
    roughly chopped
15g (½oz) **dill, chopped**
5g (⅛oz) **mint leaves, roughly chopped**
5g (⅛oz) **oregano leaves, roughly chopped**
250g (9oz) **ricotta cheese**
2 **eggs**
300g (10½oz) **feta cheese**
½ **lemon**
100g (3½oz) **filo pastry (11 sheets)**
sea salt and freshly ground black pepper

1. Preheat the oven to 180°C (160°C fan), 350°F,
Gas mark 4. Remove any tough stalks from the
greens, saving the chard stalks. Cut the chard stalks
into 1cm (½in) pieces and steam for 3–4 minutes,
then remove to a bowl. Steam the chard and spinach
leaves for 3–4 minutes until wilted. Alternatively,
if you don't have a steamer, boil in plenty of water,
which will take about a minute less. Strain the leaves
and stalks and, when they are cool enough to handle,
squeeze them thoroughly to remove all excess water,
then roughly chop.
2. In a large saucepan, heat 3 tablespoons of the oil
and sweat the onions with a large pinch of salt for
about 5 minutes until softened. Add the herbs, stir,
then add the greens. Season and cook for a minute.

3. In another large bowl, beat the ricotta and
eggs together, then crumble in large chunks of the
feta. Grate the zest from the lemon half and add
1 tablespoon of its juice. Fold the greens into the
cheese mixture and season well.
4. With the remaining oil, brush the inside of your
baking dish and lay a sheet of filo pastry so that it
covers the bottom and comes up the sides, with any
excess hanging over the edges. Brush the top of the
sheet with oil and repeat with 6 more sheets, brushing
with plenty of oil between the layers.
5. Spoon the greens mixture into the lined dish and
cover the top with a sheet of filo, tucking it in around
the sides and brushing the top well with oil. Then fold
the hanging edges over to make a parcel. Cover this
with the remaining 3 filo sheets, brushing the tops
with oil and tucking into the sides. Don't try to make
it too smooth: a bit of rucked surface will create a
good crisp texture on the top of the dish. Using a
skewer, make a few holes in the top to allow hot air
to escape. Lightly sprinkle with water and bake for
45–50 minutes, or until the top of the pie looks golden
brown and the pastry is crisp. If it still looks pale after
40 minutes, you may need to increase the temperature
to 200°C (180°C fan), 400°F, Gas mark 6.

GREEN LASAGNE

*A good lasagne has small amounts of filling between
numerous layers of pasta. This structure adds
to the texture and flavour. There's lots of room
for alternatives too: try kale, beetroot tops or
other brassicas.*

....

SERVES 6

1kg (2lb 4oz) mixed chard and spinach
650g (1lb 7oz) broccoli, cut into small florets
4 tablespoons olive oil
1 onion, finely chopped
1 leek, trimmed, washed and finely chopped
2 garlic cloves, finely chopped
1 teaspoon fennel seeds, crushed
15 lasagne sheets (ideally fresh)
200g (7oz) Parmesan cheese, grated
sea salt and freshly ground black pepper

For the béchamel
700ml (1¼ pints) full-fat milk
1 bay leaf
50g (1¾oz) butter, plus extra for greasing
4 tablespoons plain flour
a few gratings of nutmeg
½ teaspoon cayenne pepper

1. Strip the chard and spinach leaves from the stalks.
Fill your largest pan with water (about 5 litres/9 pints)
and add 1 tablespoon of salt. Bring to the boil and cook
the broccoli for about 4 minutes, or until completely
tender. Remove with a slotted spoon, drain and lay flat
on a tray to cool while you cook the green leaves in the
same water for 2–3 minutes. Remove, drain and lay on
another tray to cool. Keep the pan of water for later.
2. Heat 2 tablespoons of the oil in large pan and
sweat the onion and leek with a good pinch of salt for
about 10 minutes until soft but not coloured. Add the
broccoli, more salt and some pepper, and stir well.
Fry for a minute, then tip into a food processor and
blitz briefly to make a semi-smooth but still chunky
mixture. Scrape into a bowl and set aside.

3. In the same frying pan, heat the remaining oil and
fry the garlic and fennel seeds until the garlic begins
to brown. Add the cooked leaves, with salt and pepper,
and fry for a minute. Briefly blitz in the food processor,
then add to the bowl and stir.
4. For the béchamel, put the milk and bay leaf in a pan
and heat to just below boiling. In another pan, melt
the butter, add the flour and stir. Cook for 1 minute,
then add all the milk, stirring briskly. Bring to the boil,
stirring. Add the nutmeg, cayenne pepper and salt and
pepper. Remove the bay leaf.
5. Preheat the oven to 160°C (140°C fan), 325°F,
Gas mark 3. Boil the pasta sheets in the greens water
until al dente (according to the packet instructions),
then drain, leaving just enough water on them to stop
them sticking together.
6. Butter a 30 × 20cm (12 × 8in) baking dish. Cover the
base with a layer of pasta and dot with the vegetables,
then pour over a ladle of béchamel, season and
scatter over 2 tablespoons of the Parmesan. Repeat
for another 4 layers. For the fifth layer, spread with
béchamel and Parmesan only. Bake for 40 minutes.

COURGETTES

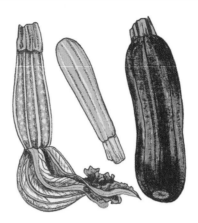

Of all Mediterranean vegetables, courgettes seem to grow most abundantly in the UK. In the last few years I've noticed many different varieties for sale – striped, yellow and round like small balloons – and often courgettes are sold with their pretty and edible flowers still attached.

When dealing with a glut of courgettes, I keep the smaller ones, which are less watery, for dishes like risotto, to fry and stir into pasta with Pecorino; or sliced thinly, fried and dressed with a dash of red wine vinegar, chopped chilli and torn mint. And if I have flowers, I'll use them too, torn over salads or cooked dishes as you might apply herbs. Larger courgettes are good for slow-cooking – sliced and fried gently with garlic until they collapse. I add lots of basil and serve these as a side or freeze batches to add to soups or frittatas when I'm in need of a quick fix.

RECIPES

Courgette fritti

Marinated courgettes and aubergine with burrata

Courgette, olive and preserved lemon salad

Courgette, broad bean, sheep's cheese and mint risotto

Courgette and goats' cheese risotto

COURGETTE FRITTI

These crisp-coated matchsticks with soft centres can be handed around on pretty plates or presented at the table as a delicious seasonal alternative to fries.

SERVES 4 AS A SMALL PLATE

300g (10½oz) 00 flour
4 tablespoons olive oil
250ml (9fl oz) warm water
12 small courgettes
1 egg white
2 litres (3½ pints) sunflower oil
sea salt

1. Mix the flour, olive oil and warm water together in a large bowl to make a batter. Set aside for 20 minutes.

2. Cut the courgettes into thin batons.

3. In a separate bowl, whisk the egg white to soft peaks and fold into the batter.

4. Heat the sunflower oil in a deep pan and test the temperature with a drop of the batter – it should sizzle and turn brown in a few seconds. Dip the courgette batons in the batter and drop into the oil, in batches. Fry for a minute, then scoop out and do the next batch. Sprinkle liberally with salt and serve.

5. Once the frying oil is cooled, strain and bottle to use another time when needed.

MARINATED COURGETTES AND AUBERGINE
WITH BURRATA

At the River Café, we used to prepare a wonderful Italian antipasti called zucchini scapece – *crisp courgette coins marinated in vinegar, chilli and mint. I've added aubergines, whose dense, meaty flavour tastes so good with the sweet courgettes, and the acidity of wine vinegar and mint to brighten the dish. Serve with burrata or mozzarella as a starter, or with tomato bruschetta for a light lunch.*

SERVES 6

2 medium courgettes (about 300g/10½oz)
1 aubergine (about 300g/10½oz)
olive oil, for frying and drizzling
small bunch of mint
1 red chilli, finely chopped
1–2 tablespoons best-quality red wine vinegar
6 balls of burrata cheese (or mozzarella)
sea salt and freshly ground black pepper

1. Cut the courgettes into 2mm (1/16in) discs and the aubergine into 4mm (¼in) slices. Lay these on kitchen paper with another sheet on top to dry them slightly.
2. Heat a large frying pan and add oil to generously cover the base. Add as many aubergine slices as you can without overlapping them, and fry over a medium–high heat for a minute or so before turning the pieces over so that they become golden brown on both sides. Remove to a piece of kitchen paper while you cook the rest. Use the same pan, with slightly less oil, to cook the courgettes in the same way.
3. Put the vegetables in a bowl, tear over the mint and scatter with the chilli, vinegar (start with half and add more later if necessary) and some salt. Gently turn everything with your hands and leave to marinate for 10 minutes, or all day if preferred.
4. Taste and add more vinegar and salt if necessary before arranging on 6 plates with a ball of burrata on each. Finish with a grinding of black pepper and a drizzle of oil.

COURGETTE, OLIVE AND PRESERVED LEMON SALAD

This Moroccan salad was inspired by a recipe served to me while staying with friends on the coast south of Casablanca. Preserved lemons are in every Moroccan kitchen, packed in salt, sometimes with additional spices. They are rinsed before use and the flesh and seeds are scooped out and discarded, leaving only the skin, so when a Moroccan recipe calls for 'finely chopped lemons', it generally means the chopped skin rather than the whole fruit. If you don't have preserved lemons, cut thin slices of fresh lemon and roast until soft and caramelized, then toss those through instead.

SERVES 6

about 750g (1lb 10oz) medium–large courgettes
2 tablespoons olive oil
2 garlic cloves, finely chopped
4 tablespoons finely chopped preserved lemon skin
100g (3½oz) Moroccan (purple or black brine-cured) olives, pitted and roughly torn
2 tablespoons mixed chopped flat-leaf parsley and mint leaves
juice of ½ lemon
sea salt and freshly ground black pepper

1. Top and tail the courgettes and grate using the largest holes of your grater. Put them in a colander and toss with 2 teaspoons of salt. Drain for 5 minutes, then squeeze well to remove any excess liquid.
2. In a large, heavy-based sauté pan or saucepan, heat the oil and cook the garlic over a medium heat until it just starts to colour. Add the courgettes and fry for about 5 minutes, stirring regularly so that they soften without taking on any colour. Add the chopped preserved lemon and the olives, stir well and cook for another minute or so.
3. Add the herbs and the lemon juice to taste, and season with pepper. Serve warm or at room temperature, either with some bread or a selection of other Moroccan vegetable dishes, or as a side dish with a tagine (see page 250) or kefte (see page 124).

COURGETTE, BROAD BEAN, SHEEP'S CHEESE AND MINT RISOTTO

At this time of year the vegetables are so tender and small and barely need any cooking, but if you're using larger beans, peel them first. Try to find courgettes with their flowers attached, or at least buy the flowers separately, as they make the dish look so pretty. Use any firm and creamy feta-style sheep's or goats' cheese.

40g (1½oz) butter
1 tablespoon olive oil
1 onion, finely chopped
1.5 litres (2⅔ pints) vegetable stock
700g (1lb 9z) risotto rice, such as vialone nano
125ml (4fl oz) white wine
400g (14oz) courgettes, very finely sliced, preferably using a mandoline
300g (10½oz) podded broad beans, any large ones peeled
150g (5½oz) sheep's or goats' cheese, cut into cubes
large sprigs of mint leaves, roughly chopped
courgette flowers, torn into strips
zest of ½ lemon
sea salt and freshly ground black pepper

1. In a large, heavy-based saucepan, heat 20g (¾oz) of the butter and the oil. Add the onion and a generous pinch of salt. Cook gently for about 10 minutes until soft but not coloured. Meanwhile, in a separate pan, heat the stock to boiling and then turn off the heat.
2. Add the rice to the onion, increase the heat slightly, stir well and then fry for a minute before adding the wine.
3. When the wine has been absorbed, add a ladle of hot stock and stir. Continue to do this, stirring regularly and always keeping the rice liquid enough so that it doesn't stick on the bottom. When it is starting to look creamy but the rice still has a chalky bite, add the courgettes, broad beans and a good pinch of salt.
4. Continue adding the stock and stirring. When the rice is soft with a bit of bite but no chalkiness, turn off the heat – this will usually take about 20 minutes. Cube the remaining 20g (¾oz) butter and beat in – with a little more stock, if needed – to make a creamy texture that is loose enough to drop from a spoon. Taste for seasoning and add salt and pepper if required. Finish by gently stirring in the cheese and the chopped mint leaves. Sprinkle over the courgette flowers and the lemon zest to serve.

COURGETTE AND GOATS' CHEESE RISOTTO

The late William Yeoward, greatly celebrated furniture designer, style maker and decorator, provided recipes for an issue of the magazine that were shot in his beautiful country home. These were dishes he served to his guests, and in his generous and hospitable way, he was graciously tolerant of dietary requirements! 'When the need arises, it's so important to be able to think outside the box and adapt. Some folk don't eat cows' milk products, so there's no Parmesan in the recipe and you can omit the butter and use more oil at the beginning.'

....

SERVES 6

2 tablespoons olive oil
25g (1oz) butter (optional)
1 onion, finely diced
300g (10½oz) risotto rice
1.25 litres (2 pints) hot chicken stock
4 medium courgettes
1 tablespoon chopped thyme
1 tablespoon chopped flat-leaf parsley
150g (5½oz) soft goats' cheese
zest of 1 lemon
sea salt and freshly ground black pepper

1. In a shallow, heavy-based pan, heat the oil and the butter (if using) until the butter has completely melted. Add the onion and a good pinch of salt and cook over a medium–low heat for several minutes so that the onion softens but doesn't colour.

2. Add the rice, stirring to coat in the oil and butter. Cook for a minute so that the rice almost begins to fry. Add a ladle of hot stock and, stirring occasionally, allow it to be absorbed before adding another.

3. Meanwhile, slice the skins of the courgettes into long strips by sliding them lengthways against the widest teeth of a grater. Roughly grate the insides of the courgettes and keep separate.

4. After about 10 minutes of cooking the rice, add the grated courgette cores to the risotto, along with some salt and pepper, the thyme and most of the parsley.

5. Continue to cook the rice, adding another ladle of the stock and allowing it to be absorbed before adding the strips of courgette skin. Season well with salt and pepper and cook for a further 5 minutes to soften the courgette cores. By this stage, the rice should be al dente; if not, continue cooking.

6. Add 1 tablespoon of the goats' cheese and vigorously stir this into the rice to create a creamy sauce. Add a little more stock or water if the risotto is looking sticky. Taste and season as necessary.

7. Sprinkle with the remaining parsley and the lemon zest, divide between 6 bowls and dot the surface with teaspoonfuls of the remaining goats' cheese.

ANCHOVIES

I'm talking about salted anchovies here – those plump meaty fillets that are preserved in salt and sold in jars or cans, sometimes still in salt or sometimes in oil. The oil tastes good too, so you shouldn't throw it away; add it to whatever you're cooking the anchovies with or use it to drench the toast they then lie on.

As an ingredient, salted anchovies are divisive: people fall into either category of lovers or haters of their umami-packed taste. But when it comes to using them as a seasoning, used with a light touch in the base of a tomato sauce, mixed with breadcrumbs to stuff sweet roasted peppers or

as part of a salad dressing, most people only notice a deep, flavoursome improvement to the dish.

I happen to love them as they are and happily eat them on toast with butter, if not straight out of the jar or can.

RECIPES

Chard soufflé with anchovy sauce

Runner and green beans with anchovy vinaigrette

Crostini with anchovies and butter

Roast artichokes with anchovies and aioli

CHARD SOUFFLÉ
WITH ANCHOVY SAUCE

Soufflés are immensely comforting – pillowy mouthfuls with a buttery sauce. You can prepare a soufflé to the last steps and keep it in the refrigerator for an hour or so before baking. Use a shallow serving dish: the rise will not disappoint and it will cook in less time.

SERVES 6 AS A STARTER OR SMALL MAIN COURSE

For the anchovy sauce
400ml (14fl oz) white wine
6 garlic cloves, halved
10 salted anchovy fillets in oil
200g (7oz) very cold unsalted butter, cubed

For the soufflé
400g (14oz) Swiss or rainbow chard
400ml (14fl oz) full-fat milk
50g (1¾oz) unsalted butter
4 tablespoons self-raising flour
½ teaspoon cayenne pepper
a few gratings of nutmeg
4 egg yolks, plus 6 whites
sea salt and freshly ground black pepper

1. For the anchovy sauce, put the wine and garlic into a small saucepan, bring to the boil, then cook until reduced by half (you want at least 200ml/7fl oz). Strain through a sieve into a bowl and set aside, then return the garlic to the pan.

2. Roughly chop the anchovies and add to the garlic. Cook over a low heat until they begin to melt, squashing the garlic against the side of the pan so that it breaks up a little.

3. Add the wine reduction and chunks of butter, 1–2 at a time. Whisk as they melt into the sauce to form an emulsion. When all are incorporated, push the sauce through the sieve, pressing through the garlic and discarding any tough bits. Set aside.

4. Preheat the oven to 200°C (180°C fan), 400°F, Gas mark 6. Remove the stalks from the chard and boil in a pan of salted water for 1–2 minutes until floppy. Drain, refresh under cold water and then squeeze out as much moisture as you can. In a food processor, chop the chard very finely and set aside.

5. Warm the milk in a small pan until just below boiling. In a large saucepan, melt the butter. Use some to brush the insides of a soufflé dish up to the rim.

6. Add the flour to the remaining butter and cook, stirring, for 1–2 minutes over a low heat. You want the flour to cook slightly without the butter browning. Pour all the hot milk over the flour and butter, and stir to combine and form a smooth liquid. Increase the heat so that it bubbles, stirring with a wooden spoon, until the mixture thickens to the consistency of thick cream.

7. Add this to the chopped chard in the food processor with the cayenne and nutmeg. Add the egg yolks and season with plenty of salt and pepper – it should taste full of flavour. Decant into a large bowl and set aside.

8. In another bowl, whisk the egg whites with a pinch of salt until they form stiff peaks. Fold them carefully into the chard béchamel and pour the whole mixture into the prepared soufflé dish.

9. Bake for 20–25 minutes until the top is risen and browned, and the middle feels wobbly. Warm through the anchovy sauce to serve. This is delicious with a lettuce and shaved fennel salad to mop up the sauce.

2 large or 4 small shallots
2 tablespoons best-quality red wine vinegar
flaked sea salt
300g (10½oz) green beans
700g (1lb 9oz) runner beans
8 salted anchovy fillets in oil (try to find an Italian
    or Spanish brand)
2 teaspoons Dijon mustard
4 tablespoons extra virgin olive oil
10g (¼oz) basil leaves
10g (¼oz) flat-leaf parsley leaves
sea salt and freshly ground black pepper

RUNNER AND GREEN BEANS
WITH ANCHOVY VINAIGRETTE

Delicious served warm or cold, this makes an excellent accompaniment to chicken or lamb chops, or eat it on its own as a light meal with added soft-boiled eggs on top. It's a particularly English thing to grow runner beans and those who love them describe the texture as 'buttery'. Try to choose smaller beans, as the larger ones can be stringy, or use any mixture of beans, including podded fresh borlotti or cannellini, although these will need a longer cooking time. Pictured on page 131.

1. Peel, halve and finely slice the shallots. Put them in a small bowl and pour over the vinegar, add a pinch of flaked sea salt and toss them until well coated in the vinegar. Leave to macerate for at least 15 minutes.
2. Cut just the tops off the beans and leave the tails on. Cut the runner beans into shorter lengths, about the same length as the green beans. Cook in salted boiling water for 2–3 minutes until tender (or steam for 3–4 minutes). Drain and cover to keep warm.
3. To make the dressing, roughly chop the anchovies and pound them to a rough paste using a pestle and mortar. Stir in the mustard and then strain the vinegar from the shallots, keeping the shallots aside, and mix this into the anchovies. Using a fork or a small whisk, add the oil in a thin stream, whisking constantly to make a thick emulsion. Season with a little salt and pepper to taste (the anchovies will provide plenty of salt).
4. Put the beans in a salad bowl with the shallots. Roughly chop or tear the basil and parsley, and add to the beans. Pour over the anchovy dressing and toss well. Taste a bean for seasoning and add more salt and pepper as necessary.

CROSTINI
WITH ANCHOVIES AND BUTTER

There is a small restaurant near where I used to live in Florence that serves this dish – the simplest but most delicious combination of three perfect ingredients. It reminds me of the importance of 'less is more' in summer cooking, the love that Italians have for anchovies and the pleasure that can be derived from assembling these simple ingredients.

SERVES 6

6–12 slices of best-quality white sourdough bread
6–12 anchovy fillets (preserved in salt or oil)
30g (1oz) cold unsalted butter (Italian if possible, which is lighter and creamier)
1 lemon

1. Grill or toast the bread so that it is coloured on both sides. Allow to cool (you want the butter to remain firm).

2. If you are using salted anchovies, run them under cold water and gently open the 2 fillets to expose the backbone. Remove this and discard so that you are left with 2 clean fillets. Pat dry on a piece of kitchen paper and repeat with the others. For anchovy fillets in oil, just remove from the oil and dab off the excess with kitchen paper.

3. Cut the butter into enough slices for each piece of bread and lay it on top. Lay 1–2 anchovy fillets on top of each slice and grate over a few strands of lemon zest before serving.

ROAST ARTICHOKES
WITH ANCHOVIES AND AIOLI

It's characteristic of Sally Clarke to write such a simple and elegant recipe, and she echoes my feelings when she says 'artichokes and anchovies attract both lovers and haters – I love them – and especially together in the same dish, as below! In the summer, we buy the purple-leaf artichokes from Italy and France. I am a great fan of anchovies too – raw fillets, simply sprinkled with lemon juice and olive oil, make a perfect "appetizer".'

SERVES 6

9–12 baby violet artichokes
1 lemon, sliced
2–3 bay leaves
extra virgin olive oil, for drizzling
1 teaspoon finely chopped rosemary
sea salt and freshly ground black pepper

For the dressing
12 salted anchovy fillets in oil
zest of 1 lemon
1 garlic clove, crushed to a paste with a little salt
about 4 tablespoons extra virgin olive oil

To serve
2 tablespoons chopped flat-leaf parsley
Quick Aioli (see opposite)
crusty bread

1. Remove and discard the outer leaves from the artichokes and peel the stems. Trim the coarse bases at an angle so that all are about the same length. Place them in a pan of salted cold water with the lemon slices and bay leaves, and bring to the boil. Cover with a small plate or saucer to keep them submerged during cooking. Simmer for 5–7 minutes until almost tender when pierced with a sharp knife. Drain, cut in half lengthways and carefully remove the central 'choke' (if any) with a small, sharp knife.
2. Preheat the oven to 160°C (140°C fan), 325°F, Gas mark 3. Lay the artichoke halves cut-side up in a baking dish. Drizzle with oil and sprinkle with salt, pepper and the rosemary. Roast for 5–7 minutes, or until they start to colour at the edges.
3. To make the dressing, roughly chop the anchovy fillets, then add the lemon zest and garlic, with salt and pepper and enough olive oil to make a pouring consistency. Remove the dish from the oven and spoon the dressing over each artichoke. Return to the oven and roast for 3–5 minutes.
4. Remove from the oven, scatter with the chopped parsley and serve warm or at room temperature with the aioli and crusty bread.

QUICK AIOLI

While not a classic aioli recipe, this one is simple to prepare and the right balance of lemon juice cuts the richness. Be sure to use a flavourful olive oil.

SERVES 6

2 egg yolks
150ml (5fl oz) extra virgin olive oil
juice of ½ lemon
1 garlic clove, crushed to a paste with a little salt
sea salt and freshly ground black pepper

1. Whisk the yolks in a medium bowl until smooth. Pour the olive oil into the yolks drop by drop, while continuously whisking, until a thick mayonnaise is created. If the mixture curdles at any stage, start again with fresh yolks in a fresh bowl.
2. Once all the oil has been incorporated, add the lemon juice and garlic, and season with salt and pepper to taste.

TOMATOES

Many tomatoes are grown in the temperate summer climate of the Isle of Wight, which allows us to eat UK produce earlier in the season, but most of the tomatoes that appear on the shelves earlier in the year come from southern Europe or further afield. If you can wait until the natural season for tomatoes and not buy year round, you will be rewarded by sweet, ripe flavours and myriad varieties. Look for heritage tomatoes in farmers' markets to experience a spectrum of colours, textures and shapes.

Ripeness is the key to flavour. Big bull's heart tomatoes are good for sauces – they have denser flesh and fewer seeds than other varieties. Cherry tomatoes are generally sweeter and travel well, but try to buy them on the vine. I never keep my tomatoes in the refrigerator, as it dulls the flavour.

For rustic tomato bruschetta, halve a big fleshy tomato and drag it, cut-side down, over toast rubbed in garlic, douse with olive oil and salt and serve with mozzarella or slices of cured ham.

If you grow tomatoes and have a glut, or just want to buy them up from the market at a reduced price when they are at the height of their season, you can preserve them as passata or slow-roast them with thyme and oil to keep in the freezer for winter.

It seems obvious, but if you don't have really tasty, fresh tomatoes to cook with, use good-quality jarred or tinned tomatoes to make a cooked sauce.

RECIPES

Tomatoes, marjoram and salted ricotta salad

Roast aubergine, tomatoes and fregola

Baked tomato gratin

Tomato-braised green beans

Charmoula chicken with potatoes and tomatoes

TOMATO, MARJORAM
AND SALTED RICOTTA SALAD

This salad looks and tastes even better with a mixture of tomato varieties, sizes and colours. Some of my favourites to look out for or grow myself are classic plum-shaped San Marzano, juicy ribbed Costoluto, beefsteak Marmande, sweet Golden Boy and tiny Yellow Pear. Store tomatoes out of the refrigerator and always eat them at room temperature; you'll get much more flavour out of them. Salted ricotta is hard enough to grate and is noticeably salty, so it adds to the seasoning of the other ingredients. You could use feta or even a salty hard cheese like Pecorino or Parmesan, or British Berkswell.

SERVES 6

1kg (2lb 4oz) mixed tomatoes (the ripest and
    sweetest you can find)
1 garlic clove, peeled
80g (3oz) Kalamata or other strong black olives,
    pitted and roughly torn
1 tablespoon mint leaves
2 tablespoons marjoram leaves
1 tablespoon best-quality red wine vinegar
3 tablespoons extra virgin olive oil
100g (3½oz) salted ricotta cheese
sea salt and freshly ground black pepper

1. Cut the tomatoes into wedges of various sizes, removing any hard white cores as you go.
2. Cut the garlic clove in half and rub it around the inside of your salad bowl.
3. Put the tomatoes in the bowl with the olives and herbs. Pour over the vinegar and oil, season with salt and pepper and toss. Shave thin slices of the ricotta and scatter over the salad. Serve as a side dish or on its own with toasted sourdough rubbed with garlic and olive oil.

ROAST AUBERGINE, TOMATOES AND FREGOLA

This is a robust salad with flavours reminiscent of a caponata. Fregola are small pearls of semolina flour dough, a speciality of Sardinia. They have a firm, nutty bite that contrasts well with the soft vegetables, but you could use giant couscous, small pasta or rice. The extra starch makes this salad into a proper meal.

SERVES 6

450g (1lb) cherry tomatoes, halved
4–6 tablespoons olive oil
1 large aubergine, cut into cubes
3 celery sticks, cut into batons
150g (5½oz) fregola
sea salt and freshly ground black pepper

For the dressing
20g (¾oz) flat-leaf parsley, chopped
20g (¾oz) basil, chopped
10g (¼oz) mint, chopped
½ tablespoon red wine vinegar
2 tablespoons extra virgin olive oil
pinch of chilli flakes

1. Preheat the oven to 180°C (160°C fan), 350°F, Gas mark 4. Lay the tomatoes in one layer on a roasting tray, pour over 1 tablespoon of the oil and season well with salt and pepper. Roast until they slightly collapse – about 30 minutes. Carefully spoon on to a plate.
2. Increase the oven temperature to 200°C (180°C fan), 400°F, Gas mark 6. Using the same tray, lay the aubergine cubes in a single layer. Drizzle with 2–3 tablespoons of the oil and add plenty of salt. Roast for about 20 minutes until soft and coloured, then remove. Using the same tray, roast the celery with most of the remaining oil for about 15 minutes until soft and starting to colour.
3. Boil the fregola in well-salted water for 7 minutes. Drain, then toss in a bowl with the last splash of oil. Mix together all the dressing ingredients. Add the vegetables to the fregola, then the dressing and toss together.

BAKED TOMATO GRATIN

I admired the late William Yeoward's thrifty attitude to home cooking, but he never forfeited quality and his table decorations elevated every meal. 'I come from the school of waste not, want not: ripe tomatoes, stale bread and that last glass of wine goes into a big terracotta pot and becomes something wonderful.'

SERVES 6

4 garlic cloves, halved
1 large red onion, roughly chopped
120ml (4fl oz) extra virgin olive oil
250g (9oz) white sourdough or ciabatta, torn into
    roughly 6cm (2½in) chunks
1.5kg (3lb 5oz) large, very ripe tomatoes
125ml (4fl oz) red wine
20g (¾oz) basil, chopped
25g (1oz) Parmesan cheese, grated
sea salt and freshly ground black pepper

1. Preheat the oven to 200°C (180°C fan), 400°F, Gas mark 6. Put the garlic, onion, 6 tablespoons of the oil and 1 teaspoon of salt into the bottom of an earthenware or heavy baking dish (large enough to fit the rest of the ingredients later) and cook for 15 minutes.
2. While the onion is softening, put the torn bread on to a baking tray and place it on the lower shelf of the oven for 5–8 minutes to dry out slightly.
3. Cut the tomatoes into quarters, removing any tough white cores.
4. Remove the onion dish from the oven and add the tomatoes, wine, bread and lots of black pepper, stirring everything together well. Bake for 45 minutes, stirring the mixture occasionally so that the top doesn't get too brown.
5. Remove from the oven, add the remaining olive oil and the basil and stir well. Increase the oven temperature to 250°C (230°C fan), 500°F, Gas mark 10, sprinkle the grated Parmesan all over the top and bake for another 10 minutes so that the top becomes crisp and brown. Serve in the dish.

TOMATO-BRAISED GREEN BEANS

I have never been a fan of squeaky, al dente green beans. I much prefer vegetables that are cooked to the point where they are yielding their softer characteristics. Here they are bathed in a sweet tomato sauce and the flavours of both suit each other well. Pile it high in a serving bowl and serve hot with roast lamb or fish, or cook ahead and leave to cool to room temperature for an easy outdoor lunch.

SERVES 6

4 tablespoons olive oil
1 onion, finely sliced
1kg (2lb 4oz) really ripe, large tomatoes
800g (1lb 12oz) green beans, topped but not tailed
sea salt

To serve
small bunch of herbs, such as flat-leaf parsley, basil,
   oregano, mint or dill, chopped
extra virgin olive oil

1. Heat the oil in a wide-bottomed, lidded casserole or deep frying pan with a lid. Fry the onion with a generous pinch of salt over a medium heat for at least 10 minutes, or until soft and sweet.
2. Meanwhile, put the tomatoes in a large bowl and cover with boiling water. Leave for 30 seconds, then drain, refresh under cold water and slip off the skins. Cut the tomatoes in half, scoop out the seeds and cut out any white cores. Roughly chop the flesh.
3. When the onion is cooked, add the tomatoes and some more salt and cook for 5 minutes or so until you have a thick sauce. Add the beans, some more salt and a splash of water, and stir to coat everything before covering with a lid. Cook for up to 20 minutes, stirring occasionally so that the bottom doesn't catch. When the beans are ready, they should be completely soft and well coated in sauce. Remove from the heat and add the herbs and a good glug of oil. Serve hot, warm or at room temperature.

40g (1½oz) coriander
20g (¾oz) flat-leaf parsley
4 garlic cloves, crushed
2 tablespoons ground cumin
1 tablespoon smoked sweet paprika
juice of ½ lemon
3 tablespoons extra virgin olive oil
6 chicken legs
1kg (2lb 4oz) large waxy potatoes, peeled
500g (1lb 2oz) large tomatoes
100g (3½oz) Kalamata olives
sea salt and freshly ground black pepper

To serve
**herb salad of rocket, Little Gem lettuce and
coriander, mint and parsley leaves, seasoned and
dressed with extra virgin olive oil and lemon juice**

CHERMOULA CHICKEN
WITH POTATOES AND TOMATOES

*Chermoula is a North African marinade made
using coriander, smoked sweet paprika and cumin.
The chicken and potatoes are cooked together in
one pot, allowing the flavours to seep into each other.
At the height of the tomato season it seems natural
to use fresh tomatoes to make a sauce, even if it
requires a little more preparation. It will taste
lighter and fresher with fresh tomatoes, especially
if you don't cook the sauce for too long. Canned peeled
tomatoes are a perfectly acceptable substitute;
just drain them from their juices before you cut
them up, and cook them a little bit longer.*

1. Preheat the oven to 180°C (160°C fan), 350°F, Gas
mark 4. Put the herbs, garlic, cumin, paprika, lemon
juice and 1 tablespoon of the oil into a blender with
1 teaspoon of salt and some pepper. Blend to a paste.
Cut 4 slits in each chicken leg and put them in a bowl.
Add all the paste and rub it into the chicken.

2. Cut the potatoes and the tomatoes into 5mm (¼in)
thick discs. Choose an ovenproof dish large enough
to fit all the chicken pieces in a single layer, with room
underneath for 2–3 layers of potatoes and tomatoes.
Pour a little of the remaining oil in the bottom of the
dish and spread the potatoes and tomatoes into layers,
seasoning with salt and pepper, and scattering with
the olives.

3. Lay the chicken pieces, and any remaining
paste, over the potatoes. Drizzle with the rest of
the oil and bake on the lower shelf of the oven for
1¼–1½ hours. The chicken skin should be crisp and
brown and the potatoes tender to the point of a knife.
Serve with the herb salad.

SPICE CUPBOARD

Spices are like magic dust that transform and enhance flavours; an easy trick to turn simple ingredients into something different and special. Some spices sweeten, some add heat and others add fragrance.

A little goes a long way; try adding a teaspoon of cumin or coriander seeds to a dish of braised lentils, some cardamom pods and a cinnamon stick cooked with plain rice, caraway seeds in a cabbage salad or a mix of turmeric, paprika and black pepper rubbed into chicken skin or fennel seeds rubbed into pork add instant flavour.

You can buy most spices already ground, although they will stay fresh longer if you buy them whole and grind them as you need them. I take great pleasure in crushing spices in a pestle and mortar and smelling the released aromas.

When a recipe calls for a spice blend, make extra and use it to enliven other dishes.

RECIPES

Moroccan carrot salad

Spiced cauliflower salad

Spiced potatoes

Smacked cucumber salad

Mechoui lamb with harissa, preserved lemon and goats' curd

Lamb kefte with herb salad and spicy yogurt

MOROCCAN CARROT SALAD

There's a great Moroccan shop on London's Golborne Road where I buy painted dishes and plates. Colourful, gently spiced dishes such as this are lovely eaten together like mezze with lots of things to choose from on the table. I love the way the sweetness of the carrots tastes with the fragrant spices.

....

SERVES 6

4 medium carrots, peeled and left whole
2 tablespoons olive oil
1 onion, diced
1 teaspoon ground coriander
1 teaspoon ground cumin
20g (¾oz) coriander, leaves roughly chopped
1 teaspoon honey
1 tablespoon lemon juice
sea salt and freshly ground black pepper

1. Cook the carrots in a pan of boiling water for 3–4 minutes until softened but still retaining a little crunch. You can test them by piercing with a skewer – it should meet some resistance. Drain and leave to cool, then slice thinly on a diagonal.

2. Heat the oil in a sauté pan and fry the onion with a pinch of salt for 5 minutes, or until soft and sweet but not coloured. Add the ground spices and the carrot slices to the pan with a splash of water and more salt and some pepper, and continue to cook for 3–5 minutes until the carrots are completely soft.

3. Add the chopped coriander, honey and lemon juice, season and mix well before serving. This can be eaten warm or cold, either on its own or as part of a mixture of dishes.

SPICED CAULIFLOWER SALAD

This delicious recipe by restaurateur and cookbook author Stevie Parle is good served hot or at room temperature, as a lunch or part of a bigger meal.

SERVES 4–6

35g (1¼oz) currants
pinch of saffron strands
1 large cauliflower, broken into florets
1 large red onion, thinly sliced
3 garlic cloves, thinly sliced
4 tablespoons olive oil
½ mild red chilli, deseeded and thinly sliced
1½ teaspoons cumin seeds
1½ teaspoons coriander seeds
1 teaspoon allspice berries
2 large plum tomatoes, chopped
handful each of mint, flat-leaf parsley and coriander
   leaves, roughly chopped
squeeze of lemon juice
sea salt

1. Bring a large pan of salted water to the boil. Put the currants in a bowl and cover with a ladleful of the boiling water. Put the saffron in another bowl with 1 tablespoon of boiling water. Soak for 10 minutes.
2. Blanch the cauliflower for 3 minutes in the boiling water until just tender, then drain in a colander.
3. Place the onion and garlic in a large frying pan along with 3 tablespoons of the olive oil and a pinch of salt. Fry gently for about 7 minutes until soft. Add the chilli to the pan.
4. Meanwhile, grind the cumin, coriander and allspice into a powder, then stir into the onion and cook for a few minutes until they smell fragrant.
5. Stir in the cauliflower, then drain the currants and add, along with the saffron water. Stir in the tomatoes, along with the remaining oil and a splash of water.
6. Cook for a few minutes until the water starts to evaporate and the cauliflower has absorbed the flavours, then leave to cool. Season well with salt, then stir through the herbs with the lemon juice.

SPICED POTATOES

Simple fried potatoes are made extra special with a dusting of spices and this recipe is excellent served with the lamb recipes on pages 123–4 or as part of a selection of other vegetable dishes.

SERVES 6

1.5kg (3lb 5oz) large waxy potatoes, such as
   Charlotte or Linzer Delikatess
200ml (7fl oz) olive oil
1 teaspoon ground turmeric
2 teaspoons ground cumin
½ teaspoon ground cinnamon
1 teaspoon ground ginger
1 teaspoon sweet paprika
sea salt

1. Peel the potatoes and cut into 2cm (¾in) cubes. Heat the oil in a large, wide, shallow pan until very hot and fry the potatoes until brown and crisp on all sides.
2. Add 1–2 teaspoons of salt and the spices and toss well, frying for about another minute so that the potatoes can absorb the flavours. Taste for salt and add more as needed.

SMACKED CUCUMBER SALAD

This is messy feasting food – big bowls of rice, maybe the Lu rou fan (see page 42), paper tablecloths and bottles of beer, chopsticks and lots of plates. Amy Poon, who wrote this recipe as part of a selection of Chinese dishes to serve together, says 'whenever I think of smacked cucumber salad, my mouth salivates. The perfect smacked cucumber is salted where the moistures are drawn out from the cucumber, giving it a refreshing crunch. If you don't want to make the chilli oil, you can find one in lots of local deli shops or Chinese supermarkets such as SeeWoo and Loon Fung in Chinatown. Tiger dressing also works well as a salad dressing for the hardier leaves such as kale.'

....

SERVES 4

2 cucumbers, preferably ridged

1 tablespoon caster sugar

1 garlic clove, peeled

sea salt

1 tablespoon finely chopped coriander, to serve

For the tiger dressing

1 garlic clove, peeled

1 green jalapeño chilli

80ml (2½fl oz) Chinkiang black rice vinegar

2 tablespoons sesame oil

25g (1oz) caster sugar

2 tablespoons rapeseed oil

pinch of white pepper

For the chilli oil

75g (2½oz) dried red chillies

¼ teaspoon fennel seeds

1 star anise

350ml (12fl oz) cold-pressed rapeseed oil

5–6 garlic cloves, finely sliced

1 small shallot, finely diced

75g (2½oz) Korean chilli flakes

40g (1½oz) caster sugar

70ml (2½fl oz) dark soy sauce

1. Cut the cucumbers in half lengthways and use a spoon to remove the seeds. Turn cut-sides down and crush with the flat part of a knife or a rolling pin. Rub with the caster sugar and 1 tablespoon of salt and leave the cucumber to macerate for at least 1 hour, ideally overnight, to draw out the moisture.

2. Rinse the salt and sugar from the cucumbers and pat dry. Crush the garlic clove with a knife and rub on to the cut sides, then chop the cucumbers into 2cm (¾in) chunks.

3. For the tiger dressing, crush the garlic clove and cut the jalapeño chilli lengthways. Mix the remaining ingredients together with ½ teaspoon of fine sea salt and the white pepper. Add the crushed garlic and chilli, then let it infuse for a few hours, preferably overnight. Give it a good whisk to emulsify before using, or put into a sterilized bottle to shake.

4. For the chilli oil, toast the dried red chillies in a pan over a medium heat, taking care not to burn them. When fragrant and turning light brown, set aside to cool and, once cool, blitz to a powder in a spice grinder. Toast the fennel seeds and star anise for about a minute and set aside to cool.

5. Heat the rapeseed oil in a pan. Add the toasted fennel seeds and star anise, garlic and shallot. Fry until golden, then strain the oil, discarding the solids.

6. In a pan, heat the oil to 160°C (325°F) and tip in the Korean chilli flakes and blitzed chilli powder. Stir and allow to infuse for 5 minutes before splashing some cold water into the oil to extract the red pigments (sometimes the oil is a little pale, but this will ensure that glistening redness). Season with 1½ teaspoons of salt and add the sugar and soy sauce. Pour the oil into a sterilized glass bottle and allow to infuse overnight in the refrigerator.

7. In a bowl, combine the cucumber with 160ml (5½fl oz) of the dressing, 60ml (4 tablespoons) of the chilli oil, 80g (3oz) chilli pulp from the oil and the coriander. Serve in bowls, spooning over the liquid.

MECHOUI LAMB

WITH HARISSA, PRESERVED LEMON
AND GOATS' CURD

Sam and Sam Clark's succulent dish of slow-cooked
lamb shoulder smothered in a spicy marinade is
inspired by the dishes they discovered in the souks of
Morocco. Serve with the spiced potatoes on page 119.

....

SERVES 6

about 2kg (4lb 8oz) shoulder of lamb, skin on but
    fat trimmed
4 tablespoons olive oil
200g (7oz) goats' curd or fresh, soft goats' cheese
150g (5½oz) Harissa (see opposite), plus 50g
    (1¾oz) to serve
20g (¾oz) coriander
2 tablespoons finely chopped preserved lemon
2 tablespoons ground cumin
freshly ground black pepper

1. Preheat the oven to 250°C (230°C fan), 500°F, Gas
mark 10. With a sharp knife, slash the skin of the lamb
in a few places, then transfer to a large roasting tray.
2. In a food processor, combine the olive oil, goats'
curd or goats' cheese, the 150g (5½oz) harissa,
coriander, preserved lemon, cumin and some pepper,
and blitz until completely smooth. Pour the mixture
over the lamb and rub all over. Pour 150ml (5fl oz)
water into the tray, cover tightly with foil and place the
lamb in the oven, reducing the temperature to 160°C
(140°C fan), 325°F, Gas mark 3. Slow-roast for about
4 hours until the meat is soft and falling off the bone –
remove the foil after 3 hours and baste the lamb with
the cooking juices several times.
3. When the meat is tender, remove from the oven
and transfer to a large wooden board, retaining the
cooking juices to use as a gravy. Leave to rest, loosely
covered in the foil, for 20–30 minutes.
4. Make a gravy by pouring off any excess fat from
the juices and then adding a little water for a thinner
consistency. Serve with the gravy and the extra harissa
on the side.

HARISSA

This recipe makes enough for the mechoui lamb, plus
an extra jar, which will keep, covered with a little olive
oil, for 10 days in the refrigerator.

....

200g (7oz) red chillies, halved lengthways and
    deseeded
1 garlic clove, crushed to a paste with a little salt
1 red pepper, roasted or grilled, skin peeled and
    deseeded
2 tablespoons caraway seeds, toasted and ground
1½ tablespoons cumin seeds, toasted and ground
4 tablespoons olive oil
1 teaspoon smoked sweet paprika
2 tablespoons sweet red wine vinegar
sea salt

1. Put the chillies and 1 teaspoon of salt in a food
processor and blitz until very smooth. Add the garlic,
red pepper, caraway and cumin, and process again
briefly until well mixed.
2. Transfer to a bowl and add the oil, paprika and
vinegar. Stir and season with salt.

LAMB KEFTE
WITH HERB SALAD AND SPICY YOGURT

These are an interpretation of the wonderful street food snacks I've eaten in the rural markets of Morocco, where stallholders cook these skewers over charcoal braziers. They are then sold rolled in flatbreads with handfuls of herbs and chopped onion. You will need 6–12 metal skewers, or you can use wooden ones, but soak in water for at least 15 minutes beforehand to stop them singeing.

....

SERVES 6

For the kefte
1.5kg (3lb 5oz) minced fatty lamb
1 medium onion, grated
3 tablespoons ground cumin
2 tablespoons ground turmeric
1 teaspoon smoked sweet paprika
½ teaspoon chilli powder
10g (¼oz) mint leaves, finely chopped
10g (¼oz) flat-leaf parsley, finely chopped
2 eggs, beaten
sea salt and freshly ground black pepper

For the herb salad
40g (1½oz) each of coriander, flat-leaf parsley
    and mint, leaves picked
½ medium red onion, finely chopped
1 tablespoon lemon juice
3 tablespoons extra virgin olive oil

For the spicy yogurt
600g (1lb 5oz) thick Greek-style yogurt
1 garlic clove, crushed
2 teaspoons ground cumin
1 tablespoon harissa

To serve
flatbreads

1. Put the minced lamb into a large bowl with the other kefte ingredients and some salt and pepper, and mix well; this is best done with your hands so that you can get all the spices and flavours incorporated into the meat.

2. Take a small handful of mince in the palm of your hand and shape it into a long sausage shape around a skewer. Press it quite firmly to make it stick. You could make either 1 large skewer or 2 thinner skewers per person. Cover and refrigerate for at least 30 minutes.

3. For the herb salad, put the herb leaves and onion into a bowl and set aside. Mix the lemon juice and oil to make a dressing and season well with salt and pepper. Just before you are ready to serve, dress the leaves and toss well.

4. To make the spicy yogurt, mix together all the ingredients and season well. Refrigerate until needed.

5. Cook the skewers under a medium grill (or in a griddle pan or on a barbecue) for 2–4 minutes on each side, depending on their thickness (try not to overcook or they will dry out). Serve hot with the herb salad, spicy yogurt and warmed flatbreads.

CHICKEN

These are some of my favourite chicken recipes: delicious and simple ways to really appreciate the qualities of a good bird. Boneless chicken makes for easy carving and the poached chicken dish provides more than one meal.

Choosing high-welfare chickens – those that have been slow-grown in a free-range environment – really pays off. The meat will be more succulent and the bones produce an infinitely better stock than quick-reared, indoor-bred, cheaper birds. They may cost more, but they're excellent value because you can utilize every part. Use the carcass from the roast chicken recipe overleaf to make stock for a soup in the following days, while the recipe for poached chicken produces the broth for you.

If you're only cooking joints, buy a whole bird and ask the butcher to joint it for you, or get them to remove the bones for the Boneless chicken with lemon and thyme salt recipe, then use them to make stock; you'll get more than you paid for.

RECIPES

Roast chicken with lemon and tarragon mayonnaise
Poached chicken with summer vegetables and garlic mayonnaise
Chicken, lemon and potatoes with wild oregano
Boneless chicken with lemon and thyme salt

ROAST CHICKEN

WITH LEMON AND TARRAGON
MAYONNAISE

I love this summery recipe, which the late William Yeoward served us in his beautiful garden in the Cotswolds. Inside the dining room were shelves stacked high with plates and bowls and glasses, designed by him or bought as inspiration for his collections. It was warm enough to eat outside, so the table was laid among pots of summer flowers. A version of roast chicken for hot days, this omits butter but instead uses the richness of mayonnaise infused with the roast chicken juices to make a dish, good served hot or cold.

SERVES 6

For the roast chicken
2kg (4lb 8oz) organic, free-range chicken
1 lemon
20g (¾oz) tarragon
2 tablespoons olive oil
sea salt and freshly ground black pepper

For the mayonnaise
2 egg yolks
1 teaspoon Dijon mustard
290ml (9¾fl oz) light olive oil
1 tablespoon lemon juice
3 tablespoons chicken cooking juices
zest of ¼ lemon
2 tablespoons chopped tarragon

To serve
boiled Cornish early potatoes with steamed carrots
    and fennel, or a green salad

1. Preheat the oven to 200°C (180°C fan), 400°F, Gas mark 6. Season the chicken inside and out and stuff the cavity with half the lemon and half the tarragon. Roughly chop the rest of the tarragon and push it under the skin of the breast. Cut the remaining lemon half into 6 slices. Lay 2 long strips of foil over the bottom of a roasting tray, with enough extra to cover the whole bird. Arrange the lemon slices in a layer on the foil, then sit the chicken on top. Pour the olive oil all over the skin of the chicken and wrap the bird completely in the foil (you may need to use more to cover the top) so that it is covered like a parcel. Roast for 1½–2 hours, or until the legs feel wobbly in their sockets and the juices run clear when a knife is inserted between the thigh and body.

2. Unwrap the bird and pour all the juices into a saucepan. Put the chicken on a plate to cool slightly (it will be served at room temperature). If any juices have escaped the package, you can deglaze these in the pan with a little water or wine and add them to the saucepan too. Remove any excess fat from the juices before bringing to the boil and reducing to 3 tablespoons. Cool in a bowl over iced water.

3. To make the mayonnaise, put the egg yolks and mustard in a bowl and slowly begin to add the oil, drop by drop, while whisking. As the mixture begins to emulsify and thicken, increase the flow of the oil. When you have added about 75ml (2½fl oz) oil, whisk in the lemon juice and the cooled cooking juices, then continue to add the rest of the oil. When all the oil has been added, you should have a thick emulsion. Stir in the lemon zest and tarragon and season to taste. The chicken juices may make it quite salty, but you might want to add a little more salt, along with some pepper.

4. Tear or carve the cooled chicken into portion-sized pieces, removing the skin if you prefer. Serve with the mayonnaise on the side amd your choice of vegetables or salad.

POACHED CHICKEN

WITH SUMMER VEGETABLES
AND GARLIC MAYONNAISE

This is a dish that keeps giving: there will be plenty of broth left over for making soups or risottos, so you'll get many meals out of this one. Making broth is a good way to use up peelings and vegetable trimmings too. If you pod your own peas, add the pods to the broth. Likewise with fennel fronds, carrot peelings and herb stalks. You will need a large pot so that everything fits comfortably. The whole dish can be done a day ahead if necessary; it's easy to reheat the vegetables and chicken in the broth.

....

SERVES 6

For the broth
2.5kg (5lb 8oz) organic, free-range chicken
large bunch of flat-leaf parsley (use the stalks for
    the broth and the leaves to garnish)
4 large carrots, peeled and left whole
1 head of garlic, halved horizontally
4 celery sticks, cut into batons
1 large fennel bulb, halved vertically
1 large oxheart tomato, halved
small bunch of thyme
1 bay leaf
5 black peppercorns
zest and juice of ½ lemon
300g (10½oz) fresh peas or broad beans
sea salt and freshly ground black pepper

For the mayonnaise
3 eggs yolks
2 teaspoons Dijon mustard
375ml (13fl oz) extra virgin olive oil
juice of ½ lemon

To serve
crusty bread
boiled potatoes

1. Put the chicken and parsley stalks with the other broth ingredients – except the lemon zest and juice and peas or broad beans, which you will add later – in a large pot. Cover with water by at least 2.5cm (1in).
2. Bring to the boil. Keep an eye on it and, as soon as it boils, scoop off any scum that has risen to the surface. Reduce to the gentlest simmer. Half-cover with a lid and cook for 2 hours. Check occasionally to make sure everything is submerged. Add more water if needed.
3. Remove the chicken and vegetables and set aside. Strain the broth and return to the pot.
4. Boil the broth rapidly until reduced by half – this will take at least 30 minutes. Taste and season well with salt and pepper, and add the lemon juice and zest.
5. To make the mayonnaise, pick out all the garlic cloves that were cooked in the broth and mash them to a paste with a pinch of salt using a pestle and mortar.
6. Scoop into a big bowl and add the egg yolks and mustard. Add the oil, drop by drop, whisking constantly until it thickens. Then increase the oil low to a steady stream until it is all used and you have a thick emulsion. Add salt and pepper, and the lemon juice.
7. Just before serving, heat the broth and cook the peas or broad beans for a couple of minutes until soft.
8. Remove the chicken from the bones and cut into large pieces. Cut the carrots into batons, the fennel into wedges and the tomato into large pieces.
9. Arrange the vegetables (including the celery and peas or broad beans) with the chicken on a platter. Chop the parsley leaves and sprinkle on top. Ladle over some of the broth and pour the rest into a jug to offer at the table. Serve with the mayonnaise, and crusty bread and boiled potatoes.

CHICKEN, LEMON AND POTATOES
WITH WILD OREGANO

There's a small Greek island that I go to in the summer where you can find a family-run restaurant on a beach, only accessible by foot or boat. After scrambling down from a high coastal path you will discover some tables sitting under the trees on the sand by a small stone building, from which appear dishes of simply prepared local food. A plate of crisp-skinned chicken for the table to share comes bathed in oil, juicy with lemons and fragrant with mountain oregano, flavours that I will always associate with hot summers on sun-drenched islands. Serve with the tomato-braised green beans and a simple green salad.

SERVES 6

6 organic, free-range chicken legs and thighs,
  skin on
small bunch of dried wild oregano
1 large lemon
1kg (2lb 4oz) potatoes (use a versatile variety,
  not too waxy or floury, such as Désirée)
4 tablespoons olive oil
sea salt
green salad, to serve

1. Put the chicken pieces in a bowl and season with salt and the oregano. Cut the lemon into 8 chunks, leaving the skin on, and add to the chicken. If you have time, you can do this the day or night before and leave it in the refrigerator, covered, to marinate, which will add to the flavour.

2. Put the potatoes, whole and unpeeled, in a pan of well-salted water and bring to the boil. Boil for 10 minutes, or until just tender on the outside and uncooked in the middle. Drain and run under cold water until cool enough to handle, then peel off the skins with your fingers. Cut into large pieces (halves or quarters).

3. Preheat the oven to 180°C (160°C fan), 350°F, Gas mark 4. Pour some of the olive oil into the bottom of a large roasting tray and lay the chicken, lemon pieces and potatoes in one layer with no overlapping pieces (if your tray isn't big enough, use 2). Turn the potatoes so that they are lying flat-side down, to encourage maximum contact with the cooking surface. Drizzle the remaining olive oil over the top.

4. Cook for 1½ hours until the chicken skin looks golden and crisp. Use a metal spatula to lift the potatoes and chicken on to a warmed serving dish, then deglaze the roasting tray with a splash of water and pour this over the meat. Serve with a green salad.

BONELESS CHICKEN

WITH LEMON AND THYME SALT

Cooking a whole chicken under a weight produces a succulent bird with a uniformly golden skin. It also takes less time than roasting it. You will need a frying pan at least 30cm (12in) in diameter and a weight of 3–4kg (6lb 8oz–9lb). I use a large pestle and mortar, but a stone, brick or any heavy object will do. I like to sauté thinly sliced potatoes in the remaining chicken fat in the pan. Alternatively, you can pour off the excess fat and add a splash of wine and boil it for a second to make a light gravy.

1.75kg (3lb 14oz) organic, free-range chicken
1 lemon
10g (¼oz) thyme, chopped
1 garlic clove, crushed
1 tablespoon flaked sea salt
2 tablespoons olive oil

To serve
sautéed potatoes
Gratin of greens (see page 89)

1. Lay the chicken breast-side down on a board with the legs facing you. With scissors, cut along both sides of the backbone through the ribs to release it (save the bone for stock). Turn the bird over and press down hard on the breast to flatten it. Choose a frying pan large enough to fit the flattened bird in it and another pan a bit smaller to place on top.

2. Grate the zest from the lemon into a bowl, then squeeze in 1 tablespoon of the juice. Add the thyme with the garlic and salt. Mix well.

3. Lay the bird skin-side up on a board and gently prise away the skin from the flesh at the top of the breasts and around the thighs. Using your fingers, push 1 teaspoon at a time of the mixture under the skin, massaging to spread it around. Rub the rest of the mixture into the underside of the bird.

4. Heat the oil in the large frying pan until sizzling hot. Lay the chicken skin-side down and reduce the heat to medium–low. Place the smaller pan on top and press down firmly, placing the weight on top of the pan for extra pressure. Cook like this for 30 minutes, then remove the weight and check that the bird is not getting too brown. Reduce the heat if necessary. Continue cooking skin-side down for up to another 30 minutes, or until the juices run clear when a knife is inserted into the thickest part of the thigh. When the bird is nearly cooked, turn it over to brown the underside for a few minutes.

5. Remove the chicken to a warm place to rest for 15 minutes before carving.

DESSERTS

Summer is the time for soft fruit: ripe raspberries that burst and bleed their colour into pools of cream, jewel-like redcurrants, dark sticky figs, plump apricots and peaches. Eating in the warmth means dishes needn't be piping hot, so they can often be made in advance or packed to take on a picnic. And for the days when you don't feel like doing much, the joy of ripe summer fruit is that it doesn't need cooking. Sometimes a pretty bowl of juicy strawberries and raspberries on the table with a jug of cream is enough.

RECIPES

Apricot and rosemary galette

Apricot custard

Baked apricots with raspberries and almond biscuits

Raspberry jellies with pistachio and thyme biscuits

Poached peach and currant strudel

Blackberry and peach clafoutis

Fig and walnut tart

Roast figs with mascarpone

APRICOT AND ROSEMARY GALETTE

I could eat some sort of galette every day of the week and a glut of seasonal fruit is the perfect excuse to make one. The rosemary provides a subtle background flavour, which works beautifully with the tart, sweet apricots. You could use peaches or nectarines instead, or even raspberries. It can be eaten hot, warm or cold.

SERVES 6

For the pastry
100g (3½oz) plain flour, plus extra for dusting

1 tablespoon caster sugar

75g (2½oz) cold unsalted butter, cut into 1cm (½in) cubes

2–4 tablespoons iced water

For the frangipane
30g (1oz) unsalted butter, softened

50g (1¾oz) ground almonds

2 tablespoons caster sugar

For the topping
½ tablespoon chopped rosemary, plus a few flowers to decorate (optional)

8 apricots, or more if small

15g (½oz) unsalted butter

1 tablespoon caster sugar

2 tablespoons apricot jam

To serve
crème fraîche or double cream

1. To make the pastry, mix the flour and sugar together in a bowl. Add the butter and gently rub in with your fingertips, or blitz briefly in a food processor, until the pieces are the size of petits pois.

2. If you have used a food processor, transfer the mixture to a bowl. Add the iced water, a tablespoon at a time, mixing lightly until the dough comes together. Small pieces of butter should be visible throughout the dough – this will give it a flaky texture when cooked.

Press it into a disc, wrap in clingfilm and rest in the refrigerator for at least 30 minutes.

3. For the frangipane, beat the butter until creamy, add the almonds and sugar and mix to a smooth paste.

4. To assemble, preheat the oven to 190°C (170°C fan), 375°F, Gas mark 5. Line an oven tray with baking parchment. Roll out the pastry on a lightly floured surface to form a 30cm (12in) circle, about 2mm (⅟₁₆in) thick. Carefully lift it on to the prepared tray.

5. Spread the frangipane in an even, thin layer over the pastry (you probably won't need it all, so freeze any left over). Sprinkle with the chopped rosemary. Cut the apricots in half, discarding the stones. Finely slice 4 apricot halves and lay them in a thin line around the edge of the pastry, about 4cm (1½in) from the outside edge. Fold the edges of pastry over the chopped ring of apricots to form a crust.

6. Quarter the remaining apricots and arrange them over the base. Melt the butter and brush it over the crust. Sprinkle the sugar over the crust and apricots. Bake for 25–30 minutes on the middle shelf of the oven until the pastry is brown and crisp and the apricots are soft. Melt the jam in a small pan and sieve it to make a smooth glaze. Brush this all over the cooked apricots. Scatter with rosemary flowers, if using.

APRICOT CUSTARD

Rowley Leigh's 'very, very simple to make but a delicate and clean way to use the "precocious" early apricots, one of the first fruits of summer'. I like the simplicity of this cooked in an earthenware dish and brought to the table.

....

SERVES 6

2 eggs, plus 3 egg yolks
75g (2½oz) caster or golden caster sugar
300ml (10fl oz) full-fat milk
300ml (10fl oz) double cream, plus extra, whipped,
　　to serve
4 drops of almond extract
12 apricots
100g (3½oz) amaretti biscuits

1. Whisk the eggs, egg yolks and 5 tablespoons of the sugar together well in a large bowl, then add the milk, cream and almond extract. Leave to stand.
2. Preheat the oven to 220°C (200°C fan), 425°F, Gas mark 7. Halve the apricots and remove the stones. Place in rows, cut-side up, in a large oven dish. Sprinkle over the remaining caster sugar and add 2 tablespoons of water. Bake for 5–10 minutes, depending on the ripeness of the apricots. They should be softened but not collapsed.
3. Crush the amaretti biscuits with a rolling pin (not to a fine powder but to a thick crumb) and sprinkle over the apricots.
4. Reduce the oven temperature to 140°C (120°C fan), 275°F, Gas mark 1. Pour the custard over the apricots and return to the oven (you don't have to wait for the temperature to come down). The custard should cook in about 40 minutes, but be vigilant. Test by giving the dish a little shake to see if it has set. Eat hot, cold or, best of all, lukewarm, with whipped cream.

BAKED APRICOTS

WITH RASPBERRIES AND
ALMOND BISCUITS

Cook this in the dish you'll serve it in and you won't
have to worry about disturbing the very soft fruit.
The rosé wine in the recipe gives you an excuse to
open a bottle that you can drink with the meal.
Sugar quantities will vary depending on the
sweetness of the fruit, so do adjust as necessary.

....

SERVES 6

100ml (3½fl oz) rosé wine
6 tablespoons caster sugar
1 bay leaf
1 vanilla pod, split in half and seeds scraped out
about 750g (1lb 10oz) ripe apricots
200g (7oz) raspberries

To serve
whipped cream or crème fraîche
Almond biscuits (see page 279)

1. Preheat the oven to 180°C (160°C fan), 350°F, Gas
mark 4. Put the wine, sugar, bay leaf and vanilla pod
and seeds in a small saucepan and slowly bring to the
boil to dissolve the sugar. After a minute of boiling,
remove from the heat.

2. Halve the apricots by cutting along the natural
indentation on the fruit. Remove the stones. Lay the
apricots cut-side down in a baking dish and pour over
the wine mixture, including the vanilla pod and bay
leaf – tuck these among the fruit.

3. Bake for 20–30 minutes. The timing will depend
on the ripeness of the fruit and you can test them by
occasionally inserting a skewer – it should meet no
resistance. Remove from the oven and scatter the
raspberries over the top so that they warm up in the
residual heat.

4. Serve with whipped cream or crème fraîche and
the almond biscuits.

RASPBERRY JELLIES
WITH PISTACHIO AND THYME BISCUITS

I'd love to have a collection of copper jelly moulds, but instead I make do with a variety of glasses I've picked up at antique markets here and there. These jellies are probably easier and quicker to make in individual moulds, but you can use a large bowl and turn the jelly out on a plate. The biscuits and cream make the whole thing into something of a special pudding. Use 150ml (5fl oz) moulds if you're making individual jellies.

SERVES 6

For the jellies
800g (1lb 12oz) raspberries
350g (12oz) caster sugar
3 fresh bay leaves, roughly torn
4 tablespoons Martini Bianco (or other sweet white vermouth)
1 tablespoon lemon juice
9 gelatine leaves

To serve
Pistachio and thyme biscuits (see page 279)
double cream (optional)

1. Put the raspberries, sugar, bay leaves and vermouth in a saucepan and add 300ml (10fl oz) water. Heat slowly until the sugar has dissolved, then bring to the boil. Turn off the heat and stir in the lemon juice.
2. Sieve the raspberry mixture over a bowl to produce a smooth liquid. Discard the solids.
3. Measure the liquid: you need 900ml (1½ pints), so top up with water if necessary. Put the gelatine leaves in a bowl and cover with cold water. Leave for 5 minutes until soft, then gently squeeze out any excess water and add to the raspberry liquid. Return the mixture to a clean saucepan and heat gently to dissolve the gelatine. If using jelly moulds, rinse them in cold water and shake them out. Pour the jelly mixture into the moulds or glasses and chill for at least 6 hours to ensure they set properly.
4. If using jelly moulds, dip each into hot water and invert on to individual plates to serve. Serve with the biscuits, along with double cream, lightly whipped, if you like. These intense, vibrant jellies work well with a very sweet wine with good acidity, such as a late-harvest Riesling or, especially if serving with cream, a fine Sauternes.

POACHED PEACH AND CURRANT STRUDEL

The late William Yeoward describes his memories of visiting his grandmother's house, where he would eat this dish. 'As a child I always remember the marvellous scent of half-baked strudel filling the air in the kitchen. This is my re-enactment.'

....

SERVES 6

For the poached peaches
about 780g (1lb 11oz) ripe peaches
1 vanilla pod, split in half and seeds scraped out
1 tablespoon lemon juice
60g (2¼oz) caster sugar
300g (10½oz) mixed blackcurrants and redcurrants, plus extra to decorate

For the strudel
4 sheets of filo pastry
60g (2¼oz) unsalted butter, melted
50g (1¾oz) ground almonds
50g (1¾oz) demerara sugar
25g (1oz) flaked almonds

To serve
clotted cream or crème fraîche

1. Preheat the oven to 180°C (160°C fan), 350°F, Gas mark 4. Cut each peach into 6 or 8 wedges, discarding the stones. Put them into a large, shallow pan with the vanilla seeds, lemon juice and sugar. If the peaches aren't very juicy, add 1–2 tablespoons of water. Cook over a low–medium heat, partially covered, for about 5 minutes until the peaches are really soft but still holding their shape. Add the currants and stir well, then cook together for another minute so that they begin to release their juices. Remove from the heat and strain, keeping any juices.

2. Brush both sides of a sheet of filo pastry with melted butter and lay it on a large baking sheet. Mix the ground almonds and demerara sugar together and sprinkle about a quarter of the mixture over the sheet of pastry. Repeat with the next 3 sheets, making sure you butter generously on both sides, and top with the sugar almond mixture.

3. Arrange the peaches and currants in a line along one of the long sides of the top filo sheet and roll them up, like a Swiss roll, ending with the seam on the underside. Sprinkle the flaked almonds all over the top and sides, and tuck any escaping fruit back inside at either end. Using a skewer or the tip of a sharp knife, pierce holes along the length of the roll. This will help the filo layers crisp up in the oven.

4. Bake for 25 minutes until crisp and brown. Cut into thick slices and decorate with the extra currants as desired. Serve while it is still hot.

BLACKBERRY AND PEACH CLAFOUTIS

Picking wild blackberries on a warm late summer day is one of life's great pleasures. The excitement of discovering a prolific patch, popping the first softest, juiciest berries straight into your mouth; the stain of dark purple fingers. I often find myself stretching perilously over the brambles to reach the plumpest ones at the back, but that's part of the fun. We once had a pet whippet who would nuzzle her nose into the bush and pop the berries into her mouth. Wild blackberries are much smaller and more complex-tasting than cultivated varieties, so it's worth the effort. What I like about this recipe is that you don't need a huge number to get a good effect. The blackberries can be dotted among the peach pieces, their flavours combining and accentuating each other. It's also an incredibly simple pudding to make: basically just a batter poured over fresh fruit and baked. A good reward for an energetic harvest.

....

SERVES 6

small knob of butter, softened
150g (5½oz) caster sugar, plus 2 tablespoons for the dish
3 eggs
50g (1¾oz) plain flour
pinch of salt
1 teaspoon vanilla bean paste
150ml (5½floz) full-fat milk
170g (6oz) crème fraîche
3 peaches
200g (7oz) blackberries
pouring cream, to serve

1. Preheat the oven to 200°C (180°C fan), 400°F, Gas mark 6. Brush the inside of an ovenproof pudding dish with the soft butter and sprinkle to cover with the 2 tablespoons of sugar.

2. In a large bowl using a hand-held electric whisk or in a stand mixer, whisk the eggs until they are voluminous and foaming. In a separate bowl, mix the remaining 150g (5½oz) sugar and the flour with the salt and add to the eggs, along with the vanilla, milk and crème fraîche. Whisk briefly just to combine. Rest for 10 minutes.

3. Remove the stones from the peaches and cut into large chunks. Arrange the peaches and the blackberries on the bottom of the prepared dish.

4. Pour the batter over the fruit and bake for 30 minutes until risen and firm. Serve warm with pouring cream.

FIG AND WALNUT TART

If you have access to a fig tree, take a leaf to infuse in the honey glaze. It gives it a unique and aromatic flavour. Or spread out the leaves on a board for decoration and serve the tart on top.

....

SERVES 6

For the dough
200g (7oz) plain flour, sifted, plus extra for dusting
2 tablespoons caster sugar
pinch of sea salt
150g (5½oz) cold unsalted butter, cut into small
    chunks
2–4 tablespoons iced water

For the topping
80g (3oz) walnuts
60g (2¼oz) unsalted butter, softened
4 tablespoons caster sugar, plus extra for sprinkling
½ teaspoon vanilla extract
1 egg yolk
450g (1lb) figs, stems removed
3 tablespoons honey

1. To make the pastry, mix the flour, sugar and salt together in a bowl. Add the butter and gently rub in with your fingertips, or blitz briefly in a food processor, until the pieces are the size of petits pois.

2. Tip the mixture into a bowl. Add the iced water, a tablespoon at a time, mixing and pressing lightly until the dough comes together. It should feel slightly dry, not wet or sticky. Press it into a disc, wrap in clingfilm and chill for at least 30 minutes.

3. Meanwhile, grind the walnuts in a pestle and mortar or a food processor. Add 40g (1½oz) of the butter to the sugar, vanilla and egg yolk and mix to a paste. Set aside at room temperature. Put the figs in a small saucepan for later, adding a fig leaf if you have one. Cut all but 2 of the figs into quarters (or sixths if very large). Finely chop the 2 figs to use for the stuffed crust.

4. Preheat the oven to 190°C (170°C fan), 375°F, Gas mark 5. When the pastry has rested, lay it on a sheet of baking parchment and dust with flour. Roll it into a rectangular shape about 3mm (⅛in) thick.

5. Spread the walnut mixture in a thin layer over the pastry, leaving a gap of at least 5cm (2in) around the edge. Arrange the sliced figs in tightly packed rows to cover the walnut mixture and then lay the finely chopped fig around the edge of the pastry and roll the pastry over it, concealing it under the dough.

6. Melt the remaining 20g (¾oz) of the butter and brush it all over the dough crust of the tart, then sprinkle liberally with caster sugar – this will give the pastry additional crunch. Place the tart, still on the baking parchment, on a baking sheet and bake for about 25–30 minutes, or until the crust has turned golden brown and crisp.

7. To make the glaze, add the honey and 1 tablespoon of water to the saucepan with the fig stems and slowly bring to the boil. Reduce the heat and simmer for a minute or so until you have sticky syrup. Dip a brush into the syrup, avoiding the fig stems, and brush the glaze all over the top of the figs on the tart, but not the pastry. Best served warm with thick yogurt.

ROAST FIGS
WITH MASCARPONE

As the juicy stone fruits of summer come to an end, I start to look forward to late-ripening figs. We have a fig tree that grows against a sunny wall in our garden, and I watch it eagerly as the fruit matures throughout August and September. In years when the harvest has not been great, I appreciate the tree for its leaves. Crushed between your fingers, they have a sweet, green coconut fragrance that seeps out during cooking. Sometimes I toast them, then steep them in homemade custard to make ice cream; or I use them to wrap fillets of fish or chicken before roasting them. You can even use them as a display under cheeses on a board. I like to cook figs simply – this recipe is one of the easiest – and I find the almond flavour of Amaretto suits the fruit well.

....

SERVES 6

12 ripe figs
200g (7oz) mascarpone cheese
1 tablespoon runny honey
1 tablespoon Amaretto liqueur
handful of amaretti biscuits

1. Preheat the oven to 200°C (180°C fan), 400°F, Gas mark 6. Cut a cross in the top of each fig, open them up slightly and place in a baking dish.

2. Mix the mascarpone, honey and Amaretto liqueur together, then spoon a dollop into each fig. Bake for 15–20 minutes until oozing and soft.

3. Remove the figs to a plate, spooning over the sauce. Crush the amaretti biscuits over the figs and serve.

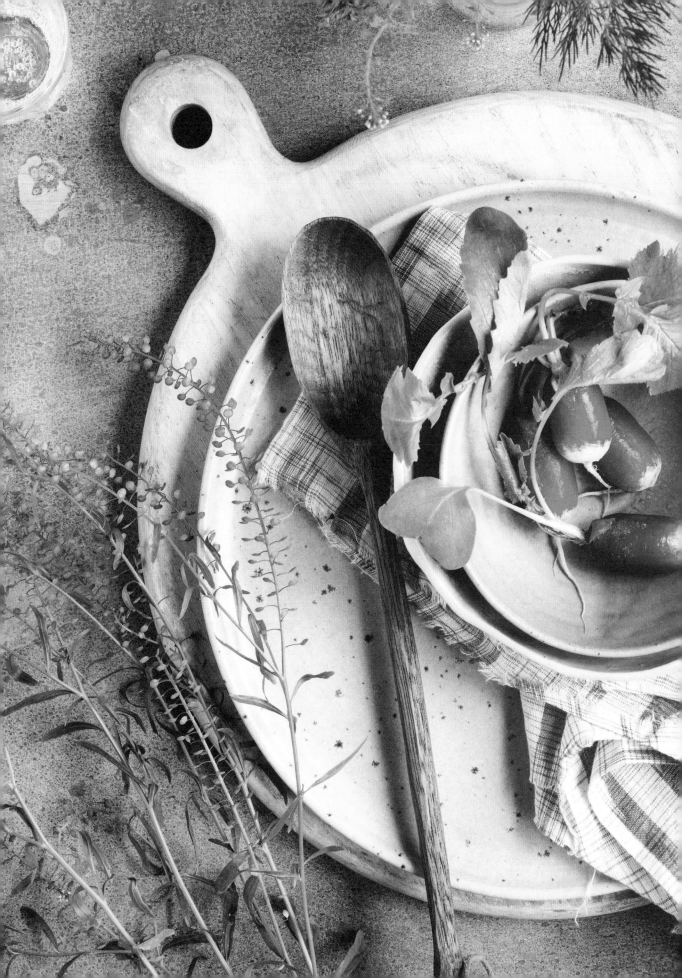

SUMMER MENUS

QUICK VEGETARIAN
Courgette fritti page 93
Broad bean spaghetti with Pecorino page 83
Roast figs with mascarpone page 144

Fritti are good to serve with a drink while you're cooking the pasta, and the roast figs take no time and can keep warm in the oven. Even if people aren't vegetarian, they often don't notice if there's no meat.

A SUMMER PICNIC
Roast aubergine, tomatoes and fregola page 111
Lamb kefte with herb salad and spicy yogurt
page 124
Apricot and rosemary galette page 133

Two of these dishes can be eaten in the hands – I provide proper napkins and glasses, and all you need are forks and plates for the salad. Melamine or enamel are excellent lightweight picnic plates. These things still taste good even after a journey in a basket – the salad will have infused its flavours and the lamb, wrapped in foil, will keep warm. Even better, if I'm lighting an outdoor fire, I cook the lamb on that.

A TABLE IN THE GARDEN
Marinated courgettes and aubergine
with burrata page 95
Poached chicken with summer vegetables
and garlic mayonnaise page 128
Raspberry jellies with pistachio and
thyme biscuits page 139

I don't want to be worried about keeping things piping hot when we eat outside and I put everything on the table, for guests to help themselves. The food becomes part of the scene and it adds to the informality.

COOKING IN ADVANCE
Asparagus, feta and dill page 74
Mechoui lamb with tomato-braised green beans
pages 123 and 112
Baked apricots with rapsberries and almond
biscuits page 136

Cook the asparagus in advance and arrange just before serving – I get guests to help if they're asking for something to do. The lamb can be cooked the day before; likewise the beans and the fruit.

FLOWERS AND TABLE DECORATIONS
I pick as many flowers as I can and fill tiny vases to scatter all over the table, such as sweet peas, roses, honeysuckle – everything that smells delicious, even bunches of flowering herbs. This is the time of year for undyed linen tablecloths and napkins, or vintage crockery finds from French markets and bric-a-brac shops. If we're eating outside in the evening, I serve wine in colourful tumblers and put tall candles among the flowers on the table.

Autumn

The summer growing season is over, but autumn continues to deliver an abundance of food

It's a cold, clear day in mid-October, and the leaves are still clinging to the chestnut trees that line the road, but they've changed from green to golden russet. After a few frosty nights they will have fallen to the ground. The summer growing season may be over, but autumn continues to deliver an abundance of food.

Even if it's not your habit, this is a wonderful time to visit a food market. As a weekend pastime, I take my daughter to look at the stalls at my local farmers' market brimming with mountains of orange- and silver-skinned squash, rainbow chard, football-sized celeriac, knobbly Jerusalem artichokes, purple beetroot with their leaves still attached and a glut of apples, pears and nuts. There are bunches of multi-coloured dahlias, like spiky pink fireworks, and pots of tiny autumn cyclamen. All the produce for sale has been grown locally, the stallholders driving in that morning to sell their wares. Connecting with the person who grows the food they are selling makes me care about it more. And believe me, they do want to drive home with an empty van, so you might well pick up a deal at the end of the day. I only buy what I can carry home on foot, so it's more about feasting my eyes than filling up the refrigerator. Buying directly from a grower is different to a supermarket transaction: it's a choice not a necessity, and the pleasure it brings makes me value my bunch of beetroot or bag of apples much more. And when it comes to cooking, good ingredients speak for themselves.

Friends staying for the weekend means a little planning ahead and I let the seasonal produce be my guide and decoration. Branches of autumn leaves, especially with berries clinging to them, make a beautiful table display, as does an assembly of various baby squash surrounded by candles.

Every Thursday we receive our organic vegetable share grown by the community farm down the road. Picked and delivered that day, there's a freshness and flavour you rarely get from a shop. Many of the recipes I cook have been born from the starting point of these ingredients – an airy Italian version of a flan made with squash and cavolo nero, which I might serve for Saturday dinner with a roast chicken. Lunch on Saturday is often a whole baked creamy white cauliflower, bathed in a sauce of tahini, sumac and chopped nuts and herbs. A green salad with shaved fennel keeps this light, leaving room for something at teatime. Dishes like this require a little preparation, then can be left in the oven, allowing us to relax or go for a walk.

SQUASH

You know autumn is here when shops' display crates are spilling with bulbous pumpkins and sunset-orange squash with hard shiny skins. Move aside butternut, this is the time for the real showmen.

These magnificent *Cucurbita* grow through the summer to swell into deep orange, silver-blue and striped yellow and green fruit, with flavours and textures as varied as their appearance. Once harvested, they are stored to 'set' or harden their skins, which allows them to store well into winter.

Their names are descriptive of their shapes: Crown Prince, Turk's Turban, Viola, Delica and Onion; and sweet dark green Acorn squash, small enough to cup in your palm. The gigantic, watery-fleshed Jack-o'-lanterns you see piled up at petrol stations are only good for carving Halloween faces (although you can roast their seeds with oil and salt to snack on).

Squash hold their shape well when roasted whole with their innards removed: you can split acorn squash in half and cook with butter inside to serve as individual portions, scooping out the creamy contents at the table. But their firm texture yields into smooth purée when peeled and cooked in stock, to melt into a risotto or make a soup. Thyme, sage and rosemary all suit their sweet, nutty flavour.

RECIPES

Crostini with pumpkin, ricotta and sage
Pumpkin soup with milk and orzo
Burrata with pumpkin and hazelnuts
Baked pumpkin soup with Gruyère and sage
Squash and cavolo flan
Pumpkin with dried red chillies

CROSTINI

WITH PUMPKIN, RICOTTA AND SAGE

Chef Charlie Hibbert's family have created a beautiful and very productive vegetable garden at Thyme hotel and restaurant in Gloucestershire. When I visited, I wandered through the neat rows of vegetables and flowers growing in the kitchen garden, and my eye was caught by an eye-watering display of squash lining the shelves of the greenhouse. Charlie, who runs their Ox Barn restaurant, created a menu of recipes for House & Garden *based on what he cooks for his family at home, using their array of produce. He makes these little crostini to serve as bites for guests while they wait for the main event. At Thyme, they deal with a glut of pumpkins by pickling some to preserve them. With the pickle made in advance, this is a quick and elegant snack or starter.*

....

SERVES 6

For the pickle
**1 small pumpkin (Onion squash or similar
    soft-rind pumpkin)**
1 teaspoon mustard seeds
1 teaspoon fennel seeds
pinch of chilli flakes
2 bay leaves
400ml (14fl oz) cider vinegar
300g (10½oz) caster sugar

For the crostini
¼ loaf of stale sourdough bread
25ml (1fl oz) olive oil
200ml (7fl oz) vegetable oil, for frying
20–30 sage leaves
300g (10½oz) ricotta cheese
freshly ground black pepper

1. Preheat the oven to 150°C (130°C fan), 300°F, Gas mark 2. Halve the pumpkin and deseed each half. Slice thinly into half-moons.

2. Put the pickling ingredients into a pan large enough for all the pumpkin, add 70ml (2½fl oz) water and bring to the boil. Add the pumpkin slices and then cover with a circle of baking parchment. Cook for 10 minutes over a medium heat, or until the pumpkin is soft. Allow to cool completely.

3. Slice the loaf as thinly as you can. Lay the slices on a baking tray and drizzle the olive oil over them. Bake in the oven for 10 minutes, or until they are golden brown and crisp. Allow to cool completely.

4. Put the vegetable oil into a small, high-sided pan over a medium heat. After 3–4 minutes, check the temperature by dropping in a sage leaf: it should fizz and cook crisp in about 30 seconds. When the oil is hot enough, fry the rest of the sage, lifting the leaves out of the oil with a slotted spoon. Drain on kitchen paper.

5. Spread some ricotta on to each crostini and top with some pickled pumpkin and a crispy sage leaf. Add a crack of black pepper and serve.

PUMPKIN SOUP

WITH MILK AND ORZO

This is Claudia Roden's version of a minestra di zucca. *The crushed amaretti garnish adds a flavour of Mantua, where pumpkins are exceptionally sweet. These are the super dry, crisp variety that keep on the shelf for months, not the chewy ones. Let your guests help themselves from a tureen and put a bowl of amaretti on the tables so that everyone can crush them in their hands over the soup. She suggests adding a little sugar if your pumpkin doesn't have enough flavour, or butternut squash can be used instead of pumpkin. You can prepare the soup in advance and add the cooked pasta when reheating, just before serving.*

SERVES 6

For the soup
900g (2lb) pumpkin or butternut squash, peeled, deseeded and diced
2 chicken or vegetable stock cubes or stock pots
120g (4¼oz) orzo
700ml (1¼ pints) full-fat milk
a little caster sugar (optional)
sea salt and freshly ground black pepper

To serve
ground cinnamon
about 9 crunchy amaretti, crumbled or whole

1. Put the pumpkin or butternut squash in a saucepan with the stock cubes or stock pots and 700ml (1¼ pints) water. Bring to the boil, then simmer, covered, over a low heat for 20 minutes until soft.
2. At the same time, cook the orzo in a saucepan of salted boiling water for about 10 minutes until is al dente, then drain immediately and set aside.
3. Blend the pumpkin or squash to a cream with a hand-held blender, then add the milk. Bring to a simmer (do not let it boil over) and season with salt, pepper and, if you like, a little sugar.
4. Add the cooked orzo to the soup and serve hot. Pass around a tiny bowl of cinnamon and a plate of crumbled or whole amaretti for your guests to scatter or crush over their soup.

BURRATA

WITH PUMPKIN AND HAZELNUTS

'The combination of pumpkin and hazelnuts is well established in the cuisine of Lombardy, where I grew up,' says Giorgio Locatelli, describing this recipe. Both ingredients are at their best at this time of year, as is burrata. Always take the cheese out of the refrigerator a couple of hours prior to serving. A fresh ricotta would also work well.

....

SERVES 6

450g (1lb) pumpkin
1 garlic clove, peeled
4 tablespoons olive oil
6 sprigs of thyme
80g (3oz) rocket
70g (2½oz) toasted hazelnuts
500g (1lb 2oz) burrata cheese
sea salt and freshly ground black pepper

For the dressing (makes enough to save for later)
1 tablespoon white wine vinegar
2 teaspoons red wine vinegar
2 tablespoons water
4 tablespoons olive oil
2½ tablespoons vegetable oil

1. Preheat the oven to 180°C (160°C fan), 350°F, Gas mark 4. Peel and deseed the pumpkin, then cut it into cubes and place on a baking tray with the garlic. Drizzle with 2 tablespoons of the olive oil, sprinkle with the thyme and season with salt and pepper. Roast for 45 minutes until tender. Leave to cool.
2. To make the dressing, mix together the white and red wine vinegars and a pinch of salt. Add 2 tablespoons of water and the olive oil and vegetable oil, then stir until combined.
3. Toss the rocket with half the dressing and arrange on plates with the pumpkin and hazelnuts. Cut open the burrata and place on top of the pumpkin. Drizzle over the remaining 2 tablespoons of olive oil and season before serving.

BAKED PUMPKIN SOUP
WITH GRUYÈRE AND SAGE

It's become an annual autumn tradition when my squash are ready to eat for me to cook Sally Clarke's 'baked pumpkin soup': a whole roast squash filled with melted Gruyère, chicken stock and cream – a soup in an edible tureen. She suggests adding roast wild mushrooms, sweetcorn or chopped walnuts to the stuffing to make it into an even more filling meal.

....

SERVES 6

For the stuffed pumpkin
2kg (4lb 8oz) Ironbark, Blue Hubbard or Onion squash, or similar pumpkin
300ml (10fl oz) double cream, plus a little extra if needed
50ml (2fl oz) vegetable or chicken stock
1 tablespoon finely chopped sage
3 garlic cloves, crushed to a paste with a little salt
100g (3½oz) Gruyère or Cheddar cheese, grated
sea salt and freshly ground black pepper

For the crisp sage
12 large sage leaves
2 tablespoons olive oil
100g (3½oz) Parmesan or extra Gruyère cheese, freshly grated

To serve
green salad
crusty bread

1. Wash the pumpkin and, with a sharp, sturdy knife, cut off the top third (ideally keeping the stalk attached to the lid). With a strong spoon, scoop out the seeds and discard. Continue to scoop out some of the flesh until about one-third has been removed. Chop this roughly and place in a pan with the cream, stock, chopped sage and garlic. Season with salt and pepper and bring gently to the boil.

2. Preheat the oven to 180°C (160°C fan), 350°F, Gas mark 4. Fold two 30cm (12in) strips of foil in half lengthways. Place them in a cross in a deep roasting tin that will hold the pumpkin snugly. Place the pumpkin in the centre of the cross. Carefully pour the hot cream mixture into the pumpkin and put the lid on top. Draw the foil up and secure the pumpkin and lid by folding the ends together. Bake for 1 hour, or until tender (different varieties of pumpkin will need different times).

3. Test with a skewer in the flesh under the lid (not the side). When it feels tender, remove from the oven, take the lid off carefully, sprinkle in the Gruyère or Cheddar cheese and add a little extra cream if needed – it should be half-full. Return to the oven with the lid to one side and continue to bake for 5–7 minutes until the cheese starts to melt and becomes stringy.

4. In a small frying pan, fry the sage leaves in the olive oil until they sizzle and become crisp – this takes seconds. Remove and drain on kitchen paper, then sprinkle with salt.

5. Use the foil to lift the pumpkin carefully out of the roasting tin, place it in a warm serving bowl, slide away the foil and serve by scooping the sides of the pumpkin 'bowl' and lid together with the cream filling on to individual plates or into bowls. Scatter with the grated Parmesan or Gruyère and sage leaves, and serve with a green salad and warm crusty bread.

SQUASH AND CAVOLO FLAN

Flan is such an old-fashioned description for this baked egg and cheese dish that rises in the oven, but less dramatically than a soufflé. It is one of my favourite dishes to cook with Crown Prince squash, a seasonal variety with a rich, sweet flesh and a low water content. The smooth, custardy texture of the squash contrasts nicely with the cavolo nero leaves inside.

....

SERVES 6

1.5kg (3lb 5oz) firm-textured squash, peeled, deseeded and cut into 3cm (1¼in) chunks
small bunch of oregano (or thyme), leaves picked
8 garlic cloves, unpeeled
3 tablespoons olive oil
200g (7oz) cavolo nero (or curly kale)
1 teaspoon softened butter
50g (1¾oz) Parmesan cheese, grated
500g (1lb 2oz) ricotta cheese
200g (7oz) crème fraîche
8 eggs
chilli flakes, to taste
a few gratings of nutmeg
sea salt and freshly ground black pepper

1. To cook the squash, preheat the oven to 180°C (160°C fan), 350°F, Gas mark 4.

2. Put the squash in a large baking tray with the oregano (or thyme) leaves, garlic cloves and oil. Toss everything together and season with salt and pepper. Arrange in a single layer and bake for 30–40 minutes, or until completely soft when pierced with a knife. Remove from the oven and set aside to cool.

3. When cool, squeeze the cooked garlic cloves from their skins (discard the skins) and pass the squash, herbs and garlic through a potato ricer or mouli-légumes. If you do not have either of these, use a sieve with large holes.

4. To make the flan, strip the cavolo nero (or kale) leaves from the stalks and discard the stalks. Boil the leaves in plenty of well-salted water for 3 minutes until tender, then drain and refresh under cold water. Squeeze dry and chop roughly.

5. Increase the oven temperature to 200°C (180°C fan), 400°F, Gas mark 6.

6. Brush a medium baking dish (around 30cm/ 12in long) with the softened butter and sprinkle with a few tablespoons of the Parmesan to coat the inside of the dish.

7. Beat the ricotta and crème fraîche in a food processor, or by hand with a wooden spoon, until creamy. Add the eggs, one by one, beating well after each addition, then add the squash, cavolo nero (or kale) and remaining Parmesan. Season to taste with chilli flakes, nutmeg and more salt and pepper.

8. Pour the flan mixture into the prepared dish and bake for 35 minutes until the top puffs up slightly and browns and the centre is just set.

PUMPKIN
WITH DRIED RED CHILLIES

Pumpkin recipes appear in cultures all over the world. This is Asma Khan's Bengali version of roast pumpkin. Known as mishti kumro, it is pumpkin spiced with panch phoron – Bengali five-spice mix – and it's eaten as a comforting seasonal dish. You can replace the cumin seeds with mustard seeds, or if you want to mix your own panch phoron, use a combination of fenugreek, nigella, cumin, black mustard and fennel seeds.

....

SERVES 6

1.2kg (2lb 10oz) peeled and deseeded pumpkin
½ teaspoon ground turmeric
1½ teaspoons sea salt
5 tablespoons vegetable oil
1 teaspoon cumin seeds
5 dried red chillies
5 garlic cloves, crushed
pinch of sugar

1. Cut the pumpkin into 2.5cm (1in) cubes. Rub with turmeric and the salt, then set aside for at least 30 minutes.
2. Heat the oil in a heavy-based saucepan or frying pan over a moderately high heat. Add the cumin seeds, chillies and garlic, and stir for a few seconds.
3. Add the pumpkin to the pan. It should have enough moisture to prevent it sticking – if not, then add a splash of water.
4. Stir the pumpkin so that it is evenly coated in the spices, then reduce the heat and cover the pan. Simmer for about 15 minutes.
5. Check to ensure the pumpkin is not disintegrating. Once it is cooked, stir in the sugar and serve.

BEETROOT

There are many varieties of beetroot beyond the deep purple we know so well. This chameleon of vegetables comes in varieties of golden, striped pink and yellow.

Sweet and earthy tasting, beetroot works in so many different dishes: soups, salads, sauces – even cakes. Think about cutting it in various ways too: on a mandoline to make a gratin with celeriac and potatoes; grated and cooked with coconut milk, Southern Indian spices and curry leaves; quartered and roasted for a salad with goats' curd and herbs; diced and sautéed as the base for soup with apple and dill. Don't forget to use the leaves as well. Treat them like chard and serve with other greens, or tangled with the cooked beets.

I often cook beetroot as soon as I've bought them, roasted whole in a tray covered with foil, then keep them in the refrigerator. This makes them a much more appealing option when you're cooking in a hurry.

RECIPES

Beetroot salad with sweet herb borani and toasted walnuts

Beetroot, apple and horseradish soup

Roast beetroot with lemon tahini and toasted seeds

Beetroot, lentils and watercress with horseradish

BEETROOT SALAD

WITH SWEET HERB BORANI
AND TOASTED WALNUTS

Sam and Sam Clark introduced me to this wonderful recipe when they wrote it for the magazine. The colour of the beetroot juices with the white yogurt and herbs is beautiful. They explain that 'A borani is a yogurt sauce from Iran, and this one, fragrant with the sweet herbs of basil, tarragon, dill and parsley, is a perfect accompaniment to beetroot and, for a bit of crunch, the toasted walnuts. Some crumbled feta on top would also be a delicious addition.'

....

SERVES 6

For the walnuts
150g (5½oz) walnuts
1 tablespoon olive oil

For the beetroot
about 1.6kg (3lb 8oz) medium beetroot
6 tablespoons extra virgin olive oil
3 tablespoons sweet red wine vinegar

For the herb borani
20g (¾oz) dill, fronds picked, plus extra sprigs
    to serve
20g (¾oz) basil, leaves picked
20g (¾oz) tarragon, leaves picked
20g (¾oz) flat-leaf parsley, leaves picked
10g (¼oz) mint leaves
½ spring onion, chopped into 3cm (1¼in) lengths
½ garlic clove, crushed to a paste with a little salt
3 tablespoons extra virgin olive oil
400g (14oz) thick Greek yogurt
1 teaspoon sweet white wine vinegar
sea salt and freshly ground black pepper

1. Preheat the oven to 180°C (160°C fan), 350°F, Gas mark 4. Toss the walnuts in the olive oil and sprinkle with salt. Roast for 5–8 minutes, or until lightly toasted. Set aside to cool.

2. Place the beetroot in a large saucepan of cold water and bring to the boil. Gently simmer for 45 minutes– 1 hour, depending on the size of the beetroots (to test if they are ready, insert a knife into the centre).

3. For the borani, put the herbs, spring onion and crushed garlic in a food processor and blitz until smooth. Add the oil, yogurt and white wine vinegar, and blitz until they are incorporated. Transfer to a bowl and season to taste with salt and pepper. Refrigerate until you are ready to serve.

4. When the beetroot is cooked, drain in a colander and cool under running water. When cool enough to handle, rub off the skin with your fingers (if cooked properly, the skin should come off easily). When the beetroot is completely cool, slice each one into 6–8 wedges and place in a bowl. Mix the olive oil and red wine vinegar together and pour over the beetroot. Season with salt and pepper, and toss gently.

5. To serve, spread the beetroot on to a plate, spoon over the herb borani and scatter with the extra sprigs of dill and the toasted walnuts.

BEETROOT, APPLE AND HORSERADISH SOUP

We are never without some sort of soup in the refrigerator at home. You could follow the order of seasonal produce through the ingredients of each soup as the months progress. This one is colourful and comforting: the earthy flavour of beetroot and sweet apple is brought to life by the hot kick of horseradish. It's worth seeking out a fresh horseradish root that you can grate directly over each bowl (the leftover root freezes well), or use horseradish from a jar, but remember it usually has added vinegar, so reduce the amount in the recipe.

....

SERVES 6 WITH LEFTOVERS

2 tablespoons light olive oil
1 medium red onion, sliced
2 celery sticks, roughly chopped
2 medium carrots, peeled and roughly chopped
1 large floury potato, peeled
1kg (2lb 4oz) beetroot (preferably organic), peeled
1 teaspoon thyme leaves
3 medium dessert apples
½ tablespoon balsamic vinegar
sea salt and freshly ground black pepper

To serve
crème fraîche or natural yogurt
freshly grated horseradish
handful of flat-leaf parsley, chopped

1. Heat the oil in a large, heavy-based pot over a medium heat and fry the onion with a large pinch of salt. Once it has started to soften, add the celery and carrots, and cook for a few more minutes.

2. Cut the potato and beetroot into walnut-sized pieces and add to the pot. Cook for a few minutes, then add the thyme, 1 teaspoon of salt, some pepper and 1.5 litres (2⅔ pints) water. Bring to the boil, then reduce to a simmer and cook for 30 minutes.

3. Grate or very finely chop the apples (removing the cores) and add to the pot. Continue to cook for another 10 minutes, by which point the beetroot should be completely soft.

4. Remove from the heat and carefully (it will be very hot) liquefy using a blender, then push all the soup through a wide-meshed sieve to make a silky liquid. Add the vinegar and taste for seasoning.

5. Serve with a dollop of crème fraîche or yogurt, a little grated horseradish and chopped parsley on each bowl.

ROAST BEETROOT

WITH LEMON TAHINI SAUCE AND
TOASTED SEEDS

*A bowl of home-roasted beetroot always comes in
handy, but if you're using shop-bought ready-cooked,
watch out for the added vinegar – you may wish to
reduce the amount in the sauce. This is quick to put
together – after a bit of slicing and whisking you'll
have an excellent lunch.*

SERVES 6

6 medium beetroot, scrubbed
3 tablespoons olive oil
sea salt and freshly ground black pepper

For the dressing
3 tablespoons tahini
1 tablespoon lemon juice
1 tablespoon cider vinegar
1 teaspoon honey

For the toasted seeds
2 teaspoons cumin seeds
2 tablespoons sunflower seeds
2 tablespoons pumpkin seeds
1 tablespoon dark soy sauce

To serve
small bunch of coriander, chopped
handful of pomegranate seeds

1. Preheat the oven to 180°C (160°C fan), 350°F, Gas
mark 4. Put the unpeeled beetroot into a baking dish.
Coat with 1 tablespoon of the olive oil and some salt,
and cover with foil. Roast for 40 minutes, or until
completely cooked (a skewer should slide through the
flesh easily). Set aside to cool.
2. For the dressing, mix together all the ingredients,
adding enough water to make it a pourable
consistency. Add salt and pepper according to taste.
Stir in 1 tablespoon of the remaining olive oil.
3. Cut the beetroot into wedges, peeling off any tough
skin if necessary.
4. Heat a dry frying pan over a medium heat and add
the cumin seeds. Toast for a few seconds before adding
the other seeds. After about 30 seconds – when they
just start to colour – add the remaining 1 tablespoon
of olive oil and the soy sauce. Stir vigorously to coat
everything. Remove from the heat.
5. To serve, arrange the beetroot wedges on a serving
platter. Add the dressing and mix well. Sprinkle with
the chopped coriander, the pomegranate seeds and the
toasted seeds. Serve warm.

BEETROOT, LENTILS
AND WATERCRESS
WITH HORSERADISH

*We used to make a lentil dish like this, minus
the beetroot, during my time at London's St John
restaurant. They served it as a vegetarian main course
option with a great dollop of goats' curd on top. I love
the earthy, peppery flavours of this combination. The
watercress wilts in the hot lentils and becomes more
like a green vegetable than a salad. You can eat this
as a meal in itself, or serve as a side dish.*

SERVES 6

about 600g (1lb 5oz) medium beetroot
4 tablespoons olive oil
about 200g (7oz) medium carrots, peeled and diced
1 onion, diced
2 celery sticks, diced
350g (12oz) brown lentils, rinsed and drained
bouquet garni (bundle of thyme, parsley stalks
    and rosemary)
2 tablespoons Dijon mustard
1 tablespoon sweet white vinegar
100g (3½oz) watercress, thick stalks removed
sea salt and freshly ground black pepper

To serve
horseradish sauce
good olive oil

1. Preheat the oven to 180°C (160°C fan), 350°F,
Gas mark 4. Put the beetroot in a roasting dish, rub
with 2 tablespoons of the olive oil and season with salt.
Wrap tightly with foil and roast for at least 1 hour, or
until completely tender.

2. In a large, lidded casserole, fry the carrots, onion
and celery in the remaining oil with ½ teaspoon of salt
over a medium heat until they are very soft and slightly
coloured. I like to take my time over this, as getting
the base really sweet and a bit caramelized gives so
much flavour. It can take at least 30 minutes and the
vegetables should be stirred only occasionally.

3. Add the lentils and bouquet garni, and cover
with 5cm (2in) water. Bring to the boil and cook,
partially covered, for 20–30 minutes until the lentils
are completely soft. Top up with water if necessary –
it should be saucy rather than dry.

4. When the beetroot are cooked and cool enough, slip
off their skins and cut into half-moons or large wedges.

5. When the lentils are cooked, remove the bouquet
garni. Add the mustard and vinegar, and season well.
Return the casserole to the heat and add the cooked
beetroot and the watercress, stirring so that the
watercress wilts through the lentils.

6. Serve in warm bowls with a dollop of horseradish
and a slick of good olive oil on top.

A SALAD, AND SIDES

As a gathering of seasonal ingredients combined to show off the textures and flavours of each component, a salad can be so much more than just a bowl of leaves. Creamy ripe pears with crumbled blue cheese and chewy walnuts scattered among peppery watercress, or rocket and soft lambs' lettuce; apples and celeriac with mustardy, creamy dressing. A dish like this is a meal in its own right, with a hunk of bread or sliced ham.

These side dishes are also substantial enough to be the main part of the meal. As a vegetarian option in restaurants, large slices of cauliflower are called 'steaks', and protein-rich tofu and meaty mushrooms are good substitutes for meat. Lentils and other pulses make excellent protein alternatives – filling, nourishing and inexpensive.

RECIPES

Braised lentils and dried porcini

Braised tofu with mushrooms

Chicory, persimmon and hazelnut salad

Roast cauliflower wedges with gremolata lentils

Whole roast cauliflower with tahini and roast chickpeas

BRAISED LENTILS
AND DRIED PORCINI

*The dried porcini and long-cooked vegetables give
simple lentils a great depth of flavour. This makes an
excellent side dish for fish or lamb, or can be eaten as a
meal in itself – serve hot with braised spinach, or cold
with sliced sausages like you're in a mountain refuge.*

SERVES 6 WITH LEFTOVERS

500g (1lb 2oz) Puy or Castelluccio lentils
4 tablespoons olive oil
1 onion, diced
2 celery sticks, finely chopped
1 leek, trimmed, washed and finely sliced
a few sprigs of thyme
1 bay leaf
a few parsley stalks
1 parsnip, peeled and diced
10g (¼oz) dried porcini mushrooms
½ tablespoon red wine vinegar
sea salt and freshly ground black pepper

1. Rinse the lentils. Heat a large, heavy-based
casserole and add the oil. When it is hot, add the onion
and a large pinch of salt and fry over a medium heat for
at least 5 minutes so that the onion begins to soften.
Add the celery and leek and another pinch of salt and
cook until everything is softened, just starting to
colour and tasting sweet.

2. Tie the herbs together, then add to the vegetables
with the parsnip, lentils and 1.5 litres (2⅔ pints) water.
Bring to the boil, then reduce to a gentle simmer.

3. While the lentils are cooking, place the porcini in
a bowl, cover with boiling water and leave to soak for
5 minutes. Remove from the water (you can add this
water to the lentils, but watch out for any grit at the
bottom) and chop the porcini finely before adding to
the lentils. When the lentils are soft but not mushy
(this takes 20–30 minutes), remove from the heat,
add the vinegar and season well with salt and pepper.

BRAISED TOFU

WITH MUSHROOMS

Amy Poon writes Chinese recipes, many of which she has learned from years spent assisting her restaurateur father at home. Tofu and mushrooms are both meaty-textured and nourishing, full of protein and umami taste; perfect for vegetarians or to make as part of a Chinese feast. Before starting the preparation for this recipe, you will need to rehydrate the dried mushrooms in 400ml (14fl oz) warm water for half an hour and then drain, reserving the soaking liquid.

SERVES 6

900g (2lb) firm tofu

3 spring onions

6 dried shiitake mushrooms, soaked (see above)

3 tablespoons oyster sauce

2½ tablespoons light soy sauce

1½ tablespoons dark soy sauce

½ teaspoon sugar

pinch of sea salt

1½ tablespoons cornflour or potato starch

6 tablespoons vegetable oil

25g (1oz) fresh root ginger, peeled and cut into thin slices

4 garlic cloves, crushed

1½ tablespoons Shaoxing rice wine

1 teaspoon sesame oil

coriander, to serve

1. Cut the tofu into 2cm (¾in) thick, triangular pieces. Lay flat and pat dry with kitchen paper.

2. Cut the spring onions at an angle into 4cm (1½in) long pieces and then separate the green and white parts.

3. Remove the stalks of the rehydrated mushrooms using a pair of scissors and rinse away any grit that may be caught in the gills. Slice each mushroom in half or, if large, into thirds.

4. In a medium bowl, mix the oyster sauce, light and dark soy sauces, sugar, salt and 400ml (14fl oz) of the reserved soaking liquid from the mushrooms (strained to remove any grit). Set aside.

5. In a bowl, mix the cornflour or potato starch with 2 tablespoons of water to make a slurry (runnier than a paste).

6. Heat a wok or shallow frying pan over a medium heat. Add the vegetable oil. Gently slide the tofu into the hot oil and shallow-fry on both sides until crisp and golden. Remove to a plate lined with kitchen paper.

7. Pour away the excess oil until you are left with about 2 tablespoons in the pan. Add the ginger to the hot pan and stir-fry for about 30 seconds. Stir in the crushed garlic, the white part of the spring onions and the mushrooms.

8. Increase the heat and stir-fry briskly for about 30 seconds, then add the Shaoxing wine. Stir-fry for another 30 seconds, then add the sauce mix.

9. Combine thoroughly and bring to the boil. Once bubbling, add the cornflour or potato starch slurry and stir until it starts to thicken.

10. Return the fried tofu to the pan, together with the green parts of the spring onions. Carefully fold the mixture until the tofu is well coated, taking care not to break up the pieces. Let your braised tofu cook for another 15–20 seconds. If the sauce is not sufficiently thick, add a little more slurry.

11. Finish by adding the sesame oil. Give the dish a final stir through. Plate, garnish with some coriander and serve.

CHICORY, PERSIMMON AND HAZELNUT SALAD

The pretty leaves of the chicory and radicchio bring
some autumnal colour to the table. I choose the firm
persimmons, which are sweet and have a good texture.
If you really can't find persimmons, try using pears,
apples or even slices of roasted squash. Serve this
as a starter or a simple lunch with a few cheeses on
a board and bread.

....

SERVES 6

For the salad
3 heads of white chicory
3 heads of red chicory
1 head of radicchio
small bunch of flat-leaf parsley
a few sprigs of tarragon
3 persimmons
100g (3½oz) hazelnuts, roughly chopped

For the dressing
1 small garlic clove, crushed
3 teaspoons balsamic vinegar
4 tablespoons extra virgin olive oil
sea salt and freshly ground black pepepr

1. Cut the chicory in half lengthways and separate the
leaves. Halve the radicchio, remove the core and slice
finely. Roughly chop the herbs. Lay the leaves in a large
serving bowl.
2. Slice the persimmons into small wedges, removing
the cores and any stones.
3. To make the dressing, mix the garlic and balsamic
vinegar in a bowl and whisk in the oil. Season with
salt and pepper. Toss the leaves in the bowl with most
of the dressing and more salt and pepper to taste.
Lay the persimmon wedges on the leaves and scatter
over the hazelnuts, drizzling the remaining dressing
over the top.

For the cauliflower
3 medium cauliflowers, or use
    1 cauliflower, broccoli and romanesco
1 tablespoon salted capers, rinsed
1 large red onion, sliced
1 lemon, thinly sliced
2 tablespoons olive oil
sea salt and freshly ground black pepper

For the lentils
350g (12oz) brown lentils
large bunch of flat-leaf parsley, chopped
zest of ½ lemon
1 tablespoon red wine vinegar
1 tablespoon extra virgin olive oil

ROAST CAULIFLOWER WEDGES
WITH GREMOLATA LENTILS

*Creamy white heads of cauliflower or fractal spires
of romanesco are delicious roasted until golden and
sweet. The caramelized lemons and capers add a sweet
acidity and a rich depth of flavour. If you don't have
lentils, or don't have time to cook them, use a jar or can
of cooked beans instead.*

....

SERVES 6

1. Preheat the oven to 180°C (160°C fan), 350°F,
Gas mark 4. Cut the cauliflower (and other brassicas,
if using) into quarters, using the stems as a guide.
2. Lay the pieces in one layer in a roasting tray and
scatter with the capers, the sliced red onion and lemon
and the olive oil. Season well with salt and pepper.
3. Roast for 25–30 minutes, then turn and roast for
another 20 minutes until lightly browned and soft.
The onion and lemon slices should be caramelized
and crisp.
4. Meanwhile, rinse the lentils and put them in a
saucepan with about double the amount of water
and 1 teaspoon of salt. Bring to the boil and cook,
uncovered, for 25 minutes, or until soft. There should
be just a little liquid left in the pan – do not drain.
5. Add the remaining ingredients to the lentils, mix
well and taste for seasoning. Serve the wet lentils on
a plate with the cauliflower wedges arranged on top.
Scatter with the onion and lemon slices and the capers.

WHOLE ROAST CAULIFLOWER
WITH TAHINI AND ROAST CHICKPEAS

*How to make a prosaic vegetable look impressive –
serve it whole. The sauce ingredients, once gathered,
just need to be fed into a blender, and before you know
it, you have a vegetable dish worth celebrating to
put in the middle of the table, for everyone to carve
out their own portions. Cook this in a big Le Creuset-
type pot and either serve it in that or transfer it
whole to a dish, sitting on the lemon slices, the sauce
poured over the top and decorated with the nuts,
chickpeas and pomegranate seeds. It should be soft
enough to serve with a spoon.*

....

SERVES 4–6

1 cauliflower
1 lemon, thinly sliced
1 tablespoon sumac
1 tablespoon za'atar
3 tablespoons olive oil
sea salt and freshly ground black pepper

For the sauce
3 tablespoons tahini
3 tablespoons natural yogurt
1 teaspoon cider vinegar
juice of ½ lemon
1 teaspoon honey
1 garlic clove, crushed
2 tablespoons olive oil

For the topping
50g (1¾oz) hazelnuts, chopped
50g (1¾oz) flaked almonds
300g (10½oz) cooked chickpeas
seeds of 1 pomegranate

1. First steam the whole cauliflower. Put 5cm (2in)
water in the bottom of a large, lidded, ovenproof
casserole. Sit the cauliflower on an upturned heatproof
plate in the pot and steam for 15 minutes until just
tender at the core.

2. Preheat the oven to 180°C (160°C fan), 350°F,
Gas mark 4. Tip out the water from the casserole and
remove the cauliflower and the plate. Lay the lemon
slices on the bottom of the casserole and place the
cauliflower on top. Sprinkle with the spices and lots
of salt, and pour over 2 tablespoons of the oil. Cover
and cook in the oven for 30 minutes, then remove the
lid and cook for another 20 minutes. Insert a skewer
into the stem – it should meet no resistance. Leave in
a warm place.

3. Combine all the sauce ingredients, season well
and add enough water to create a loose, runny sauce.

4. For the topping, toast the nuts in the oven for
15 minutes, or until golden. Increase the oven
temperature to 200°C (180°C fan), 400°F, Gas mark
6. Rinse and dry the chickpeas. Lay them flat on a
roasting tray, cover with the remaining 1 tablespoon
of olive oil and season well. Roast for 5–10 minutes
until they crackle and colour slightly.

5. Put the whole cauliflower on a large serving
plate, pour some of the sauce over the top and scatter
with the hazelnuts, almonds, roast chickpeas and
pomegranate seeds. Serve the rest of the sauce in
a jug at the table.

CHICKEN

The cooler days in autumn make me crave soups and braises and glossy-skinned roast chicken. Whenever I buy meat I'd rather spend more and get better quality, and then make the most of it. If you get a whole bird, you can use every part of it: the leftover flesh from the cooked bird is perfect for a salad or sandwich, or to add to noodles or soup; the giblets and bones or carcass can be used for stock.

If a recipe calls for jointed pieces, ask the butcher to do it for you and take home the bones.

RECIPES

Chicken marinated in pomegranate molasses, yogurt and spices
Nourishing chicken broth with noodles
Chicken with sweet wine and grapes
Flattened chicken with lemon, garlic and herbs
Alternative (no rice) Hainan chicken

CHICKEN MARINATED IN POMEGRANATE MOLASSES, YOGURT AND SPICES

Pomegranate molasses has a sweet-sour flavour, a little like tamarind. This is softened by the yogurt, which also helps to tenderize the meat, particularly if you leave it to marinate overnight. It's an easy dish if you're entertaining – pop it in the oven and leave it to do its thing. Good with rice, but I like it served with wilted spinach tossed with white beans and olive oil, and leeks halved lengthways and roasted until they are soft and a little crispy around the edges.

SERVES 6

For the marinade
2 garlic cloves, peeled
1 tablespoon cumin seeds
1 tablespoon coriander seeds
1 teaspoon smoked sweet paprika
1 teaspoon ground cinnamon
1 tablespoon cider vinegar
2 tablespoons pomegranate molasses
3 tablespoons natural yogurt
1 teaspoon honey
sea salt

For the chicken
2 large chicken breasts, skin on
2 large chicken legs and thighs, joined (or buy a 2.5kg/5lb 8oz chicken and ask the butcher to remove the legs and thighs and keep the carcass for stock)
2 tablespoons olive oil

To serve
10g (¼oz) coriander leaves, chopped

1. Crush the garlic with a large pinch of salt using a pestle and mortar. In a dry frying pan, toast the cumin and coriander seeds for a minute until wisps of smoke rise and they smell toasty. Add these to the mortar and grind with the pestle. Add all the other marinade ingredients along with 1 tablespoon of fine salt and mix to a paste.

2. Place the chicken pieces in one layer in a roasting tin and massage the marinade into the pieces. Try to leave it in the refrigerator, covered, for at least 2 hours, or overnight. Preheat the oven to 180°C (160°C fan), 350°F, Gas mark 4.

3. Pour the olive oil over the chicken and cook for 40 minutes. Then increase the oven temperature to 200°C (180°C fan), 400°F, Gas mark 6 and cook for 10 minutes to brown the skin. Remove from the oven and rest for up to 20 minutes in a warm place.

4. To serve, slice the breast meat, separate the drumsticks from the thighs and cut the thighs in half along the bone. Arrange on a plate with the chopped coriander leaves sprinkled on top. Pour the juice from the roasting tin into a jug and serve alongside.

NOURISHING CHICKEN BROTH
WITH NOODLES

*Use the carcass from a roast chicken to make a cheap
and delicious broth. For a deeper-flavoured stock,
roast the carcass before making. Add any vegetables
you feel like eating, even cooked leftovers to make it
super quick.*

....

SERVES 6

For the stock
1 roast chicken carcass
vegetables, such as carrots, onions, celery, fennel,
    celeriac and parsnips, peeled and chopped
1 bay leaf
1 sprig each of thyme, sage and rosemary
6 black peppercorns
sea salt

For the broth
2 carrots, peeled and diced (keep the peelings for
    your next stock)
1 sweet potato, peeled and finely diced (keep the
    peelings)
knob of fresh root ginger, peeled and grated
4 small spring onions, finely chopped
1 red chilli, finely chopped
300g (10½oz) leftover roast chicken pieces,
    shredded
340g (11¾oz) packet rice vermicelli or soba noodles
leftover cooked vegetables (optional)
4 tablespoons dark soy sauce
juice of 1 lime or lemon
20g (¾oz) coriander, chopped
a few sprigs of mint, chopped
20g (¾oz) flat-leaf parsley, chopped

1. To make the stock, place the chicken carcass and
the other stock ingredients in a large pot or pan. Add
2 litres (3½ pints) water and bring to the boil. Skim off
any foam and turn down to a simmer. Cook for at least
2 hours. Strain to remove the vegetables, return to the
pan and boil until reduced to about 1.2 litres (2 pints).
Season with salt to taste.

2. If the vegetables for the broth are raw, cook them in
the stock for 3–4 minutes. (Cooked vegetables can be
added to the hot broth to reheat just before you serve
it.) Add the ginger, spring onions, chilli and leftover
chicken pieces.

3. Boil the noodles according to the packet instructions.

4. Add any cooked vegetables along with the soy
sauce, lime or lemon juice and the herbs to the broth
and taste for seasoning.

5. Distribute the cooked noodles between 6 bowls and
ladle the broth over the top.

CHICKEN

WITH SWEET WINE AND GRAPES

This traditional Tuscan dish comes from Claudia Roden who explains that she discovered it in Florence in a trattoria-fiaschetteria called Il Latini, where it was served on a slice of grilled polenta. One large chicken thigh per person is usually enough, but one or two people may want a second piece, so she suggests using eight.

....

SERVES 6

6 tablespoons olive oil

4 sprigs of rosemary, leaves picked and chopped

8 chicken thighs, skin on, bone in

6 garlic cloves, peeled

30g (1oz) butter (optional)

150ml (5fl oz) sweet Muscat wine

750g (1lb 10oz) mixed seedless white and red grapes, rinsed and drained

sea salt and freshly ground black pepper

1. Heat 3 tablespoons of the oil in a lidded sauté pan or casserole wide enough to hold the chicken pieces in a single layer. Add the chopped rosemary and then the chicken thighs, skin-side down.

2. Sprinkle with salt and pepper and cook over a medium heat until lightly browned. Turn over the pieces and season again, then cook until the other side is lightly browned.

3. Add the whole garlic cloves. When they have only just begun to colour on one side, add the butter, if using – it gives a lovely creaminess to the sauce – and pour in the Muscat wine.

4. Put the lid on and simmer over a low heat for about 25 minutes until the chicken thighs are tender, moist and juicy, turning them over at least once and removing the lid towards the end to reduce the sauce. Taste for seasoning – you need enough salt and pepper to balance the sweetness of the wine.

5. At the same time, heat the remaining 3 tablespoons of oil in a wide frying pan and add the grapes. Cook over a medium heat for about 20 minutes, shaking the pan and turning the grapes over, until they have collapsed and their juice is much reduced. Pour them over the chicken pieces and heat through together.

FLATTENED CHICKEN
WITH LEMON, GARLIC AND HERBS

This is the easiest way to cook chicken, either in the oven or on a grill. By completely deboning it, the meat lies flat and cooks evenly. Deboned chicken cooks more quickly too, and when it comes to serving, just cut it into slices; no complicated carving needed. It's tricky to debone a chicken at home, so ask the butcher to do it for you, then keep the bones for stock. Serve with chips and a green salad for an easy supper.

....

SERVES 6

2.5kg (5lb 8oz) organic, free-range chicken, deboned
2 sprigs of rosemary
small bunch of thyme
handful of sage leaves
2 garlic cloves, crushed
1 lemon, halved
2 tablespoons olive oil
sea salt and freshly ground black pepper

To serve
chips
green salad

1. Lay the chicken flat skin-side down on a tray or clean work surface. Finely chop the herbs and mix with the garlic and the juice of one lemon half. Rub this mixture all over the flesh of the chicken before seasoning generously with salt and pepper.
2. Slice the other half of the lemon into thin circles. Lay the lemon slices on the base of a large roasting tin and flip the chicken over to lay it skin-side up on top of the lemon slices, flat in the roasting tin. Season the skin generously with salt. Leave to marinate, covered, in the refrigerator for as long as you can – overnight is best.
3. Preheat the oven to 220°C (200°C fan), 425°F, Gas mark 7. Pour the oil over the chicken and roast for 20 minutes, or until the skin is well browned. Then reduce the oven temperature to 160°C (140°C fan), 325°F, Gas mark 3 and cook for another 20 minutes. Remove from the oven, cover with foil and leave to rest for 20 minutes.
4. Place on a board and cut into slices. Pour off the juice collected in the roasting tin and serve with chips and a green salad.

ALTERNATIVE (NO RICE) HAINAN CHICKEN

This is family food, everyone crowded around the table with a bowl of chicken, chopsticks and maybe a dish of smacked cucumber on the side (see page 120). 'Every Chinese family has its own method of making this quintessential comfort dish,' writes Amy Poon. 'Traditionally, one would serve the chicken skin on, bone in with rice cooked with the poaching liquid of the chicken. I have omitted the rice here. My children dislike poached chicken skin and are lazy with bones, so I shred the chicken and take the skin off. If you take the skin off, you can crisp it in the oven with salt and serve as a snack.'

....

SERVES 6

For the chicken
50g (1¾oz) fresh root ginger, peeled
3 spring onions, left whole
about 1.2kg (2lb 10oz) corn-fed chicken
sea salt

For the sauce
150g (5½oz) fresh root ginger, peeled
250g (9oz) spring onions, finely chopped
pinch of white pepper
150ml (5fl oz) groundnut or vegetable oil

To serve
coriander
dark soy sauce

1. Bring 1.5–2 litres (2⅔–3½ pints) water to the boil in a lidded saucepan and add 2 tablespoons of salt. Crush the ginger and add to the pot with the spring onions.

2. Hold the chicken by its wing and gently lower it into the boiling water, dunk, then lift out. Repeat 3 times. This regulates the temperature of the chicken inside and out to produce a silkier texture.

3. Bring the water back to the boil and immerse the chicken, then pop on the lid, turn off the heat and leave undisturbed on the hob for 25–30 minutes.

4. Check the meat is cooked through by inserting a skewer into the thigh: the juices should run clear. Prepare a large bowl of iced water with a couple of handfuls of ice cubes. Lift the chicken out of the pan and plunge into this ice bath to arrest further cooking. Discard the poaching liquid and the spring onions and ginger in it.

5. For the sauce, finely grate the ginger. This can be done with a food processor. Then finely chop the spring onions – I don't recommend that you do this in a food processor, as it becomes a slimy mess. Combine both in a heatproof bowl. Add ½ teaspoon of salt and the white pepper.

6. Heat the oil in a pan over a medium heat until smoking. Gently pour the hot oil over the ginger and spring onion mixture. Take care – it will spit and splatter, and the bowl becomes very hot. Mix well.

7. To serve, shred the chicken into bite-sized pieces and place in a bowl. Pour over the ginger and spring onion sauce, and combine. Garnish with coriander and serve with a dish of soy sauce for dipping.

A FOCUS ON JAPANESE FLAVOURS

Looking for inspiration on an autumn day, I'm tempted by the wooden and earthenware ceramic dishes I find in a Japanese shop.

There are many delicious flavours used in Japanese cooking – the sweet, earthy taste of miso, mirin, rice vinegar and soy sauce can now be found easily, yet often I find people say they are intimidated by them. I am asked 'What is mirin?' (a sweet, syrupy rice wine) or 'How can I use miso other than in soup?'

With these recipes, I want to show how easy it can be to take everyday ingredients – like spinach, salmon and aubergines – in a different flavour direction.

The basic Japanese flavours tend to balance sweetness, saltiness, acidity and umami tastes, and these few ingredients will bring those characteristics to the food. Mirin for sweetness; soy sauce for salt; rice vinegar for acidity; and the deep flavour of fermented soya beans in miso for umami.

I'm not trained in Japanese cookery, but I adore eating in Japanese restaurants and these recipes are inspired by the simpler dishes I've enjoyed. When I cook this food, I make a selection of dishes and put them all on the table at once. Stoneware bowls and plates and simple pottery dishes suit this food.

Dashi is the simplest of stocks, used in many Japanese dishes. It is made using dried bonito flakes and kelp, sometimes with mushrooms. You don't need to make it yourself; sachets of instant dashi dissolved in water are as common as stock cubes. It also lasts for ages in the cupboard.

White miso is sweeter and lighter (it has been fermented for less time). Red or dark miso is earthier tasting and stronger.

Sake (Japanese rice wine) is available in most supermarkets and some wine merchants. It is delicious to drink and goes well with all these dishes, which makes it worthwhile buying a bottle.

RECIPES

Smoked mackerel miso

Mussels and miso

Spinach gomae

Salmon teriyaki

Glazed miso aubergine

Easy Japanese rice

Quick cucumber pickle

Japanese salad dressing

SMOKED MACKEREL MISO

*This is inspired by a game-changing miso soup
I once ate at a chef's residency in London. Chef and
restaurateur David Chang was cooking at the St John
hotel for a week and one of the dishes on his menu was
a miso made using broth infused with smoked eel
bones. I use both smoked eel and smoked mackerel
when I make this and it has become something of a
store-cupboard supper.*

....

SERVES 4

2–4 sachets instant dashi (according to your
   preference), dissolved in 1 litre (1¾ pints) water
4 tablespoons dark miso paste
1 smoked mackerel fillet or smoked eel, cut into
   small pieces
150g (5½oz) firm tofu, cut into small cubes
large pinches of dried wakame seaweed (optional),
   soaked in cold water according to the packet
   instructions and drained
2 spring onions, finely sliced

1. Bring the dashi to a simmer in a pan. Put the miso
in a small bowl and thin it using 1 tablespoon of the
broth to help it disperse more easily. Then stir this
mixture into the remaining dashi.
2. To serve, put the smoked mackerel or eel in the
bottom of 4 bowls with the tofu and wakame (if using),
and pour over the broth. Finish with the finely sliced
spring onions.

MUSSELS AND MISO

A steaming bowl of mussels is just what one feels like at this time of year. Adding miso and ginger introduce a great depth of flavour, and for a more substantial meal, serve with soba noodles on the side, to add to the liquid left in the bowl.

....

SERVES 2

1kg (2lb 4oz) mussels
2 tablespoons light oil, such as groundnut
　　or sunflower
5cm (2in) piece of fresh root ginger, peeled
　　and chopped
1 garlic clove, chopped
1 red chilli, finely chopped
2 spring onions, finely chopped
1½ tablespoons white miso paste
3 tablespoons rice wine
20g (¾oz) coriander, chopped
seaweed sprinkle, such as furikake or shredded nori

1. Wash the mussels and then remove any 'beards' attached to the shells. Discard all shells that are broken or open.
2. Heat the oil in a large pot with a lid and add the ginger, garlic, chilli and spring onions. Fry for a few minutes until soft.
3. In a bowl, whisk the miso and rice wine to combine, then add 3–4 tablespoons of water.
4. Add the miso mixture to the pot and increase the heat, stirring well before adding the prepared mussels. Cover with the lid and cook for 5–10 minutes, or until the shells have opened.
5. Serve with the coriander and seaweed sprinkle scattered on top.

SPINACH GOMAE

This is a dish found in many Japanese restaurants and I always order it. There is something moreish and magical about the flavour combination of spinach and a salty-sweet sesame sauce. What's more, it couldn't be simpler to make. You could use this dressing on steamed broccoli too.

SERVES 4

1.5kg (3lb 5oz) spinach leaves, stalks removed
sea salt
2 tablespoons ground sesame seeds, to serve

For the sesame sauce
2 tablespoons dark soy sauce
2 tablespoons rice vinegar
4 tablespoons mirin
2 tablespoons white tahini

1. Wash the spinach and put it into a large bowl, still dripping. Heat a large, lidded pan with nothing in it and add the wet spinach and a generous pinch of salt. Cover the pan and allow the heat to steam the leaves for a couple of minutes – you will need to occasionally toss the spinach to distribute the heat.
2. When it is all wilted and cooked, drain and refresh under cold water. Squeeze it dry and then gently try to open out some of the leaves so that it isn't too compacted. Shape into golf-ball-sized spheres.
3. To make the sauce, mix all the ingredients together in a bowl, then pour into a shallow dish.
4. To serve, place the spinach balls in the sauce and sprinkle the ground sesame seeds over the top.

SALMON TERIYAKI

*This well-known sauce tastes so much better
homemade, and when you know how simple it is to
make, you will never need to buy the bottled version.
Salmon and chicken are most commonly cooked in
this way, but for a vegetarian option, I cook firm tofu
slices as I would the salmon. Apart from the fresh fish,
all of the other components can be kept for ages in the
cupboard, so it makes a great last-minute dish to cook.
You can even make double quantities of the sauce
and keep that in the refrigerator for another time.
Sometimes I add a teaspoon of grated ginger, but if
I'm serving it with other recipes that contain ginger,
I tend to omit it.*

....

SERVES 4

1 tablespoon grapeseed oil
4 salmon fillets, skin on
sea salt

For the teriyaki sauce
10g (¼oz) caster sugar
100ml (3½fl oz) sake
50ml (2fl oz) mirin
50ml (2fl oz) dark soy sauce

1. Put all the teriyaki ingredients into a frying pan
and bring to the boil. Let the sauce bubble and reduce
by almost half until it becomes syrupy. You can do this
ahead of time and keep it covered in the refrigerator
for up to a month until needed.

2. To cook the salmon, heat the grapeseed oil in a
nonstick frying pan. Sprinkle the salmon fillets with
salt and fry for a minute on each side to brown the skin
and flesh.

3. Add the teriyaki sauce and continue to cook until
the salmon fillets are no longer translucent, basting
as they finish cooking. Remove the fish to a plate and
pour over the sauce to serve.

GLAZED MISO AUBERGINE

Miso has an extraordinary depth of flavour and can be used in all sorts of dishes: dressings, sauces, marinades and glazes. This is a good vegetarian dish and the aubergine flesh almost tastes meaty when cooked with the miso. Try to find the freshest aubergines you can for this – I use either the round Violetta varieties or long aubergines. Make sure the skin is taut and the flesh is firm.

....

SERVES 6

3 large or 6 small aubergines
2 tablespoons grapeseed or sesame oil
sea salt

For the glaze
1 teaspoon honey
90g (3¼oz) white or red miso paste (see page 190)
1 teaspoon grated fresh root ginger
1 tablespoon rice vinegar
2 tablespoons sake
1 tablespoon dark soy sauce

1. Preheat the oven to 220°C (200°C fan), 425°F, Gas mark 7. Cut each aubergine in half lengthways and score the flesh in a crisscross pattern about 2cm (¾in) deep. Sprinkle over a few pinches of salt.

2. Pour the oil into a large roasting tin and roll the aubergine halves in the oil, finally laying them flesh-side down. Roast for 30–40 minutes until completely soft.

3. In a saucepan, mix together all the ingredients for the miso glaze and heat gently, stirring.

4. Remove the aubergines from the oven, turn them over so that they are flesh-side up and spread the glaze over the surface.

5. Heat the grill to high and grill the aubergines for about 5 minutes until the glaze is bubbling.

EASY JAPANESE RICE

Japanese rice is short-grain and usually sold in supermarkets as sushi rice. I love rice cooked simply like this and it makes such a good side dish or even the main part of a meal, sprinkled with sesame seeds or furikake and seasoned with some soy sauce or rice vinegar.

SERVES 6

For the rice
300g (10½oz) Japanese short-grain rice

For the dressing
1 tablespoon rice vinegar
2 tablespoons mirin
½ teaspoon fine salt
½ teaspoon sugar

1. Wash the rice in several changes of water until the water is no longer cloudy. Drain well.
2. Put the rice in a medium saucepan and add 360ml (12½fl oz) water (or 360g/12½oz – I find it easier to weigh it than to use a measuring jug).
3. Cover and bring to the boil, then reduce the heat and cook, covered, for 12 minutes until the water has been absorbed. Each grain should be plump and soft but retain its shape.
4. Turn off the heat and leave covered for 10 minutes before serving.
5. Mix the dressing ingredients together and spoon through the rice before serving.

QUICK CUCUMBER PICKLE

This is a refreshing side dish to serve with Salmon teriyaki (see page 195), or any of the other vegetable dishes. You could even just eat it with some rice for a light meal.

SERVES 6

1 cucumber, peeled, halved lengthways and seeds scraped out
2 tablespoons dark soy sauce
2 tablespoons rice vinegar
1–2 teaspoons sugar or agave nectar
3cm (1¼in) piece of fresh root ginger, peeled and cut into thin matchsticks
sea salt

1. Slice the cucumber halves and toss the slices with a large pinch of salt.
2. Mix the other ingredients together in a bowl and add the cucumber. Leave to marinate for 30 minutes before serving.

JAPANESE SALAD DRESSING

I use this to dress soaked seaweed or peppery leaves such as mizuna or rocket. They make a great refreshing side dish to a Japanese meal.

MAKES ENOUGH FOR 6 LARGE HANDFULS OF SALAD

1 tablespoon rice vinegar
1 tablespoon dark soy sauce
1 tablespoon toasted sesame oil

1. Simply stir all the ingredients together in a small bowl and pour over the salad just before serving.

APPLES

Some years our apple trees produce enormous amounts of fruit and we rush to try to preserve it all – stored in a shed or made into purées and apple juice – the ground littered with windfalls that end up in the compost heap. Our apples keep quite well in the shed on wooden slatted drawers for several months and I'm greeted by the sweet, dense, musk smell of apple whenever I walk in the door.

Autumn is the season for apples, one of the UK's finest and most abundant fruits. Hanging from trees and filling baskets at the market, you'll see red, green, golden and russet brown varieties, each with a different flavour and texture from crisp to soft, tart to sweet.

I tend to use 'eating' apples when cooking desserts and save the less sweet 'cooking' apples for sauces or chutney. You can make foolproof *tartes fines* with thinly sliced apples arranged on puff pastry, brushed with butter and sprinkled with sugar, then baked in a hot oven for 30 minutes. Or core apples and bake, stuffed with butter and doused with a splash of cognac.

When I'm dealing with a glut, I make apple purée to eat with yogurt for breakfast, or spicy apple chutney to put in sandwiches with cheese.

RECIPES

Bircher muesli

Apple, quince, prune and cinnamon pie

Apple and blueberry cobbler

Apple and almond Welsh cakes

Toffee apples for Bonfire Night

BIRCHER MUESLI

I like to make a batch or double batch of this for the weekend. It's something I often don't get around to during the week, despite my best intentions, and it's always enjoyed by all. You could also use poached quinces, fresh pears or even soaked prunes, served chopped up on top.

....

SERVES 6

250g (9oz) **porridge oats**
2 tablespoons **pumpkin seeds**
2 tablespoons **sunflower seeds**
2 tablespoons **sesame seeds**
400ml (14fl oz) **almond milk**
2 **apples**
200g (7oz) **full-fat natural yogurt**
honey, to taste

1. Put the oats, seeds and almond milk into a bowl large enough to leave room for the other ingredients and leave to soak overnight. If the kitchen is cool, I leave it out of the refrigerator.
2. In the morning, grate the apples and add them to the oats with the yogurt and honey. Stir well and serve.

APPLE, QUINCE, PRUNE
AND CINNAMON PIE

*Sally Clarke, whose recipe this is, says that filo
pastry is the only item they buy ready-made at
the restaurant, so no one should feel guilty about
doing the same!*

....

SERVES 6–8

about 700g (1lb 9oz) medium-ripe quinces

juice of 2 oranges

70g (2½oz) caster sugar, plus extra for sprinkling

½ vanilla pod, split in half

2cm (¾in) cinnamon stick

zest of ½ lemon

4 large Braeburn, Cox or Jonagold apples

75g (2½oz) demerara sugar

pinch of ground cinnamon

zest of 1 orange

8 prunes, soaked in water for 20 minutes, then
    drained, halved and stones removed

125g (4½oz) unsalted butter

pinch each of ground cinnamon, cloves, allspice
    and ginger or 1 level teaspoon mixed spice

12 sheets of filo pastry

To serve

whipped cream or ice cream

1.   Peel, quarter and core the quinces. Cut each piece
in half and place in a pan with 250ml (9fl oz) water,
the orange juice, 50g (1¾oz) of the caster sugar, the
vanilla pod, cinnamon stick and lemon zest. Bring to
the boil, cover, then simmer for up to 30 minutes, or
until tender when pierced with a knife. Allow to cool
in the juices.

2.   Peel, quarter and core the apples, and add to a
bowl with the demerara sugar, ground cinnamon and
orange zest. Add the prune halves and toss together.

3.   For the pastry, warm the butter, the remaining
20g (¾oz) sugar and the spices together over a low
heat. Place one filo sheet on a clean tea towel. Using
a pastry brush, brush the spiced butter on to the filo
and place a second sheet on top. Place this into a 20cm
(8in) tart tin or a shallow cake tin with a removable
base, pressing the pastry into the corners and allowing
the ends to fall over the outside rim. Continue with the
remaining sheets, placing them in a star pattern so
that the outside edges are irregular.

4.   Drain the quince well, reserving the juices, and
add the quince to the apple mix. Pile the fruit into the
centre of the tart, then scoop the pastry edges over
and around the tart decoratively. This will make the
finished tart look attractive, so do not worry if it looks
a bit like crumpled sheets at this stage.

5.   Preheat the oven to 180°C (160°C fan), 350°F,
Gas mark 4. Brush the top with the remaining spiced
butter, sprinkle with a little extra sugar and bake in
the oven for 1 hour, or until the pastry is crisp, golden
brown and firm at the edges as well as underneath.

6.   Meanwhile, reduce the quince juices over a high
heat until syrupy and pour into a serving jug. Allow
the tart to cool a little before removing from the tin,
sliding the base away and serving on a flat dish. Serve
warm or cool with the syrup and cream or ice cream.

APPLE AND BLUEBERRY COBBLER

A cobbler is made with a batter or dough, or in this case a scone topping over a pie filling, making a change from a crumble or pie crust. If you prepare this quantity of topping, it will give you a batch of scones to have up your sleeve for another day (keep them in the freezer and cook from frozen for 15 minutes at 200°C/ 180°C fan/400°F/Gas mark 6). You could use other fruit (plums or rhubarb), but the colour of blueberries with apples is lovely and the flavour works well with the fragrant bay leaves.

....

SERVES 6

For the filling
1kg (2lb 4oz) cooking apples (about 7 large)
250g (9oz) blueberries
1 tablespoon plain flour
1 bay leaf
100g (3½oz) dark soft brown sugar
zest of lemon, plus juice of ½

For the topping
500g (1lb 2oz) plain flour, plus extra for dusting
4 teaspoons baking powder
large pinch of salt
200g (7oz) unsalted butter, cut into cubes
300ml (10fl oz) buttermilk, or single cream mixed with 1 teaspoon lemon juice
1 egg, beaten, for brushing

For the custard
3 eggs, plus 2 egg yolks
40g (1½oz) caster sugar
1 teaspoon vanilla extract or seeds of 1 vanilla pod
200ml (7fl oz) full-fat milk
200ml (7fl oz) double cream

1. Peel, core and thinly slice the apples. Put them in a bowl with the other filling ingredients and mix well. Leave them to macerate for 1 hour or more, then fill a pie dish with the mixture.

2. Preheat the oven to 190°C (170°C fan), 375°F, Gas mark 5. Sift the dry ingredients for the topping into a bowl and stir well to combine. Add the butter and gently rub in with your fingertips to form rough crumbs, or blitz briefly in a food processor.

3. Pour in the buttermilk or cream mixture and bring together to form a soft dough. Press into 2 discs, wrap in clingfilm and leave to rest in the refrigerator for at least 30 minutes.

4. Roll out the dough to about 2cm (¾in) thick on a floured surface. Cut into small circles (about the diameter of a shot-glass rim) and lay the scones, not quite touching, on top of the pie filling. Brush with beaten egg.

5. Bake for 40–45 minutes until golden on top and bubbling inside. If the top is getting too brown before the apple is cooked, cover with foil.

6. Meanwhile, whisk the eggs and the extra yolks for the custard in a bowl with the sugar and vanilla.

7. Heat the milk and cream in a saucepan until it is almost boiling, then pour it in a thin stream into the egg mix in the bowl, whisking to combine.

8. Return to the pan and cook over a very gentle heat, stirring constantly until the custard thickens enough to coat the back of a spoon. This takes about 10 minutes. You can keep it warm over a pan of hot water until it is needed.

9. Serve the cobbler hot with the custard.

APPLE AND ALMOND
WELSH CAKES

*These are what I make when we decide we want
something for tea but there isn't time to bake a cake.
They are incredibly simple to put together and are
fried on the hob, so they're fun to cook with children.
Like scones straight from the oven, they're best eaten
straight away.*

....

MAKES ABOUT 12

130g (4¾oz) self-raising flour, plus extra for dusting
100g (3½oz) cold unsalted butter, cut into cubes,
    plus extra for frying
pinch of salt
50g (1¾oz) ground almonds
40g (1½oz) caster sugar, plus extra to serve
½ teaspoon ground cinnamon
a few gratings of nutmeg
40g (1½oz) raisins
1 sweet apple, peeled, cored and finely diced
1 egg, well beaten

1. Sift the flour into a mixing bowl, add the butter
and gently rub in with your fingertips, or blitz briefly
in a food processor, until the pieces are no smaller
than petit pois.
2. Add the rest of the ingredients, except the egg,
and mix together well. Stir in the beaten egg with a
fork until the mixture starts to form clumps. Bring
the mixture together to form a dough, handling it
as little as possible.
3. Wrap the dough in clingfilm and refrigerate for
at least 30 minutes.
4. Dust a work surface with flour and roll out the
dough to about 1cm (½in) thick. Using a 6cm (2½in)
round cutter, cut out 12 circles, pressing any offcuts
together and re-rolling as necessary.
5. Melt some butter in a frying pan over a
medium heat and fry the Welsh cakes in batches
for 2–3 minutes on each side until golden brown.
Sprinkle with caster sugar to serve.

TOFFEE APPLES
FOR BONFIRE NIGHT

*This childhood treat is easy to make and fun to eat –
bonfire or not. Make the most of the many UK-grown
apples available at this time of year; I like to use small,
Cox-like Herefordshire Russets for this, for a good ratio
of toffee to apple.*

....

SERVES 6

6 small apples
light oil, such as groundnut or sunflower,
    for greasing
225g (8oz) demerara sugar
1 teaspoon white wine vinegar
1 tablespoon golden syrup
30g (1oz) unsalted butter
½ teaspoon vanilla extract
100g (3½oz) hazelnuts, finely chopped

1. Wash the apples and remove the stalks. Skewer
each apple with a wooden stick, pushed down through
the core. Lightly oil a baking tray.
2. Dissolve the sugar in 110ml (3¾fl oz) water in a
pan over a moderate heat. When dissolved, add the
vinegar, syrup and butter. Bring the mixture to the
boil and boil rapidly for about 8–10 minutes. If you
have a jam thermometer, the temperature at hard-
crack stage will be 140°C (275°F). Otherwise, you can
test it by putting a drop in a glass of cold water – if it
hardens to a ball, it is ready; if it is still soft and tacky,
it will need longer. Be careful not to burn the mixture,
otherwise it will taste very bitter.
3. When the toffee is ready, remove the pan from the
heat and add the vanilla extract. Put the chopped nuts
on a flat plate. Dip each apple into the toffee using the
stick and twist around to cover completely. Allow the
excess toffee to drip off before rolling the apples in the
chopped nuts.
4. Place the apples on the oiled baking tray and leave
to cool and harden. They will be ready to eat in just a
matter of minutes.

AUTUMN MENUS

SIMPLE IDEAS FOR THE WEEKEND
Breakfast – Bircher muesli page 201
Lunch – Squash and cavolo flan page 162
Tea – Apple and almond Welsh cakes page 209
*Dinner – Flattened chicken with lemon, garlic
and herbs* page 186

If we have friends staying, I like to have some sort of plan of what we will eat. These are all simple seasonal dishes that don't take long to make.

AN AUTUMN FEAST
Baked pumpkin soup with Gruyère and sage page 161
Chicken with sweet wine and grapes page 185
Apple, quince, prune and cinnamon pie page 204

Soup cooked inside a whole pumpkin and displayed on the table for everyone to dig into is a celebratory sight. I make this dish every year; it's become a sort of seasonal marker. Claudia Roden's Tuscan chicken is traditionally made at the end of the grape harvest, and apple and quince pie is a showcase for autumn fruit.

GET AHEAD (VEGETARIAN)
Beetroot, apple and horseradish soup page 169
*Whole roast cauliflower with tahini and
roast chickpeas* page 179
Apple and blueberry cobbler page 207

A soup ready to heat up when you need it is a very reassuring thing to have in the kitchen. And I often make this cauliflower dish, leaving it cooking in the oven while I do other things.

REFRESHING SPICY FLAVOURS
Alternative (no rice) Hainan chicken page 188
Braised tofu with mushrooms page 174
Mussels and miso page 193
Quick cucumber pickle page 199
Easy Japanese rice page 199

Occasionally I crave the spices and flavours of Japanese, Chinese and Taiwanese food. They offer the earthy tastes that autumn represents and these are all a simple introduction to using ingredients and techniques that might not usually be part of your repertoire.

FLOWERS AND TABLE DECORATIONS
Autumn offers a particular colour palette in both food and flowers: burgundy dahlias and deep orange pumpkins, red apples and burnished copper leaves. I put rows of squash on side tables and fill wooden bowls with apples and walnuts. Branches of autumn leaves make a magnificent display, and earthenware plates and bowls for serving suit these earthy colours.

Winter

*Cooking can be a meandering pleasure
during the long dark evenings or days that
are too cold to be outside*

Time spent cooking in winter, especially during the long dark evenings or days that are too cold to be outside, pays greater dividends than at any other time of the year.

One lesson I learned cooking in restaurants is that there is always something one can do ahead of time. 'The 30-minute meal ain't all it's cracked up to be. Slinging dinner on the table may feed us, but such hurried gestures often bypass the pleasure that real cooking offers,' says chef David Tanis. Slow-braised meat dishes using cheaper cuts that release their flavoursome potential over hours in the oven taste even better reheated the next day, as do soups, baked vegetable dishes and the base for various fish stews. While there's something in the oven, this is the time to tend to things bubbling on the stove: pots of orange-scented marmalade to fill the kitchen with aromas; stocks made with leftover bones and vegetables; pans full of chickpeas, beans or lentils that become the base or star turn in future meals.

Stew some onions, roast some vegetables; a few hours spent like this in the kitchen and you'll have made your way through half of the prep time for any number of dishes you might want to cook another day. Then cooking can be a meandering pleasure, not a last-minute dash to get everything ready from start to finish in time for dinner.

If you choose to eat seasonally, you'll be overwhelmed by the abundance of root vegetables and brassicas at this time of year. These are plants that can handle our cold climate. They'll cost you less too, an especially satisfying economy if you buy locally produced. If they're farmed organically, you don't even need to peel these roots. Carrots, parsnips, swede and potatoes – many of the nutrients are in their skins, which makes chopping up a bundle feel like a breeze compared to podding a box of peas in summer. Vegetarian or not, you can fill yourself up with very little when it comes to root vegetables. Think baked potatoes oozing with butter and the melted remnants of the cheeseboard, served with a cheerfully coloured winter slaw, or, as a majestic accompaniment to an egg or some slices of ham, a mountain of greens baked in a gratin topped with crisp golden breadcrumbs.

Make a little effort with how the table looks and your work in the kitchen will reap double rewards. Small things make a big difference, and eating food together becomes an enjoyable ritual rather than a human necessity. Throw on a tablecloth, light some candles and arrange some sprigs of evergreen leaves – holly, sage, rosemary or pine branches – in vases. Put a pile of pomegranates, tangerines or walnuts in a bowl as a centrepiece, and guests can nibble on them during dessert.

RED LEAVES

Tight-headed purple cabbages, violet-fingered radicchios, crisp chicories from Belgium, Italian pink-speckled Castelfranco – these bitter and sweet colourful leaves turn a basic salad into an explosion of colour.

Many of these radicchio varieties are mainly cultivated in Northern Italy, hence their names: radicchio di Chioggia, the tight-leaved ball-shaped one, and Treviso tardivo, with the stiff straight stalks that curl at the end. These red-leaved salads have stronger stalks and firmer leaves than their summer lettuce cousins. Chicories retain their bite even when cooked, and thinly sliced cabbage, made into the Winter slaw overleaf, can be prepared in advance and still retains its crunch.

One of the most prized varieties of chicory, radicchio di Castelfranco is often called 'winter rose', describing the soft folds of leaves that resemble yellow and freckled pink petals.

The beautiful wine-red colours of these leaves indicate their high levels of polyphenols, which are excellent for gut health. They can be expensive, but you can stretch what you have by combining them with other ingredients: add quinoa to bolster from salad to meal, or stir into creamy risotto.

RECIPES

Winter slaw with pomegranate and pumpkin seeds
Radicchio and red wine risotto
Quinoa, radicchio, fennel and pomegranate salad
Salad of winter leaves

WINTER SLAW

WITH POMEGRANATE AND PUMPKIN SEEDS

Sally Clarke's colourful, textural dish makes the most of the season's ingredients. You can prepare the first five vegetables for this robust salad and refrigerate, covered, for up to 48 hours.

....

SERVES 6

For the slaw

½ small red cabbage, halved and white centre removed
1 large fennel bulb
2 celery sticks
1 medium parsnip, peeled
small handful of curly kale, stalks removed
2 apples, such as Russet or Cox
juice of 1 lemon
small handful of dried cranberries or sultanas
1 tablespoon pumpkin seeds
1 pomegranate
large bunch of watercress, thick stalks removed
sea salt and freshly ground black pepper

For the dressing

1 teaspoon Dijon mustard
1 teaspoon honey
4 tablespoons good-quality olive oil
1 tablespoon soured or double cream

1. Slice the cabbage very finely and place in a bowl.
2. Cut the fennel in half from the root end to the leaf, lay cut-side down and slice as thinly as possible lengthways. Slice the celery finely, slightly on the angle. Cut the parsnip into ribbons with a peeler, then slice the kale as finely as possible. Grate the apples on the wide side of the grater.
3. Place these ingredients in a bowl with the cabbage and lemon juice, mixing the salad until well amalgamated. Season with salt and pepper, then add the cranberries or sultanas and pumpkin seeds.
4. Whisk the dressing ingredients together until smooth. Pour over the salad and mix well.
5. Cut the pomegranate in half around the equator, then hold one half over a bowl. Knock the shell with a rolling pin and the seeds will drop out. Remove the white membrane and keep the juices with the seeds in a small bowl. Repeat with the other half.
6. Leave the salad, covered, in the refrigerator (for up to 24 hours), then toss again and scoop into a serving bowl. Garnish with the watercress and scatter the pomegranate seeds and juice on top.

RADICCHIO AND RED WINE RISOTTO

The slight bitterness of radicchio contrasts beautifully with the creamy, cheesy risotto. In Northern Italy they make this with locally produced Gorgonzola, which is a lovely alternative to Parmesan, if you have it.

SERVES 6

6 rashers of thin streaky bacon
50g (1¾oz) butter
1 red onion, finely chopped
small handful of rosemary, chopped
300g (10½oz) risotto rice
200ml (7fl oz) red wine
1.5 litres (2⅔ pints) hot chicken stock
1 small head of radicchio, thinly shredded,
    core removed
80g (3oz) Parmesan cheese, grated
sea salt and freshly ground black pepper

1. Finely chop the bacon and fry to a crisp in a wide, heavy-based pan over a medium heat. Add half the butter, the onion and a large pinch of salt and fry for 5 minutes until soft but not browned. Add the rosemary and the rice, stirring to coat the grains in butter. Fry for a minute.
2. Pour in the wine; it should sizzle and bubble. Keep stirring as the wine is absorbed. When it is nearly all gone, add a ladleful of stock. Stir a few times, but not constantly, to allow the rice to absorb the stock before you add the next ladle, continuing to stir between each addition of stock. After 15 minutes, the rice should feel soft on the outside with a little resistance to the bite.
3. Add the shredded radicchio with a ladle of stock and another large pinch of salt, cooking and stirring until the leaves wilt. The rice should be surrounded by enough liquid to make a sauce. If it is too dry, add more stock.
4. Remove from the heat and add the remaining butter, Parmesan and some pepper, stirring vigorously with a wooden spoon to create a creamy sauce. Serve on warm plates.

QUINOA, RADICCHIO, FENNEL AND POMEGRANATE SALAD

During my time at Moro on London's Exmouth Market many years ago, I was introduced to the beguiling flavour of pomegranate molasses – an ingredient that is now fairly commonplace. At the restaurant, it was used in this dressing, which gives a sweet-sour tang and spicy warmth to the vegetables. I love the textures and colours of this salad: it's cheerful, comforting and fresh all at the same time.

SERVES 6

350g (12oz) quinoa
1 fennel bulb
½ head of radicchio
1 pomegranate
large bunch of coriander and flat-leaf parsley
small bunch of mint and dill
3 tablespoons pistachios, roughly chopped

For the dressing
1 garlic clove, peeled
¼ teaspoon ground allspice
½ teaspoon ground cinnamon
1 teaspoon lemon juice
2 tablespoons pomegranate molasses
6 tablespoons extra virgin olive oil
sea salt and freshly ground black pepper

1. Put the quinoa in a saucepan and add enough water to cover it by about 4cm (1½in). Bring to the boil and cook for 15 minutes (or according to the packet instructions). Drain and set aside.
2. Finely slice the fennel and radicchio. Remove the seeds from the pomegranate and chop the herbs.
3. Crush the garlic, then mix all the dressing ingredients together. Season well with salt and pepper.
4. Season the cooked quinoa and add the vegetables, herbs, chopped pistachios and pomegranate seeds. Stir in the dressing and taste for seasoning before serving. I like to eat this on its own, but it could be a side dish or part of a selection of plates.

SALAD OF WINTER LEAVES

'Baby kale leaves, Belgian endive [chicory] and curly
endive, with pineapple and pomegranate dressing.
This may be prepared the day before and all left in
separate containers in the refrigerator overnight,' says
Sally Clarke, always keeping in mind the busy cook.

....

SERVES 6

For the salad
2 handfuls of baby kale leaves (or large leaves, torn)
1 small frisée endive
½ pineapple, top or root removed
1 small pomegranate
2 heads of chicory (red and white if possible)

For the dressing
1 tablespoon pomegranate molasses
4 tablespoons good-quality olive oil
sea salt and freshly ground black pepper

1. Wash and spin dry all the salad leaves except the
chicory. Place the leaves in a sealed plastic bag in the
salad tray of your refrigerator.
2. Place the cut surface of the pineapple on a chopping
board and remove the peel using a small knife.
Carefully remove the 'eyes', if present, using the tip of
the knife. Cut into quarters through the core and then
remove the core from each section. Cut into even-sized
pieces, place in a bowl and cover.
3. Remove the seeds from the pomegranate into a
small bowl, cover in clingfilm and chill until required.
4. Mix the dressing ingredients together and season
to taste with salt and pepper.
5. To serve, drain the pomegranate juices from the
seeds and add to the dressing. Remove the root end of
the chicory, pull apart the leaves and place in a serving
dish. Add the salad leaves, pineapple and dressing,
and toss gently but thoroughly together. Sprinkle the
pomegranate seeds over and serve.

SEAFOOD

Fish can be so simple to cook and comfortingly easy to eat – a warming fish curry on a cold evening or fishcakes, made the day before and quickly fried after work. Our UK waters have plentiful supplies of superb fish, but many species are overlooked by markets in favour of foreign imports. The choice of fish can be bewildering, so ask whoever you're buying from which of their fish are plentiful, in season and caught close to our shores. Abundance means a lower price while in season, and close to our home usually indicates bountiful and fresher fish.

If you've arrived with an idea in mind of what to cook and it's not on the slab that day, ask what they can offer as a suitable alternative. I'm sure the fish seller would rather you left buying something after all.

Cooking whole fish for large numbers can be expensive, but these recipes range from extravagant to thrifty, with the simplest preparations to bring out the best from the fish that you choose.

RECIPES

Warming Madagascan curry with coconut rice
Steamed scallops with garlic and glass noodles
Scallops with sage and capers
Fishcakes with sweet potato, chilli, ginger and lime
Kedgeree
Fish chowder

WARMING MADAGASCAN CURRY
WITH COCONUT RICE

I first ate this curry in Madagascar, where they served it with whole crab that we messily dismantled with our hands at the table. This version is more genteel to eat and easier for the cook, as most of the recipe can be made in advance. Monkfish is meaty and firm, and will hold its shape while absorbing all these lovely flavours; halibut would be an excellent, if more expensive, alternative.

....

SERVES 6

3 tablespoons olive oil

1 onion, chopped

2 garlic cloves, chopped

40g (1½oz) fresh root ginger, peeled and chopped

2–3 red chillies, chopped

300g (10½oz) sweet potatoes, peeled and chopped

3 teaspoons ground cumin

3 teaspoons ground coriander

2 teaspoons ground turmeric

2 teaspoons ground cinnamon

400g (14oz) can chopped tomatoes

400ml (14fl oz) can coconut milk

600g (1lb 5oz) basmati rice, rinsed and soaked in
  water for 20 minutes

900g (2lb) monkfish fillet, cut into large chunks

sea salt and freshly ground black pepper

To serve

20g (¾oz) coriander, chopped

lime wedges

1. In a large pot, heat the oil and fry the onion, garlic, ginger and chillies with a large pinch of salt until soft and slightly coloured.

2. Add the sweet potatoes and fry for a minute, before adding the ground spices and 1 teaspoon of pepper. The mixture will dry out with the spices, so cook for a minute, stirring all the time, and then add the tomatoes and three-quarters of the coconut milk (save the rest for the rice). Bring to the boil, then reduce the heat and simmer until the potatoes are soft. Check the seasoning.

3. To make the rice, drain and put it in a medium saucepan with a lid, then pour over the remaining coconut milk, adding water to cover it by about 2cm (¾in). With the lid on, bring to the boil (about 2–3 minutes), then reduce the heat and cook for 10–12 minutes until the rice is soft. Turn off the heat and leave with the lid on to steam while you cook the fish.

4. Season the monkfish. Bring the curry mixture to the boil before adding the fish to the pot. Simmer for 5 minutes, then turn off the heat and leave for a few minutes before serving sprinkled with coriander, with the coconut rice and the lime wedges on the side.

STEAMED SCALLOPS
WITH GARLIC AND GLASS NOODLES

This simplest of dishes, contributed by Amy Poon, is a celebration of the fresh, sweet succulence of scallops. Surprisingly simple to make and impressive to serve.

SERVES 6

150g (5½oz) glass noodles (otherwise known as dried mung bean noodles)

6 garlic cloves, crushed

2 tablespoons vegetable oil

1½ teaspoons light soy sauce

1 teaspoon Shaoxing rice wine

½ teaspoon sugar

½ teaspoon sesame oil

12 scallops on the half shell

sea salt

2 spring onions, finely chopped, to serve

1. Soak the noodles in a bowl of hot water for 3–5 minutes until softened. Drain and rinse in cold water.

2. In a small bowl, combine the garlic, vegetable oil, soy sauce, Shaoxing wine, sugar and sesame oil with a pinch of salt. Mix well.

3. Add a small handful of noodles and 1 teaspoon of the garlic mixture to each scallop in the shell.

4. To steam, place the scallops in their shells on a large heatproof plate. It is unlikely that they will fit in a single layer, so you can balance the shells carefully on top of each other in the gaps between the actual scallops. Or you can steam them in 2 batches. The best way to do this is to place a steaming rack into a large pan with a well-fitting lid. Add about 4cm (1½in) boiling water to the pan, then set the plate of scallops carefully on the rack and place the lid on tightly. Alternatively, you can fashion your own rack using an empty can (of tomatoes or chickpeas) with both the ends removed. The idea is to create a platform upon which you can securely place a plate above the water to steam.

5. Steam for 3–6 minutes, depending on the size of the scallops. They are cooked once they turn opaque and spring back a little when gently prodded.

6. Carefully remove the plate from the steaming pan. Sprinkle over the chopped spring onions and serve immediately.

SCALLOPS
WITH SAGE AND CAPERS

Scallops are one of the easiest and quickest fish to cook, and my favourite way to eat these meaty, sweet-tasting shellfish is simply prepared with the robust flavours of sage and salty capers – a recipe I learned at the River Café restaurant in London. It's a good starter on pretty little plates with lemon wedges.

SERVES 4

12 large scallops, removed from the shells
   and cleaned
2 tablespoons olive oil
10g (¼oz) butter
small bunch of sage leaves
1 tablespoon capers, rinsed
sea salt
lemon wedges, to serve

1. Pat the scallops dry and season with a little salt.
2. Heat a large, nonstick frying pan and add the oil and butter. When the butter is foaming, add the sage leaves and fry on both sides until crisp. Remove to a plate. Add the capers to the pan and fry for a minute until they start to pop open. Remove to the same plate you used for the sage.
3. Fry the scallops in the sage and caper-flavoured oil and butter, in batches if necessary. Cook for a couple of minutes on each side, allowing them to brown sufficiently before turning. The cooked scallops should feel firm but yielding to the touch.
4. Serve the scallops with the sage and capers sprinkled over and a wedge of lemon on the side.

FISHCAKES
WITH SWEET POTATO, CHILLI, GINGER AND LIME

The sweet potato gives these fishcakes a lightness and creaminess, but you can substitute any floury potatoes instead. The recipe makes enough for three fishcakes per serving, but they are also suitable to freeze if you are cooking for fewer people. Try serving with the Smacked cucumber salad on page 120 or a green salad.

SERVES 6

For the fishcakes
500g (1lb 2oz) sweet potatoes
500g (1lb 2oz) floury potatoes
350g (12oz) skinless firm white fish fillets, such as
   coley, hake or haddock
2 tablespoons fish sauce
1 red chilli, finely chopped
30g (1oz) coriander, finely chopped
30g (1oz) fresh root ginger, peeled and finely
   chopped
zest of 3 limes, plus 2 tablespoons juice
sea salt and freshly ground black pepper

For the breadcrumb crust
100g (3½oz) plain flour
2 eggs, beaten
200g (7oz) panko or homemade white breadcrumbs
3 tablespoons vegetable oil

1. Peel both types of potato and cut into small cubes. Put them in a pot, cover with water and add 1 tablespoon of salt. Bring to the boil and cook for 10–15 minutes, or until they are completely soft. Drain the cooked potatoes well and squeeze through a sieve or potato ricer to make a smooth purée.

2. Cut the fish into small chunks and mix with the other fishcake ingredients, then stir through the potato. Season well with salt and pepper. Refrigerate, covered, for 1 hour until cold. Preheat the oven to 190°C (170°C fan), 375°F, Gas mark 5.

3. Line a baking tray with baking parchment. Assemble 3 large flat bowls, with one containing the flour, one the beaten eggs and one the breadcrumbs.

Take half a handful of the fish mixture (weighing about 70g/2½oz) and form into a ball, then squash gently to form a cake. First dust with the flour, then coat with egg and finally with the breadcrumbs. Lay on the lined baking tray. Repeat until you have used all the mixture, making 18 small fishcakes.

4. Drizzle the oil over the top of the fishcakes and bake them for 20 minutes until crisp and golden.

KEDGEREE

I know kedgeree is traditionally eaten at breakfast, but I like to increase the chilli and serve this for an easy supper or light lunch. Anyway, I never get up early enough to make this in the morning. It's our Friday night staple and leftovers reheat well. The purée of split peas coats the rice and keeps the mixture saucy – more like a dhal.

....

SERVES 6–8

For the split peas and rice
200g (7oz) yellow split peas
1 teaspoon ground turmeric
300g (10½oz) basmati rice
sea salt

For the haddock
500g (1lb 2oz) smoked haddock fillet, skin on
500ml (18fl oz) full-fat milk
6 black peppercorns
2 bay leaves

For the spicing
2 tablespoons light olive oil
1 onion, diced
2 green chillies, diced (seeds in or out)
6cm (2½in) piece of fresh root ginger, peeled and chopped
2 garlic cloves, finely chopped
2 teaspoons cumin seeds

To finish
small bunch of curly parsley, finely chopped
poached eggs or chutney

1. Put the split peas in a pot with the turmeric, ½ teaspoon of salt and 1 litre (1¾ pints) water. Bring to the boil, then reduce to a simmer and cook for 40 minutes until soft. Blitz the split peas and their cooking liquid in a blender to make a smooth purée.

2. Wash the rice well and put it in a separate saucepan with ½ teaspoon of salt and 250ml (9fl oz) water. Bring to the boil, then reduce to a simmer, cover with a lid and cook until soft (about 12 minutes). Turn off the heat and leave the rice to steam, covered, for at least 5 minutes before fluffing.

3. To cook the haddock, place it skin-side down in a wide, shallow pan – you may need to cut the fish into 2 pieces. Cover with the milk and add the peppercorns and bay leaves. Bring to the boil, then simmer for 10 minutes. Remove the fish to a plate and strain the milk into a jug. Clean the saucepan.

4. To make the spicing, heat the oil in the saucepan you used for the fish and, over a medium–high heat, fry the onion, chillies and ginger until soft and starting to caramelize. Add the garlic and cumin seeds, and cook until the garlic is beginning to colour.

5. To finish, remove the skin from the fish. Flake the fish and add it to the spicing. Stir in the rice and split pea purée, adding some of the reserved milk if necessary. Season and serve scattered with the parsley, and with either a poached egg or a spoonful of chutney.

FISH CHOWDER

I love the smoky, deep flavour of chowder and it's a good recipe to experiment with different fish. The key is to choose a combination of smoked and white fish, and some sort of crustacean. UK smoked haddock is excellent, and crayfish are a cheaper alternative to Scottish langoustines. This is an ideal dish to serve guests, as the preparation is mainly done in advance, with just a few minutes before serving to cook the fish.

....

SERVES 6

For the base
2 tablespoons olive oil
150g (5½oz) smoked bacon lardons
**2 medium leeks, trimmed, washed and finely
    chopped**
small bunch of thyme, chopped
700g (1lb 9oz) waxy potatoes, peeled and cubed
600g (1lb 5oz) canned sweetcorn
1.5 litres (2⅔ pints) fish or shellfish stock
300ml (10fl oz) single cream
juice of 1 large lemon
sea salt

For the fish
**650g (1lb 7oz) skinless white fish fillets, such as
    hake, coley or pollock**
270g (9¾oz) skinless smoked haddock fillet
**6 langoustines, split down the middle, or large
    crayfish, peeled**
20g (¾oz) curly or flat-leaf parsley, finely chopped

1. Heat the oil in a large pot or casserole and fry the lardons until completely crisp. Remove and set aside. Add the leeks with a generous pinch of salt and cook over a medium heat, stirring occasionally, for 10–15 minutes until soft and sweet.

2. Return the lardons to the pot. Add the thyme and potatoes, and fry for a minute, before adding the sweetcorn, stock and cream. Bring to the boil, season to taste and add the lemon juice. Simmer until the potatoes are soft.

3. Cut the white fish and smoked haddock into bite-sized pieces. Bring the pot to the boil before adding all the fish, then reduce the heat immediately and simmer for 5–10 minutes. Remove from the heat and add the chopped parsley before serving.

MEAT

Cook meat rarely and lovingly. Even if you don't eat a lot of it, when it's cold outside and the appetite calls for something filling and warm, it can be just the answer. If you eat less meat that is farmed more sustainably, you won't mind spending more.

Fattier, more muscly cuts, like pork belly or shin, are cheaper to buy and more forgiving to cook. They benefit from reheating, which makes them useful if you're entertaining. I've included James Lowe's recipe for venison loin (see page 238), which is cheap, widely available and nutritious. I think it has a superior flavour to most beef fillets.

RECIPES

Pork belly Lyonnaise

Sausage and bean hotpot with Savoy cabbage, apple, mustard and cider

Fallow deer loin with red cabbage and quince

Pork chops with baked apple ketchup

Slow-cooked beef shin with fennel and gremolata

PORK BELLY LYONNAISE

Lucas Hollweg's simple and luxurious recipe is based on a dish he spotted at a market in central France, where small pork hock joints had been cooked in giant pans with white wine and onions. Pork belly is forgiving to cook; the fat prevents it from drying out and I'm a fan of anything that can be made in advance. You can ask your butcher to score the skin of the pork. If you have time, this is best left in the refrigerator overnight to marinate.

SERVES 6

3 sprigs of rosemary
8 sprigs of thyme, leaves picked
7 garlic cloves: 1 crushed, 6 thinly sliced
1.5kg (3lb 5oz) thick piece of boneless pork belly
2 tablespoons olive oil
6 medium onions, sliced
4 bay leaves
1 tablespoon tomato purée
2 tablespoons white wine vinegar
300ml (10fl oz) dry white wine
up to 1 litre (1¾ pints) chicken stock
1 tablespoon finely chopped curly or flat-leaf parsley
sea salt and freshly ground black pepper

To serve
boiled or mashed potato, or a green salad

1. Chop the leaves from 1 sprig of rosemary and mix with the leaves from 2 sprigs of thyme, the crushed garlic and a good grinding of pepper. Scatter evenly over a chopping board. Sprinkle with salt and place the pork belly on top, flesh-side down, so that the underside is coated with the mixture. Score the skin into 6 equal pieces. Transfer to a tray and chill, uncovered, for a few hours, preferably overnight.

2. Remove the meat from the refrigerator and rub 1 teaspoon of salt into the skin. Heat the olive oil in a roasting tin on the hob and brown the meat on the flesh side. Remove.

3. Put the sliced onions and garlic in the tin with a pinch of salt, the bay leaves and the remaining rosemary and thyme. Sweat for 25 minutes, stirring often until soft and golden brown. Stir in the tomato purée for a minute, then add the vinegar and wine. Bubble until the liquid turns syrupy. Preheat the oven to 160°C (140°C fan), 325°F, Gas mark 3.

4. Put the pork on top of the onions, skin-side up, adding enough stock to come about two-thirds of the way up the side of the meat. Bring to a simmer, transfer to the oven and cook for 4 hours, or until the side of the meat is soft enough to pierce easily with a fork. Remove the meat and leave to rest for 5 minutes. Drain off the liquid into a bowl, then skim and discard the fat. Season the juices and add enough to the onions to make them sloppy.

5. Cut the meat into 6 pieces. Pour the extra juices from the bowl into a jug. Serve the pork with some of the onions, scattered with the parsley, along with boiled or mashed potato, or a green salad.

SAUSAGE AND BEAN HOTPOT

WITH SAVOY CABBAGE, APPLE, MUSTARD AND CIDER

Humble, modest, yet exceptionally good. This would also describe Phil Howard, Michelin-star-winning chef-restaurateur and creator of this recipe. I regularly make it at home; in fact, I keep cider and beans in the cupboard on standby for the purpose. It's simple comfort food at its best, literally a one-pot wonder.

....

SERVES 6

15 shallots

¼ celeriac

1 small Savoy cabbage

2 tablespoons duck fat

12 pork sausages

100g (3½oz) stale bread

2 teaspoons olive oil

6 sage leaves

1 large can dry cider (about 440ml/15½fl oz)

25g (1oz) butter

2 teaspoons plain flour

600ml (20fl oz) chicken stock

3 Granny Smith apples

1½ × 400g (14oz) cans butter beans

3 teaspoons wholegrain mustard

1 teaspoon runny honey

sea salt and freshly ground black pepper

1. Peel and lightly trim the shallots. Peel the celeriac and cut into 1cm (½in) pieces. Discard the outer leaves of the cabbage. Keep the next 6 leaves, cutting out most of the main rib of each one but leaving it intact at the top. Chop the remaining leaves into 2cm (¾in) pieces.

2. Preheat the oven to 180°C (160°C fan), 350°F, Gas mark 4. Melt 1 tablespoon of the duck fat in a heavy-based frying pan. Add the sausages and fry until coloured on all sides. Transfer to a roasting tray and bake for 20 minutes.

3. Meanwhile, blitz the bread, oil and sage in a food processor to form fine crumbs. Bake on a baking tray for 20 minutes, shaking the tray frequently. Drain on kitchen paper.

4. Remove the sausages from the oven, drain (reserving the fat), cool and slice into 1cm (½in) lengths. Pour the reserved fat into a frying pan, add the shallots and season. Add the cider and simmer until completely reduced. Remove the shallots and set aside. Add the remaining 1 tablespoon of duck fat to the pan and fry the celeriac, draining at the end and reserving the fat.

5. Preheat the oven to 150°C (130°C fan), 300°F, Gas mark 2. Place the leftover fat and the butter in a lidded, ovenproof casserole over a medium heat. Let it sizzle, then add the chopped cabbage and a pinch of salt, and fry for 3–4 minutes. Stir in the flour and then slowly add the stock, stirring continuously. Bring to the boil, then add the shallots, celeriac and sausages. Return to the boil, cover and cook in the oven for 30 minutes.

6. Peel, core and roughly chop the apples. Drain the beans. Add both to the casserole. Return to the oven for 20 minutes. Remove from the oven, stir in the mustard and honey and allow to cool for 10 minutes.

7. Bring a pan of salted water to the boil. Blanch the reserved cabbage leaves for 2 minutes, then drain and place each one in a large, shallow bowl. Spoon the hotpot over the cabbage and finish by sprinkling over the breadcrumbs.

FALLOW DEER LOIN
WITH RED CABBAGE AND QUINCE

James Lowe, chef-proprietor of Lyle's restaurant in London, cooks a lot of game. So when I wanted to find someone to write about game, James was my first choice. Thinking primarily about the home cook, he chose loin rather than another cut, as it is so straightforward to handle. James suggests choosing fallow deer venison over roe or red deer, especially at this time of year, for the best balance of size, flavour and texture. He says, 'I love the red cabbage and quince combination, so much so that we've served this entirely by itself at the restaurant. If you hold back a couple of quinces and purée the rest, you can serve pieces of pickled quince alongside the dish for a contrast in texture.'

....

SERVES 6

For the pickled quince
300ml (10fl oz) white wine vinegar
400g (14oz) demerara sugar
4 quinces, peeled, cored and quartered

For the venison
2 teaspoons juniper berries
10 black peppercorns
bunch of thyme
1 garlic clove, peeled
2 tablespoons vegetable oil
800g (1lb 12oz) trimmed venison loin
1 tablespoon duck fat
40g (1½oz) butter
1 bay leaf
sea salt

For the quince purée
1 pickled quince
splash of white wine vinegar

For the red cabbage
1 red cabbage
1 tablespoon vegetable oil
25ml (1fl oz) white wine vinegar

1. To make the pickled quince, preheat the oven to 120°C (100°C fan), 250°F, Gas mark ½. Combine 300ml (10fl oz) water with the vinegar and sugar in a large ovenproof pan and simmer to dissolve the sugar. Add the quinces and bring back to a simmer.

2. Cook in the oven for about 4 hours, or until the fruit is soft and has changed to a darker, more orange/red colour. Leave to cool, then put the quinces into a sterilized jar and add the cooled liquid to cover. Store at room temperature or in the refrigerator.

3. The day before, make the marinade for the venison. Lightly crush the juniper berries, peppercorns, 6 sprigs of thyme and the garlic in a pestle and mortar. Stir in the oil to form a marinade and rub it over the venison. Cover and refrigerate overnight.

4. To make the quince purée, in a blender, blend the pickled quince with a little of the pickling liquid and the vinegar until you achieve a smooth purée – start with just the fruit and then add the liquid a little at a time. You are aiming for the consistency of ketchup.

5. Preheat the oven to 180°C (160°C fan), 350°F, Gas mark 4 and line a roasting tray with baking parchment. Cut the red cabbage into wedges – they should be about 6cm (2½in) thick at the outside edge. Allow up to 2 wedges per person. Heat the oil in a pan and fry the wedges on one side until brown, then transfer them to the lined tray.

6. Season the cabbage well with salt and all the vinegar, then spread the puréed quince over the cabbage. Cover with 4 sprigs of thyme and bake for 10–15 minutes.

7. To cook the venison, rub off the marinade and season the loin well with fine salt. Heat a heavy-based frying pan and add the duck fat, then the loin. You may need to cut it in half in order to fit it into the pan. Brown the meat all over.

8. Add the butter, the bay leaf and remaining thyme, and continue to baste and roll the meat in the pan. When the butter turns brown, remove from the heat. To check the meat, probe the centre of the muscle using a thermometer – it should be 45–47°C (113–117°F).

9. Rest for 10 minutes in a warm place until its internal temperature reaches 53°C (127°F) for medium rare. Slice and serve with the cabbage.

PORK CHOPS

WITH BAKED APPLE KETCHUP

As quince is to venison, so apple is to pork. As in the preceding recipe, the fruit accompaniment can be made well in advance – always a bonus – and pork chops will benefit from resting in their cooking juices, giving you plenty of time to relax before settling down to eat. This recipe is by Merlin Labron-Johnson whose restaurant, Osip, in Somerset's Bruton champions use of seasonal, local produce, often grown in Osip's own kitchen garden. Pork chops can vary enormously from fatty and rich to dry and tasteless, so more than any other meat chop, it really pays to buy free-range. Excellent breeds to eat are Middle White or Mangalitza, which have a wonderfully high fat content.

SERVES 6

For the apple ketchup
500g (1lb 2oz) cooking apples (about 4)
150ml (5fl oz) cider vinegar
2 tablespoons honey
sea salt

For the pork chops
6 pork chops (about 300g/10½oz each)
olive oil, for frying
4 garlic cloves, crushed
1 sprig of rosemary (no need to strip or chop),
    plus extra sprigs to serve
large knob of butter

To serve
roast potatoes
green salad

1. Preheat the oven to 180°C (160°C fan), 350°F, Gas mark 4. For the ketchup, wash the apples and place them whole in an ovenproof dish with a lid – or seal with foil. Bake for about 40 minutes, or until they are completely cooked and soft to the touch. Remove from the oven and leave to cool.

2. Meanwhile, put the cider vinegar and honey in a saucepan and bring to the boil. Reduce the heat and simmer until reduced by two-thirds.

3. Place the unpeeled cooked apples in a blender with the vinegar reduction and blend to a purée. Use the back of a spoon to push the purée through a sieve, season with some salt and set aside.

4. One hour before cooking the pork chops, season them generously with salt. When ready to cook, give them a quick wipe with kitchen paper and pat dry.

5. Heat a large frying pan with olive oil over a high heat and add the chops, making sure that there is space for them to lie flat (in batches if necessary, keeping the first lot warm in a low oven). The pan should be slightly hotter than feels comfortable.

6. Fry for 3 minutes on one side, then add the garlic and rosemary, turn over and add the butter. Cook over a medium heat for a further 4 minutes, before removing and placing on a plate to rest.

7. Pour the cooking juices over the chops. Serve with the apple ketchup and extra rosemary sprigs on the side, plus roast potatoes and a green salad.

SLOW-COOKED BEEF SHIN
WITH FENNEL AND GREMOLATA

This recipe includes lovage, a strong-tasting herb with a flavour similar to celery. It grows in a huge bush in my herb bed and seems to withstand all weather and maltreatment. It pairs beautifully with beef, but if you can't get hold of it, use celery leaves or even celeriac leaves. The fennel and the gremolata lift the flavours of the rich meat, giving it a contrasting brightness. Make the day before and let it settle overnight.

SERVES 6

For the beef
1.5kg (3lb 5oz) beef shin
4 tablespoons olive oil
300ml (10fl oz) red wine
500g (1lb 2oz) carrots, peeled and diced
1 onion, diced
350g (12oz) celery sticks, diced
400g (14oz) can plum tomatoes
3 fennel bulbs, cut into wedges
bouquet garni (bundle of thyme, parsley stalks and rosemary)
small bunch of lovage (about 20g/¾oz), roughly chopped
500ml (18fl oz) chicken or beef stock
sea salt

For the gremolata
large bunch of flat-leaf parsley, finely chopped
1 garlic clove, finely chopped
finely grated zest of 1 lemon

To serve
creamy mashed potato
English or Dijon mustard

1. Season the meat generously with salt – preferably 1 hour before cooking – then allow it to come up to room temperature.
2. Preheat the oven to 160°C (140°C fan), 325°F, Gas mark 3. Heat 2 tablespoons of the olive oil in a large, lidded casserole and brown the meat well on both sides. (You may need to do this in batches.) Remove the meat to a bowl when browned and deglaze the pan with the wine, then pour it over the meat.
3. Using the same casserole, heat the remaining 2 tablespoons of olive oil. Add the carrots, onion and celery with ½ teaspoon of salt to make a soffritto. Cook, stirring occasionally, for about 20 minutes.
4. Sieve the tomatoes, rinsing off the can juices, then tear roughly and add to the pan with the fennel, bouquet garni and lovage. Continue to fry for another few minutes.
5. Return the meat to the pan and add the stock. Cover with the lid and cook in the oven for 3 hours. Remove the bouquet garni.
6. To make the gremolata, mix together the parsley, garlic and lemon zest. Serve the meat with mashed potato and a dollop of mustard, and with the gremolata sprinkled over.

ROOT VEGETABLES

Apart from the sturdy brassicas and winter leaves of chard and kale, this is high season for root vegetables. They are naturally sweet, filling and abundant. If I have a haul in my refrigerator, I often roast a tray of them with just oil, salt and some herbs to have on hand when I need. They make excellent additions to soups, the base for a gratin or chopped up and stirred into fritters.

Use the following recipes as a guide and substitute different root vegetables depending on what you have. Served as sides or on their own, these are colourful and easy, and provide invaluable leftovers.

RECIPES

Root vegetable gratin

Sweet potato fritters with turmeric hummus

Roast root vegetables

Vegetable tagine with couscous

ROOT VEGETABLE GRATIN

Sally Clarke suggests making this the day before and reheating to serve straight from the oven. Like cooks and hosts, many dishes are more enjoyable when they've had some time to relax.

....

SERVES 6

2 large Désirée or King Edward potatoes
2 large sweet potatoes
1 large celeriac
3 large parsnips
100g (3½oz) butter, melted
2 teaspoons finely chopped rosemary leaves
250ml (9fl oz) double cream
125ml (4fl oz) chicken or vegetable stock
3 bay leaves
2 garlic cloves, crushed
sea salt and freshly ground black pepper

1. Peel all the vegetables and rinse well with cold water. If you have one of those clever vegetable slicing machines, now is the time to get it out. Slice each vegetable and keep them separate so that the colours are not mixed up. Alternatively, cut the potatoes, sweet potatoes and celeriac in half and slice across as thinly as possible by hand, with a sharp knife. The parsnips may be sliced across whole, in thin slices.

2. Choose an ovenproof dish that will hold all the vegetables and brush with half the melted butter. In a small bowl, mix the rosemary with 1 teaspoon of salt and 1 teaspoon of pepper. Start to fill the dish with the potato slices – they should be arranged in concentric circles so that they slightly overlap one another. Add a sprinkling of the rosemary mixture.

3. Cover the potatoes with half the sweet potatoes in the same way, then add the celeriac, then the remaining sweet potatoes, then finally the parsnips. This final layer should be arranged as carefully as possible, with beautifully overlapping slices, as this will be the top of the finished dish.

4. Preheat the oven to 180°C (160°C fan), 350°F, Gas mark 4. In a saucepan, combine the double cream, stock, bay leaves and crushed garlic with ½ teaspoon of salt and ½ teaspoon of pepper. Heat until simmering. Remove the bay leaves and set aside. Gently pour the liquid over and around the sliced vegetables, allowing each addition to slowly sink into the dish before adding more. You may not need all the liquid, but any leftovers could be used to top up the dish during cooking. Drizzle the remaining melted butter over the top and garnish with the bay leaves.

5. Place the dish on a baking sheet (as the cream may bubble over while cooking) and bake for 1 hour–1 hour 20 minutes, or 10–15 minutes if reheating. If the surface of the gratin starts to colour too soon, simply cover with a piece of foil and continue to bake until a small sharp knife pierces the centre easily. The top should be golden brown all over, with a few crisp, slightly burnt edges for colour. Remove the dish from the oven and serve immediately, or cover tightly with foil to keep warm until you are ready to serve.

SWEET POTATO FRITTERS
WITH TURMERIC HUMMUS

Making hummus from scratch is only fun if you've got cooked chickpeas at the ready. You can buy excellent cooked giant chickpeas in jars that are especially creamy and make the best hummus. Or if you need dried-to-cooked in a hurry, you could use marrowfat peas instead. Serve with a bundle of herbs to pick at and eat, like loose salad.

....

SERVES 6

For the fritters
500g (1lb 2oz) sweet potatoes, peeled and grated
6 spring onions, finely chopped
20g (¾oz) coriander leaves, finely chopped
1 red chilli, finely chopped
1 teaspoon grated fresh root ginger
3 tablespoons self-raising flour
2 tablespoons lime juice
vegetable oil, for frying
sea salt and freshly ground black pepper

For the hummus
600g (1lb 5oz) cooked chickpeas (Navarrico jarred giant chickpeas are the softest)
3 tablespoons tahini
6 garlic cloves, crushed
3 tablespoons extra virgin olive oil
2 teaspoons grated fresh turmeric
2 teaspoons ground coriander
juice of ½ lemon

To serve
1 tablespoon nigella seeds
large bunch of flat-leaf parsley, mint and coriander

1. Preheat the oven to 150°C (130°C fan), 300°F, Gas mark 2. Mix together all the ingredients for the sweet potato fritters, except the oil, in a bowl and season well with salt and pepper. If the mixture seems a little dry, add a splash of water – it should be sticky but not wet.

2. Heat 1 tablespoon of oil in a large frying pan. Scoop a large spoonful of the fritter mixture and roll it in your hands, then press into a plump patty shape. Place this in the pan and repeat with a few more spoonfuls of mixture. Try not to overcrowd the pan – it is easier to cook the fritters in batches.

3. After a few minutes cooking on one side, flip them over and cook for another 3 minutes. Remove to a dish and keep warm in the oven while you cook the rest, adding more oil to the pan with each batch.

4. Next, make the hummus. Using a blender, pulse all the ingredients, except the lemon juice, with plenty of pepper until smooth, adding water to create a loose sauce. Taste and add salt and lemon juice as necessary.

5. Serve the warm fritters with a large dollop of the hummus, the nigella seeds and a bunch of herbs, still on the stem.

ROAST ROOT VEGETABLES

This recipe by Claudia Roden is a reminder of the simple pleasure a dish of roast vegetables can bring. Make more than you need and your efforts will pay great dividends. Roast vegetables are easy to reheat, served for a quick lunch with an egg on top or puréed and added to stock for a quick soup. Use whatever root vegetables you have to hand and you will have a fine dish to enjoy eating more than once.

....

SERVES 6

1 celeriac
3 sweet potatoes
3 carrots
2 red onions, cut into 6 wedges
3 sprigs of thyme, leaves picked

3 sprigs of rosemary, leaves picked and chopped
6 tablespoons olive oil
sea salt and freshly ground black pepper

1. Preheat the oven to 180°C (160°C fan), 350°F, Gas mark 4. Peel the celeriac, sweet potatoes and carrots, and cut them into 3cm (1¼in) chunks. Place these with the onions in a large roasting tin lined with foil.
2. Sprinkle over salt and pepper and the herbs and pour over the olive oil, turning the vegetables so that they are well covered.
3. Roast for about 1 hour, turning the vegetables over once, until they are tender and lightly browned.

VEGETABLE TAGINE
WITH COUSCOUS

*Warming, colourful and beautiful to serve, this dish
looks like a feast in a bowl. Although traditionally
Moroccans use a meat stock or bones to flavour their
tagines, there is so much taste in the slow-cooked
vegetables, you really don't miss it. You can vary the
vegetables you choose to use in this, but keep in mind
the overall flavours and textures – some sweetness
(squash, sweet potato, carrots), some creamy softness
(courgette, celeriac, Jerusalem artichokes) and a little
bite (turnips, kohlrabi). This is a great dish to make
in advance too, as the flavours only improve. You will
need a large, shallow pan so that you can turn the
vegetables easily without mashing them.*

SERVES 6

For the tagine
6 large carrots, peeled
6 small turnips, peeled
1 medium kohlrabi, peeled
½ celeriac, peeled
1 swede, peeled
2 tablespoons olive oil
1 onion, diced
3 teaspoons ground cinnamon
3 teaspoons ground ginger
pinch of saffron strands, crushed and soaked in
    3 tablespoons boiling water
1 teaspoon grated fresh turmeric or 1 teaspoon
    ground turmeric
3 large courgettes
100g (3½oz) dates, halved and pitted
400g (14oz) cooked chickpeas
400g (14oz) couscous
sea salt and freshly ground black pepper

To serve
large bunch of flat-leaf parsley and coriander,
    chopped
harissa (optional)

1. Cut all the vegetables, except the courgettes, into
large chunks. In a large, shallow pan, heat the oil.
Add the onion and a pinch of salt, then fry until soft
and a little coloured. Add the cinnamon, ginger and
½ teaspoon of pepper and cook for a minute while
stirring. Add the saffron, turmeric, carrots, turnips,
kohlrabi, celeriac and swede, and stir to coat. Cook for
a few minutes, then add the whole courgettes, dates
and chickpeas.

2. Season generously with salt and cover with
water. Bring to the boil, then reduce the heat and
simmer, partially covered, for 30 minutes until all the
vegetables are completely soft. Cut the courgettes into
chunks and return them to the pan.

3. Prepare the couscous according to the packet
instructions, but use the liquid from the tagine instead
of water (top up with boiling water if needed).

4. Make a bed of couscous and arrange the vegetables
over it, then sprinkle with the chopped herbs. Serve
with harissa for those who enjoy a fiery kick.

CITRUS

Winter is the season for citrus. Not only do they grow best at this time of year, it's as if nature knows that we need what they offer. The arrival of citrus brings zingy, refreshing flavours and sunshine colours to brighten the darker days.

Blood oranges develop their striking red colour in the low temperatures of the Mediterranean nights. Squeeze over rhubarb before roasting, or add peeled slices to a salad of radicchio, fennel and black olives. For a colourful dessert, pour caramel over orange slices and scatter with chopped dates, pistachios, pomegranate and mint.

Lemons are an essential ingredient. Their zest and juice balance and accentuate flavour, and brighten marinades, salads, meat dishes, pastas and cakes. Buy unwaxed Italian lemons, preferably with their large leaves attached. Risotto made with chicken stock and sharpened with lemon zest and juice is a good accompaniment to slow-cooked pork, or slices of lemon, skin on, can be roasted underneath meats or vegetables to caramelize for another layer of flavour.

Mediaeval Crusaders brought sour oranges back to Europe from the East. Seville oranges are unpalatably bitter, but the peel is high in pectins, which allows the jelly to set in marmalade. The juice is excellent made into a curd to fill sweet pastry tarts. Or use up the last of your marmalade added to sponges, chocolate almond cakes or as a filling for biscuits.

Mainly grown in Southern Italy, bergamot are round, green citrus prized for their intensely fragrant zest. The juice tastes herbal and very acidic, so I blend it with sweeter citrus. Mix zest with whipped cream to serve with puddings or make a syrup with the zest and juice to drizzle over a simple sponge.

RECIPES

Blood orange, fennel, feta and olive salad

Citrus salad

Lemon risotto with crisp sage

Bergamot and yuzu cheesecake

Orange, yogurt and olive oil cake

Shortbread ma'amoul cookies filled with marmalade and orange blossom

Treacle and marmalade tart

BLOOD ORANGE, FENNEL, FETA AND OLIVE SALAD

With sweet and juicy oranges, crisp fennel and salty feta and olives, this salad could be an elegant starter with watercress or rocket scattered on top, or served as a refreshing side dish with braised chicken. Or leave out the feta and serve it with oily fish. Salads like this make me want to choose my prettiest plates to serve them on.

....

SERVES 4

4 blood oranges
2 fennel bulbs
170g (6oz) feta cheese
100g (3½oz) Kalamata olives
2 tablespoons roughly chopped flat-leaf parsley
1 tablespoon roughly chopped marjoram leaves
1 tablespoon balsamic vinegar
3 tablespoons extra virgin olive oil
sea salt and freshly ground black pepper

1. With a sharp, serrated knife, remove the skin and pith from the oranges, then cut into thin, round slices.
2. Cut the fennel lengthways into thin strips. Slice the feta and break into pieces.
3. Toss the oranges, fennel and feta in a bowl with the olives, roughly chopped herbs, vinegar and oil, and season well.

CITRUS SALAD

Claudia Roden's recipe for this most refreshing salad uses a joyful mix of colours. Perfect to serve with fish or chicken and perhaps with cheese.

....

SERVES 6

1 large sweet orange
1 large or 2 small grapefruit
150–200g (5½–7oz) mixed small salad leaves
juice of ½ lemon
4 tablespoons extra virgin olive oil
good handful of mixed herbs, such as chives, dill and flat-leaf parsley
sea salt and freshly ground black pepper

1. Peel the citrus fruit using a serrated knife – slice off the tops, then cut down the sides, making sure you remove the pith with the skin. Cut them into slices and cut the slices into quarters, then arrange them on a wide platter. Spread the salad leaves on top.
2. Mix the lemon juice and olive oil, season with salt and pepper and pour all over the salad. Snip the herbs over the top using scissors.

LEMON RISOTTO

WITH CRISP SAGE

*This makes enough for a meal on its own, or as a starter
on smaller plates. It looks simple and pretty, and
makes me think of those little yellow-petalled winter
aconites with dark green leaves that carpet woodland
areas. If you were eating this as a main course, you
could serve it with some braised pork or pork chops.
Choose an Italian lemon with bright zest and a thick
skin – the sort of lemons with their leaves attached
that look good enough to display in fruit bowls.*

SERVES 6

1.25 litres (2 pints) **light chicken stock**
60g (2¼oz) **unsalted butter**
4 **celery sticks, finely chopped**
1 **fennel bulb, finely chopped**
1 **lemon**
300g (10½oz) **risotto rice**
100ml (3½fl oz) **Martini Bianco (or other sweet
    white vermouth)**
2 **tablespoons olive oil**
30g (1oz) **sage leaves**
20g (¾oz) **Parmesan cheese, grated, plus extra
    to serve**
sea salt and freshly ground black pepper

1. Bring the stock to the boil, set aside and keep
warm. Put a wide, shallow, heavy-based saucepan
over a medium heat. Add 40g (1½oz) of the butter and,
when it starts to foam, add the celery and fennel with
a large pinch of salt. Cook for about 10 minutes,
stirring occasionally, until the vegetables are soft.
2. Meanwhile, cut wide strips of zest from half the
lemon and slice into fine shreds. Reserve the rest of the
lemon for later. Add the zest, rice and another large
pinch of salt to the saucepan. Fry for 1 minute, stirring
well so that the edges of the rice become translucent.
Add the vermouth, stirring as it bubbles.
3. When the vermouth has been absorbed, add a
ladle of stock, stir again and cook until the stock is
absorbed. Continue adding stock and stirring, keeping
the heat high enough so that there are always a few
bubbles and enough liquid to keep the rice wet.
4. While the risotto cooks, add the olive oil to a frying
pan and fry the sage leaves for a few seconds on each
side until crisp. Drain on kitchen paper.
5. When the rice is beginning to feel al dente (after
about 15–20 minutes), turn off the heat and add the
remaining butter and Parmesan. Stir to create a
creamy sauce around the rice. Add most of the juice
of the remaining lemon and stir again. The risotto
should exude liquid when spooned on to a plate, so
add more stock (or water) if necessary. Taste for
seasoning and add salt and pepper, and more lemon
juice, if required. Scatter the sage leaves over each
plate and extra Parmesan.

BERGAMOT AND YUZU CHEESECAKE

Sometimes new fruit appear in my local greengrocer and I want to find ways to introduce them into my cooking. Yuzu is a small and deeply wrinkled orb-shaped citrus indigenous to Japan and Korea. It has a beguiling flavour – somewhere between a sweet mandarin and a fragrant grapefruit. You can buy yuzu juice in some supermarkets and I've substituted the yuzu zest with bergamot, another citrus fruit that is in season this time of year but one that is grown in Europe and is therefore more readily available! It has a slightly sweeter, more fragrant flavour than lemons. The zest is highly perfumed. Bergamot adds a freshness to the rich cheesecake mixture, balanced by the sweetness of the yuzu juice. Of course, you could make this with blood orange or lemon zest and juice instead. I sometimes add a teaspoon of crushed fennel seeds too.

....

SERVES 6

160g (5¾oz) digestive biscuits
75g (2½oz) unsalted butter, melted
3 eggs , plus 3 egg yolks and 1 egg white, beaten
300g (10½oz) thick Greek-style yogurt
300g (10½oz) mascarpone cheese
130g (4¾oz) caster sugar
4 tablespoons yuzu juice
zest of ½ unwaxed bergamot

1. Preheat the oven to 180°C (160°C fan), 350°F, Gas mark 4. Crush the biscuits to make coarse crumbs and mix with the melted butter.
2. Line the base of a 20cm (8in) springform cake tin with baking parchment and wrap the outside of the tin with 2 sheets of foil, to cover and seal the base and the sides. Press the biscuit mixture into the tin evenly. Bake for 8–10 minutes.
3. Brush the biscuit mixture with the egg white.
4. In a large bowl, beat the yogurt, mascarpone and sugar together. Add the eggs and extra yolks, the yuzu juice and bergamot zest, and continue beating until you have a smooth mixture.
5. Place the tin in a large roasting tray and pour in the cheesecake mixture. Add boiling water to the tray so that it is at least halfway up the sides of the cake tin – be careful it doesn't go over the top of the foil.
6. Bake for 40 minutes, then reduce the oven temperature to 150°C (130°C fan), 300°F, Gas mark 2 and bake for a further 10 minutes. The cheesecake top should still feel slightly wobbly.
7. Leave to cool on a wire rack and remove the foil. Chill in the refrigerator for an hour or so before removing the tin. It will keep in the refrigerator for up to 2 days.

ORANGE, YOGURT AND OLIVE OIL CAKE

I first ate this cake in Greece and was intrigued by the soft, layered texture. I then discovered that it is made with yogurt, eggs and olive oil rather than butter and flour. The result is something like lightly set custard held together with leaves of soft filo. I like to eat it warm, with crème fraîche.

....

SERVES 6

For the syrup
150g (5½oz) caster sugar
1 teaspoon ground cinnamon
juice of 1 orange

For the cake
100g (3½oz) olive oil, plus extra for greasing
150g (5½oz) filo pastry (5 sheets)
zest and juice of 2 oranges
300g (10½oz) natural yogurt
80g (3oz) caster sugar
3 teaspoons baking powder
6 eggs, whisked until bubbles appear

1. Preheat the oven to 180°C (160°C fan), 350°F, Gas mark 4. Put the syrup ingredients into a saucepan (including the squeezed orange halves) with 120ml (4fl oz) water. Heat slowly to dissolve the sugar, then boil briefly to make a thin syrup. Remove and discard the orange skins, then leave the syrup to cool.

2. Oil a 30 × 20cm (12 × 8in) baking tin. Tear the filo into pieces about the size of a business card, scrunch them up to make an airy pile, then put in a bowl. Put all the other ingredients in another bowl and whisk together. Scatter a quarter of the filo over the tin bottom, then add a quarter of the cake mixture. Repeat with the rest of the filo and cake mixture.

3. Bake for 30–40 minutes until puffy and browned. Remove from the oven, pour over the syrup and leave to soak in for at least 30 minutes before serving.

For the shortbread

120g (4¼oz) plain flour

80g (3oz) fine semolina

3 tablespoons icing sugar, plus extra for dusting
   (optional)

zest of 1 lemon

120g (4¼oz) unsalted butter, softened, cut into cubes

2–3 teaspoons orange blossom water

For the filling

2 tablespoons marmalade

SHORTBREAD MA'AMOUL COOKIES

FILLED WITH MARMALADE AND ORANGE BLOSSOM

The recipe for these zesty cookies comes from Sarit Packer and Itamar Srulovich whose Honey & Co. cookbooks, shop and restaurants are full of Middle Eastern delicacies. The crumbly semolina shortbread is filled with marmalade, and a hint of orange blossom water.

....

1. To make the dough, mix together the flour, semolina, icing sugar and lemon zest in a bowl. Add the butter and gently rub in with your fingertips until the mixture resembles fine breadcrumbs. Add 1–2 teaspoons of orange blossom water, a teaspoon at a time, to form a nice dough. Cover with clingfilm and leave for 30 minutes in a cool place, but not in the refrigerator.

2. Meanwhile, mix the marmalade with the remaining 1 teaspoon of orange blossom water.

3. Divide the dough into 12 balls and use your palm to flatten each one into a thick circle. Place 6 of these on a baking tray and top each one with 1 teaspoon of the marmalade filling in the centre.

4. Top each with a second dough circle and use a fork to press the edges down to seal them. You can also use a little tartlet tin to seal the edges, or pinch them together. Chill for 20 minutes. Preheat the oven to 190°C (170°C fan), 375°F, Gas mark 5.

5. Bake the cookies in the centre of the oven for about 15 minutes until golden, then leave them to cool before serving. You can dust them with more icing sugar if you want.

For the filling
600g (1lb 5oz) golden syrup
50g (1¾oz) butter
200g (7oz) breadcrumbs
zest of 1 lemon
large pinch of salt
150g (5½oz) marmalade or jam

To serve
crème fraîche or cream

1. Put the flour, icing sugar, butter and salt (omit if using salted butter) in a food processor. Blitz briefly to the texture of fine breadcrumbs.
2. Add the egg yolk and mix to combine. Tip the mixture into a bowl and bring together by hand into a ball. If dry, add a splash of water or egg white. Squash into a thick disc, wrap in clingfilm and chill for at least 30 minutes.
3. Roll out the pastry on a floured surface and line a 23cm (9in) tart tin, with some overhang (you can trim later). Chill for at least 30 minutes.
4. Preheat the oven to 160°C (140°C fan), 325°F, Gas mark 3. Line the tart pastry case with baking parchment and fill to the brim with baking beans (or use any dried beans from your cupboard).
5. Cook for 20 minutes. Remove the parchment and beans, and cook for another 10 minutes until golden brown. Set aside to cool. Once cool, cut off the pastry overhang.
6. Preheat the oven to 170°C (150°C fan), 340°F, Gas mark 3½. Heat the syrup and butter in a pan until runny, then add the breadcrumbs in a bowl with the lemon zest and salt. Fold together gently. Rest for 20 minutes.
7. Spread the marmalade or jam on the base of the tart. Pour in the breadcrumb mix and smooth over.
8. Bake for 30–40 minutes, or until golden and firm-ish to the touch. Serve with crème fraîche or cream.

TREACLE AND MARMALADE TART

You can use any type of sourdough, plain white, brown, brioche or even panettone for this. If you don't like marmalade, use another type of jam, but choose one that is acidic to offset the sweetness – raspberry or blackcurrant are good.

SERVES 6

For the pastry
140g (5oz) plain flour, plus extra for dusting
30g (1oz) icing sugar
75g (2½oz) cold unsalted butter, cut into cubes
pinch of salt
1 egg, separated

CHOCOLATE

When extravagance and indulgence are on the menu, chocolate puddings are the answer. And a good reason to clear out the odds and ends of leftover bars.

I always keep some bars of good-quality cooking chocolate in the cupboard, and generally all you need are some eggs and flour and you have all the ingredients for a special dessert. Chocolate is always a good store-cupboard fallback; melt it into a sauce to pour over poached pears or use pieces to stud a cake or some biscuits with. Sift a dusting over cakes or add to recipes to intensify the chocolatey flavour.

I love creating recipes off the cuff with chocolate, but I particularly like knowing what other chefs and cooks like to make. I've chosen the following by contributing *House & Garden* writers to give a sense of that range. Chocolate tastes delicious with chestnuts, nuts, dried fruit and obviously cream, although I find really rich dishes are sometimes better with yogurt.

RECIPES

Pecan, milk chocolate and ricotta cake

Chocolate rye tart

Chestnut and chocolate cake

Chocolate, amaretti biscuit and dried fig roll with toasted hazelnuts and whipping cream

Lavender Gateau St Emilion

PECAN, MILK CHOCOLATE AND RICOTTA CAKE

The addition of ricotta makes for an incredibly soft, yielding cake in this recipe by Sarit Packer and Itamar Srulovich. They suggest making it as 'a dinner party dessert, as it is a real crowd-pleaser. A cross between a proper cake and a cheesecake, it has a unique texture. Incidentally, it is also flourless and hence gluten-free, but that is not the only reason you'll be making this cake again and again.'

....

MAKES A 20CM (8IN) ROUND CAKE

110g (3¾oz) butter, plus extra for greasing
100g (3½oz) caster sugar
3 eggs
200g (7oz) pecans
2 tablespoons cornflour

200g (7oz) ricotta cheeese
1 teaspoon Chinese five-spice mix
pinch of salt
60g (2¼oz) milk chocolate, finely chopped
2 tablespoons demerara sugar

1. Preheat the oven to 190°C (170°C fan), 375°F, Gas mark 5. Grease a 20cm (8in) round cake tin, ideally loose-bottomed.
2. Cream the butter and caster sugar until light and pale. Beat in the eggs one at a time. Chop 150g (5½oz) of the pecans very finely and add to the mix. Stir in the cornflour, ricotta, five-spice mix and salt.
3. Fold in the chopped chocolate and transfer to the prepared tin. Smooth the surface, sprinkle with the remaining pecans and the demerara sugar and bake for 20 minutes. Rotate the tin and bake for a further 10 minutes. Serve hot or cold.

CHOCOLATE RYE TART

Helen Evans was head baker at Flor in London and now has her own bakery, Eric's, in Dulwich. I commissioned her to write recipes that utilized different flours in baking as a way to introduce readers to healthier and more environmentally friendly alternatives. She writes, 'the rye gives the pastry a lovely depth of flavour, and a perfectly "short" crunch. Since this recipe is such a simple one, choose a good-quality chocolate. You could also make the ganache with slightly sweeter chocolate if you prefer, although make sure the cacao content doesn't drop below 60%.' You'll need a shallow tart tin for this recipe; ideally a 30cm (12in), 3.5cm (1⅓in) deep, fluted quiche tin with a removable base. Make sure to grease the edges really well so as not to lose pastry pieces in the fluted grooves.

SERVES 6

For the pastry
120g (4¼oz) cold unsalted butter, cut into cubes
275g (9¾oz) finely milled wholemeal rye flour, plus extra for dusting
2g (¼ teaspoon) fine salt
90g (3¼oz) light soft brown sugar
1 egg, plus 1 beaten for egg wash

For the ganache
250ml (9fl oz) double cream
230g (8oz) dark chocolate (70–72% cocoa), chopped into small pieces
60g (2¼oz) unsalted butter, softened

1. Start by making the pastry. Rub the cubed butter into the dry ingredients in a bowl until the mixture resembles fine breadcrumbs. Add the egg and bring together by kneading lightly with your hands on a floured surface. Make sure that no dry spots remain, and work until homogeneous and smooth. Wrap in clingfilm and chill for at least 30 minutes.

2. Prepare your tart tin by greasing with extra butter and lining the base with a disc of baking parchment. Roll the chilled pastry out on a lightly floured surface to around 3–4mm (⅛–¼in) thick, then transfer to the tin. (My top tip for transferring the pastry – lightly dust the surface with flour, then fold your pastry disc into quarters until it resembles a large slice of pizza. Lift the 'pizza' into the tin, aligning the point exactly in the centre, then unfold.) Press lightly into all the corners and edges using a knuckle, then chill for another 30 minutes. Once chilled, you can trim the overlapping pastry edges with a small knife.

3. Crumple up a large piece of baking parchment and work it into the pastry case. Fill the paper lining with baking beans (I use dried chickpeas) and blind bake the pastry at 170°C (150°C fan), 340°F, Gas mark 3½ for about 12–14 minutes. Once the pastry is set, carefully tip out the beans, brush lightly with beaten egg and return to the oven for a further 4–5 minutes until golden brown and firm to the touch. Leave to cool slightly, but do not remove from the tin!

4. Bring the cream to a rolling boil. Little by little, pour the hot cream directly over the chocolate, stirring after each addition to combine. Once all the cream has been added, it should look smooth and shiny. Now stir in the butter. Pour the ganache into the baked pastry case straight away, before it sets in the bowl, tapping the tin lightly against a work surface to ensure it sets level. Leave to set at room temperature, then chill for at least 2 hours before cutting. Cut with a hot knife.

CHESTNUT AND
CHOCOLATE CAKE

This Catalan-inspired cake recipe by Claudia
Roden is moist and rich and truffle-like. Decadent
and seasonal.

....

SERVES 6

For the cake
125g (4½oz) vacuum-packed cooked chestnuts
125ml (4fl oz) full-fat milk
125g (4½oz) dark chocolate, broken into pieces,
    plus 5 tablespoons freshly grated, to garnish
125g (4½oz) unsalted butter, cut into cubes,
    plus extra for greasing
65g (2¼oz) caster sugar
2 tablespoons whisky
2 large eggs, beaten

For the topping
200ml (7fl oz) double cream
1–2 teaspoons icing sugar
⅛ teaspoon vanilla extract

1. Preheat the oven to 180°C (160°C fan), 350°F, Gas mark 4. Place the chestnuts and milk in a saucepan. Cover and bring to the boil over a low heat, then cook for a few minutes until soft. Remove from the heat and mash the chestnuts with a potato masher to a rough purée.

2. Place the chocolate pieces in a heatproof bowl. Sit the bowl on a small pan of barely simmering water – there should be only a little water so that the bowl doesn't touch the surface of the water. Add the butter and stir occasionally as it melts with the chocolate.

3. Add the caster sugar, melted chocolate and butter, whisky and eggs to the chestnut purée in the saucepan. Mix thoroughly.

4. Grease and line a 20cm (8in) nonstick springform cake tin with baking parchment and pour in the mixture. Bake for 30–35 minutes until slightly firm. Turn the cake out when it cools – it can be upside down.

5. To make the topping, whip the cream with the icing sugar and vanilla extract until soft peaks form.

6. To serve, cover the cake with the cream and sprinkle with the grated chocolate.

CHOCOLATE, AMARETTI BISCUIT AND DRIED FIG ROLL

WITH TOASTED HAZELNUTS
AND WHIPPING CREAM

Giorgio Locatelli, who wrote this recipe for a
Christmas issue of the magazine, suggests this as 'a
perfect dish for a Christmas feast, as it can be prepared
in advance and looks beautiful as a centrepiece to
a table.' The nuts and figs perfectly complement the
chocolate and look wonderful as you slice through.

SERVES 6

For the roll
250g (9oz) unsalted butter
225g (8oz) caster sugar
pinch of flaked salt
2 eggs, beaten
50g (1¾oz) dark chocolate (70% cocoa), broken
    into pieces
100g (3½oz) cocoa powder
300g (10½oz) amaretti biscuits, crushed
75g (2½oz) dried figs, chopped

To serve
50g (1¾oz) hazelnuts
175g (6oz) whipping cream

1. In a stand mixer, beat together the butter and sugar with the salt until creamy. Then add the eggs gradually and beat the mixture again.

2. Melt the dark chocolate in a bowl set over a pan of simmering water, then add it to the mixture all at once. Continue whisking until everything is fully incorporated.

3. Fold in the cocoa powder, the crushed amaretti biscuits and chopped figs. Mix together until all of the dry ingredients are well coated in the chocolate batter.

4. Spread the mixture across a sheet of baking parchment, then roll it into a sausage and chill in the refrigerator for 4 hours.

5. Meanwhile, preheat the oven to 180°C (160°C fan), 350°F, Gas mark 4. Place the hazelnuts on a baking tray and toast for 8 minutes while you whip the cream. Roughly chop the cooled hazelnuts.

6. To serve, slice the roll and add a dollop of whipped cream with toasted hazelnuts scattered over the top.

LAVENDER GATEAU ST EMILION

This classy chocolate mousse cake recipe by Annie Bell acquires a new lease of life with a few drops of lavender extract. The cake will keep for several days in the refrigerator.

....

MAKES A 20CM (8IN) CAKE

200ml (7fl oz) full-fat milk
225g (8oz) dark chocolate (about 70% cocoa),
    broken into pieces
10 drops of lavender extract, or more to taste
120g (4¼oz) unsalted butter, softened
75g (2½oz) icing sugar
3 egg yolks
60g (2¼oz) amaretti biscuits
2 tablespoons brandy
sprigs of dried lavender, to serve (optional)

1. Gently warm the milk and dark chocolate in a small nonstick saucepan, stirring until the chocolate melts, then give it a quick whisk so that it is smooth. Pour this mixture into a bowl and leave for 15 minutes, or until it cools to room temperature. Stir the lavender extract into the chocolate milk.

2. Meanwhile, beat the butter for 1–2 minutes in a large bowl using a hand-held electric whisk until really pale and mousse-like, then whisk in the icing sugar and the egg yolks, one at a time. Gradually whisk in the chocolate milk. Transfer the mixture to a 20cm (8in) springform cake tin, 4–5cm (1½–2in) deep, smooth the surface, then cover and chill for half a day or overnight.

3. Before serving, crush the amaretti into crumbs in a medium bowl using the end of a rolling pin, drizzle over the brandy and toss to coat. Scatter the crumbs over the top of the cake, then remove the springform collar. A few lavender sprigs around the outside will look especially pretty.

WINTER MENUS

....

QUICKER DISHES
Salad of winter leaves page 220
Fish chowder page 230
Pecan, milk chocolate and ricotta cake page 264

Get the cake in the oven first, then prepare
the base for the chowder and while it's cooking
you can assemble the salad. The beauty of fish
is that it's so quick to cook and the cake will
be warm from the oven just in time
for pudding.

A MEAL MADE IN ADVANCE
*Winter slaw with pomegranate and
pumpkin seeds* page 216
*Sausage and bean hotpot with Savoy cabbage,
apple, mustard and cider* page 237
Treacle and marmalade tart page 262

Like many slow-cooked dishes, this sausage hotpot
improves with time. The slaw can be made ahead, and
if you make extra, it's nice to have on hand for another
meal. The tart can be gently reheated before serving.

A WINTER FEAST
Radicchio and red wine risotto page 218
Fallow deer loin with red cabbage and quince
page 238
Chestnut and chocolate cake page 266

More than any other season, our appetites are keen
in winter. I usually don't serve risotto as a starter, but
if you do, you can make it daintier by serving smaller
portions. The fallow loin is exceptionally good and it's
the season for venison. Claudia Roden's Chestnut and
chocolate cake makes an indulgent finale.

WINTER CITRUS
Blood orange, fennel, feta and olive salad page 253
Lemon risotto with crisp sage page 254
Bergamot and yuzu cheesecake page 257

Just when spirits are lowest in winter, the citrus
harvest begins. These extraordinary and beautiful
bright fruits come to the rescue with colour and sweet,
sharp flavours. It's amazing how versatile they can be
too, use in both sweet and savoury dishes.

FLOWERS AND TABLE DECORATIONS
Napkins and tablecloths take up so little space in a cupboard, and particularly at
this time of year I feel like dressing the table with them; it's like giving it an extra
layer of warmth. It makes the surfaces feel softer and can be a good way of bringing
colour in on darker days. Likewise candles, which provide such gentle light and a
much cosier atmosphere. I use ferns in pots or early bulbs like amaryllis to bring
some nature to the table.

CAKES, BISCUITS AND BREAD

When I'm low on cooking inspiration, I bring myself back to my senses by baking. You need not have a reason to make a cake, a batch of cookies or even a loaf of soda bread, and that's why it's a pleasure. Unlike other food that needs to be served as soon as it's ready, cakes and biscuits can sit around, offering a solution to those moments of sweet craving or unexpected guests.

If you go to the trouble of making a batch of biscuit dough, keep it in the refrigerator so that you can cook a fresh tray every time you need a fix, or to give a homemade touch to some shop-bought ice cream. The following cakes are all moist enough to last a few days, and suitable to serve as desserts, which can be made well ahead of time.

RECIPES

Almond, pistachio and orange blossom cake

Ricotta cake

Almond biscuits

Pistachio and thyme biscuits

Pear and olive oil cake with crème Anglaise

Brown butter chocolate chip cookies

Cheddar cheese and oatmeal 'scones'

Brown Irish soda bread

ALMOND, PISTACHIO AND ORANGE BLOSSOM CAKE

I love the Middle Eastern ingredients and flavours of this cake. Because it is mainly made with nut flours, it stays tender and soft for longer. It is just as good to eat as pudding as it is at teatime and keeps beautifully for days.

....

SERVES 6

80g (3oz) fine semolina flour
100g (3½oz) ground almonds
100g (3½oz) ground pistachios
1 teaspoon baking powder
¼ teaspoon sea salt
200g (7oz) unsalted butter, softened
200g (7oz) caster sugar
zest of ½ orange
2 tablespoons orange blossom water
6 cardamom pods, green husks removed and
    seeds crushed to a fine powder
4 eggs (about 250g/9oz)

For the glaze
1 teaspoon finely grated orange zest
50g (1¾oz) caster sugar
6 tablespoons lemon juice
3 tablespoons roughly chopped pistachios
4 tablespoons pomegranate seeds
2 tablespoons dried rose petals

1. Preheat the oven to 160°C (140°C fan), 325°F, Gas mark 3 and line a 20cm (8in) round cake tin. Mix together the semolina flour, ground almonds, pistachios, baking powder and salt in a bowl.
2. In another bowl, use a hand-held electric whisk to beat the butter and sugar together until pale and creamy. Add the orange zest, orange blossom water, cardamom and the eggs, one by one, then fold in the dry ingredients.
3. Pour into the prepared tin and bake for 50 minutes– 1 hour. Test by inserting a skewer into the middle – it should come out clean. Cool slightly before turning the cake out of the tin.
4. To make the glaze, put the orange zest, sugar and lemon juice in a saucepan and heat to dissolve the sugar. Sprinkle the chopped pistachios and pomegranate seeds over the surface of the cake and pour the glaze on top. Scatter with the rose petals.

RICOTTA CAKE

Ricotta replaces butter in this cake, and adds moisture, which keeps it tasting fresh for a few days. You can eat it for breakfast with some strong coffee or enjoy at teatime or serve for pudding; I like this sort of versatility with summer recipes. To embellish it as a dessert, try serving with stewed fruit and a dollop of crème fraîche.

....

SERVES 6

4 tablespoons olive oil, plus extra for greasing
3 eggs
80g (3oz) caster sugar
230g (8oz) ricotta cheese
zest and juice of 1 lemon
170g (6oz) plain flour
½ teaspoon bicarbonate of soda
1 teaspoon baking powder
pinch of salt
4 tablespoons pine nuts

1. Preheat the oven to 180°C (160°C fan), 350°F, Gas mark 4. Lightly oil a nonstick loaf tin (or line it with baking parchment if the one you have is not nonstick).
2. In a large bowl using a hand-held electric whisk or in a stand mixer, whisk the eggs and sugar together until very light and fluffy, and they have increased in volume by at least one-third.
3. In another bowl, beat together the ricotta, lemon zest and juice and the oil until smooth. Add this to the eggs and beat to combine fully.
4. Sift the flour, bicarbonate of soda, baking powder and salt into a separate bowl and stir to distribute well.
5. Fold the flour mixture into the egg mixture and pour into the loaf tin. Scatter the pine nuts all over the top and lightly press them into the batter. Bake for 30 minutes, or until a skewer inserted into the middle comes out clean.

ALMOND BISCUITS

A batch of freshly baked biscuits makes a simple pudding into something special. I like these either with a cup of coffee or served with cooked fruit (like the Baked apricots with raspberries on page 136).

MAKES ABOUT 12

100g (3½oz) ground almonds
50g (1¾oz) whole almonds, skin on, roughly chopped
80g (3oz) caster sugar
3 egg whites
½ teaspoon vanilla extract
pinch of sea salt

1. Preheat the oven to 180°C (160°C fan), 350°F, Gas mark 4. Line a baking sheet with baking parchment.
2. Put all the ingredients in a saucepan and stir well. Cook over a low heat, stirring constantly. At first, the mixture will be quite loose, like semolina pudding, but after a few minutes it will begin to dry out and thicken. When the mixture is beginning to get lumpy and thick, remove from the heat.
3. Using a dessertspoon, drop spoonfuls of the mixture on to the baking parchment, a few centimetres apart. You should be able to make 12 biscuits. Bake for 15 minutes, or until the biscuits are golden on the outside and feel firm enough to lift off the sheet. Cool completely. These can be kept in an airtight container for up to 4 days.

PISTACHIO AND THYME BISCUITS

These are crumbly and crisp, and fragrant with spices and herbs. A homemade biscuit served with shop-bought ice cream or a plate of fruit makes such an easy dessert.

MAKES ABOUT 12

80g (3oz) unsalted butter, softened
30g (1oz) caster sugar
½ teaspoon fine sea salt
4 cardamom pods, green husks removed and seeds
    crushed to a fine powder
1 tablespoon thyme leaves, roughly chopped
50g (1¾oz) pistachios, finely chopped
100g (3½oz) plain flour, plus extra for dusting
1 egg yolk
double cream, to serve

1. For the biscuits, cream together the butter, sugar and salt. Add the cardamom, thyme, pistachios and flour to the butter mixture. Combine thoroughly, then add the egg yolk and mix until a soft dough forms.
2. With lightly floured hands, roll the dough on a board into a thick sausage. Wrap in baking parchment and refrigerate until needed.
3. Preheat the oven to 150°C (130°C fan), 300°F, Gas mark 2. Line a baking tray with baking parchment.
4. Unwrap the dough and cut into 5mm (¼in) slices (you should have 12), then arrange on the tray. Bake for 20 minutes, or until crisp and lightly coloured.

PEAR AND OLIVE OIL CAKE

WITH CRÈME ANGLAISE

I met Mafruha Ahmed when she cooked at the Rose Bakery in London's Dover Street Market. She now cooks at contemporary art organization Young Space in East London. She says, 'this dessert is one of my favourites. The cake is lovely and moist from the pears, and with the addition of custard, it gives you comfort on those colder days. I do like to use an extra virgin olive oil in this cake, as the flavour profile with the pear is delightful.'

....

SERVES 6

150ml (5fl oz) olive oil, plus extra for greasing
zest of 1 lemon
300g (10½oz) peeled and cored pears, diced
150g (5½oz) caster sugar
2 eggs
200g (7oz) plain flour
1 tablespoon ground ginger
1 teaspoon bicarbonate of soda
1 teaspoon baking powder
½ teaspoon fine salt

For the crème Anglaise
250ml (9fl oz) full-fat milk
250ml (9fl oz) double cream
60g (2¼oz) caster sugar
1 vanilla pod, split in half
3 egg yolks

1. Preheat the oven to 180°C (160°C fan), 350°F, Gas mark 4. Line and grease your loaf tin. Add the lemon zest to the diced pear and set aside. Whisk the olive oil and sugar in a stand mixer until well incorporated, then whisk in the eggs, one by one.

2. Sift all the dry ingredients together and slowly add this to the wet mixture. Fold in the pear mixture and mix until the batter is even.

3. Pour the batter into the prepared tin and bake for 45 minutes. Check at 25 minutes and turn the loaf.

4. For the crème Anglaise, stir the milk, cream, half the sugar and vanilla in a saucepan and bring to a simmer. In a separate bowl, mix the egg yolks and remaining sugar together. Pour half the milk mixture into the egg yolks and whisk until combined, then pour back into the saucepan and remove the vanilla pod. Cook, stirring constantly, until the crème Anglaise mixture thickens slightly.

5. To serve, I like to have my cake slightly warm, swimming in a pool of custardy goodness.

BROWN BUTTER CHOCOLATE CHIP COOKIES

I first discovered Helen Evans when she was head baker at Flor London in Bermondsey. This recipe for chocolate chip cookies takes them to another level by browning the butter first. In case it starts sounding too professional and cheffy, she insists the recipe is low maintenance (with no creaming of the butter).

....

MAKES 12

150g (5½oz) unsalted butter (to make 135g/4¾oz brown butter)

40g (1½oz) wholemeal flour

140g (5oz) plain flour (I use Red Lammas wheat, which is an old variety dating back to 1660)

25g (1oz) emmer, einkorn or spelt flour (or more wholemeal)

2g fine salt

125g (4½oz) light soft brown sugar

90g (3¼oz) dark soft brown sugar

2g baking powder

2g bicarbonate of soda

1 egg, beaten

165g (5¾oz) chocolate chips (we use a mixture of 65%, 75% and 85% chocolate chips)

1. Brown the butter by cooking it gently in a saucepan until it starts to give off a nutty aroma and the milk solids look caramelized and quite dark. Weigh out exactly 135g (4¾oz) and set to one side – it needs to cool before it can be mixed with the dry ingredients.

2. Weigh all the dry ingredients together (flours, salt, sugars, baking powder and bicarbonate of soda) and whisk well to ensure any lumps are broken down.

3. Once the butter has cooled, tip it on to the dry ingredients, making sure to scoop out and add all the caramelized milk solids (which will have sunk to the bottom of your pan). Mix everything together until there are no remaining dry spots and set a timer for 15 minutes. This is to ensure that the flour is properly hydrated before adding the egg, particularly the wholemeal flour.

4. Add the egg and mix gently until homogeneous, then add the chocolate chips and mix once more. Try to avoid overmixing – the dough should be 'just' brought together, and the chocolate chips 'just' distributed.

5. Divide the dough into 12 balls and flatten lightly on a tray lined with baking parchment, allowing plenty of space for spreading. Chill for at least 30 minutes.

6. Preheat the oven to 190°C (175°C fan), 375°F, Gas mark 5.

7. Bake the cookies for 5 minutes, then turn and tap the tray to aid even spreading. Bake for a further 4 minutes then remove from the oven and tap again. I like to underbake the cookies slightly, to ensure maximum fudginess.

CHEDDAR CHEESE AND OATMEAL 'SCONES'

This soda bread recipe by Sally Clarke is shaped and baked in the traditional way, with indentations formed on the top, which makes the 'breaking of the bread' easy – and each triangle becomes a portion-sized 'scone'. Serve with soup or some cheeses, pickles and salad for an easy lunch.

SERVES 6

350g (12oz) good-quality coarse wholemeal flour
150g (5½oz) rolled oats
1 teaspoon bicarbonate of soda
100g (3½oz) Cheddar cheese, grated
1 teaspoon sea salt
450ml (16fl oz) buttermilk
1 tablespoon honey
1 tablespoon melted butter

1. Preheat the oven to 200°C (180°C fan), 400°F, Gas mark 6 and cover a baking sheet with baking parchment. Put the flour, 100g (3½oz) of the oats, the bicarbonate of soda, cheese and salt in a bowl and mix well.

2. In another bowl, mix the buttermilk and honey until smooth. Stir this into the flour and mix quickly but thoroughly together – this is best done by hand. Knead gently on a clean surface until it is one mass. Shape the dough into a ball, then flatten slightly and coat with the melted butter all over – again, this is best done by hand, despite being messy.

3. Wash and dry your hands, then roll the loaf in the remaining oats and place on the baking sheet. Using the handle of a wooden spoon, mark out 6 triangular portions, pressing down 3–4 times gently but firmly.

4. Bake for 30 minutes, or until the bread is crisp on the outside and hollow sounding when knocked underneath. Allow to cool slightly before breaking into individual pieces along the indentations.

BROWN IRISH SODA BREAD

Imen McDonnell and Cliodhna Prendergast cooked this for me at the romantic and historic Glin Castle in Ireland. We were photographing their traditional Irish recipes, which they teach in beautiful locations like Glin. Imen told me that according to Irish folklore, making a cross indentation in the dough before baking will let the fairies out.

....

SERVES 6

225g (8oz) plain flour, plus extra for dusting
1 teaspoon bicarbonate of soda
225g (8oz) wholemeal flour
1 teaspoon sea salt
400ml (14fl oz) buttermilk

1. Preheat the oven to 230°C (210°C fan), 450°F, Gas mark 8. Sift the plain flour and bicarbonate of soda into a mixing bowl. Add the wholemeal flour with the salt and mix well.

2. Make a well in the centre and pour in almost all the buttermilk, mixing in big folds with your hand and adding more if necessary. The amount of buttermilk will vary from day to day, depending on how dry the flour is, or if it is very humid in the kitchen. The dough needs to be soft but able to hold its shape. If it becomes too soft, add an extra handful of flour. Try to incorporate all the dry ingredients with as few folds as possible – the more you mix, the heavier the bread will become, so keep it light.

3. Dust a surface with flour and turn the dough out on to it. Dust the dough generously with more plain flour. Shape it lightly into a circle, press gently to flatten it a little and place on a floured baking sheet.

4. Using the back of a knife, make a cross in the bread – not too deep – then pierce each quarter twice.

5. Bake the bread for 20 minutes, then reduce the oven temperature to 200°C (180°C fan), 400°F, Gas mark 6 and cook for a further 20–25 minutes.

6. To check if the bread is done, tap the bottom of the loaf. It should sound hollow. If not, bake for another 5 minutes. Remove from the oven and leave to cool on a wire rack.

CHRISTMAS

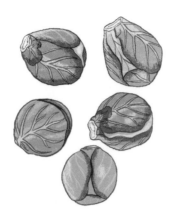

Of all the festive occasions that we cook for, Christmas can be the most joyful or the most stressful. If you choose to go down the traditional route – a roast bird and all the accompaniments – Sally Clarke's following recipes, which she wrote for *House & Garden*, will set you in good stead; they are the ones I turn to for my Christmas day feast. Turkey makes sense if you're feeding a crowd, but for fewer guests, the flavour of goose is incomparable. Because of its delicious natural fat, goose is also more forgiving for the cook and stays succulent and tender.

Like any big meal, it's always worth getting jobs done ahead of time – parboiling the potatoes and making stock for gravy, sauces and puddings. It also frees up oven and hob space for those things that need cooking on the day. Then you can enjoy decorating the table with candles and greenery and getting those potatoes golden and crisp while the bird roasts in the oven.

And don't forget to allow the meat plenty of resting time. It will improve what you've cooked and give you the valuable chance to relax before sitting down to celebrate around the table.

RECIPES

Bronze turkey crown and legs with gravy and stuffing
Roast goose with crab apple jelly glaze
Pecan stuffing

BRONZE TURKEY
CROWN AND LEGS
WITH GRAVY AND STUFFING

*The turkey crown is dry-brined and the legs are boned
and filled with a chestnut, sage and orange stuffing –
then roasted. Ideally, you should start to prepare the
turkey two days before roasting.*

....

SERVES 6–8

5.5–6.5kg (12lb–14lb 5 oz) bronze turkey,
    including giblets
50g (1¾oz) butter

For the dry brine
2 tablespoons finely chopped sage, thyme or
    rosemary leaves (or a mixture of all three)
zest of 2 large oranges
zest of 1 lemon
3 garlic cloves, crushed
½ teaspoon brown sugar
3 tablespoons olive oil
sea salt and freshly ground black pepper

For the stuffing
100g (3½oz) butter
1 medium onion, finely chopped
2 teaspoons finely chopped sage
zest of 1 orange
240g (8½oz) fresh breadcrumbs
100g (3½oz) vacuum-packed cooked chestnuts,
    roughly chopped
1 large egg
splash of cream or full-fat milk (if needed)

For the roasting vegetables
1 large onion, roughly chopped
3 carrots, peeled and roughly chopped
3 celery sticks, roughly chopped
2 outer fennel leaves, roughly chopped
a few sprigs of sage, rosemary or thyme (or all three)
50g (1¾oz) butter, cut into cubes

For the gravy
1 dessertspoon plain flour
1 large glass red wine
juice of 2 oranges
500ml (18fl oz) good-quality chicken stock

To serve
2 bunches of watercress, thick stalks removed

1. Remove the bag of giblets from the turkey and
keep in the refrigerator. Cut the legs away from
the carcass, then remove the drumstick and the thigh
bones, along with any large tendons in the drumstick
meat. Remove the wing tips from the crown. All this
sounds more complicated than it is, but if you prefer
not to struggle with it, a friendly butcher will do this
for you in 30 seconds. Place the leg meat and the
bones in the refrigerator.
2. Mix the dry brine ingredients together with
2 teaspoons of sea salt and ½ teaspoon of pepper,
forming a paste. Carefully lift the skin away from
the breasts at the cavity end and spread half the
paste under the skin all over the breast – as far as
you dare, as the skin can tear easily. Place the skin
back into position, then massage the remaining
paste over the crown and wing joints. Wrap the bird
tightly in clingfilm, or a heavy plastic bag. Keep in
the refrigerator to dry brine for 24–36 hours.
3. Next, prepare the giblets: rinse the liver and heart,
and trim away the sinew or pipes. Chop roughly and
leave in a cool place. Rinse the neck and gizzard, and
leave with the reserved bones and wing tips.

4. To make the stuffing, heat the butter in a small pan until sizzling and add the chopped onion. Cook over a medium heat until soft but not coloured. Add the sage, orange zest, ½ teaspoon of salt and ¼ teaspoon of pepper and allow to cool. In a bowl, mix the breadcrumbs and chestnuts with the chopped raw liver and heart and the cooled onion mix. Lightly whisk the egg and stir into the breadcrumb mixture. It should not be at all wet, but it should hold itself together loosely. If it seems a little dry, add a splash of cream or milk.

5. Place the turkey legs (without the bones) on a chopping board, skin-side down, and season well with salt and pepper. Divide the stuffing mix in half and spread out along the centre of each leg. Fold the meat over the stuffing and gently shape each leg into a sausage shape by hand. Using butcher's twine or thin string, tie the filled legs neatly but firmly. Roll each one neatly in a double layer of clingfilm, tying the 4 ends in a firm knot, like a Christmas cracker. Leave them in the refrigerator until ready to cook.

6. To roast the crown, preheat the oven to 190°C (170°C fan), 375°F, Gas mark 5. Place the roasting vegetables and herbs in a large roasting tin with the leg bones, wing tips, neck and gizzard, then dot with the butter. Unwrap the turkey crown and place on top of the vegetables. Roast for 1½ hours, then reduce the temperature to 180°C (160°C fan), 350°F, Gas mark 4. Continue to cook until the juices run clear when a skewer or small knife pierces the thickest part of the breast close to the wing bone – about a further 30–40 minutes. Remove the crown to a warm serving dish and cover it tightly with foil, topped with a clean tea towel. Leave to rest for up to 30 minutes.

7. While the crown is roasting, place the prepared legs (still wrapped in clingfilm) in a medium saucepan and cover with cold water. Bring to the boil, then cover and simmer for 35–45 minutes, or until a small knife goes into the leg easily. Drain the water away and allow the legs to cool a little before placing them on a chopping board. Carefully remove the clingfilm and check that the twine is still firmly in place. Re-tie if necessary.

8. Next, roast the turkey legs. Heat the 50g (1¾oz) butter in a small ovenproof pan until sizzling. Place the legs into the butter, seam-side up, and sear them over a medium heat, turning the meat over and around in the hot butter until the skin becomes golden brown all over. Place the pan in the oven (with the turkey crown still at 180°C/160°C fan/350°F/Gas mark 4) and roast the legs for 15–20 minutes, or until a small knife pierces the meat very easily and the juices run clear. Remove from the oven and cover the pan tightly with foil.

9. While the legs and crown are resting, make the gravy. Drain away the excess fat from the roasting pan, place the pan (including the vegetables) over a medium heat on the hob and add the flour, stirring continuously. Slowly add the red wine, orange juice and stock, and bring gently to the boil as it thickens. Simmer for 3–4 minutes, pour through a sieve into a small pan, then taste and adjust the seasoning. Leave over a low heat until ready to serve, skimming occasionally if needed.

10. To serve, carefully remove the twine from the turkey legs and slice across in thick slices, then arrange around the crown with watercress leaves to garnish. Serve the hot gravy separately.

ROAST GOOSE

WITH CRAB APPLE JELLY GLAZE

You can start to prepare this at least two days beforehand so that you have time to produce the goose fat and stock for the accompaniments. It will make cooking on the day a lot easier.

....

SERVES 6–8

5.5–6kg (12–13lb 4oz) goose, including giblets
50g (1¾oz) butter
1 medium onion, chopped
1 carrot, peeled and chopped
1 celery stick, chopped
3 garlic cloves, crushed
25g (1oz) plain flour
few sprigs of rosemary, thyme and sage
600ml (20fl oz) chicken or beef stock
about 100ml (3½fl oz) red wine
zest and juice of 2 oranges
1 tablespoon crab apple or redcurrant jelly
sea salt and freshly ground black pepper

1. Trim the excess fat and the 'flap' from the bird, remove the giblets from the cavity and trim the wing tips away, reserving all these items.

2. Rinse the neck, heart, gizzard and liver in cool water, then drain well. Trim away any discoloured parts from the heart and liver and chop them into small dice. Reserve in a bowl in the refrigerator for the stuffing later (see page 294).

3. Place the neck, wing tips and gizzard in a large, heavy saucepan with the butter and cook over a high heat until sealed on all sides and beginning to turn golden brown.

4. Add the chopped vegetables, garlic, flour and herbs, and continue to cook until the vegetables start to colour.

5. Add the stock, red wine and orange zest and juice, and bring to the boil, skimming away any impurities that rise to the surface. Simmer for 1 hour until flavourful. Strain (saving the stock for the gravy), discard the debris and allow to cool.

6. Meanwhile, place the excess goose fat and flap in a small pan with a splash of water and bring it to a simmer. Continue to cook as the fat renders down. This will result in the fat and some of the skin liquidizing, with a small amount of solid material left in the pan. Strain, discard the debris and allow the fat to cool. Preheat the oven to 220°C (200°C fan), 425°F, Gas mark 7.

7. Season the goose inside and out with plenty of salt and pepper. Place the bird on a wire rack, then place over a roasting tin. Roast on the middle shelf for 20 minutes. Reduce the temperature to 180°C (160°C fan), 350°F, Gas mark 4 and then continue to roast for 2–2½ hours. During this time, the fat from the skin will drip into the roasting tin, so make sure that the bird is positioned squarely over the tin to avoid spillage.

8. About 10 minutes before the end of the cooking time, spread the crab apple or redcurrant jelly over the skin of the goose.

9. To test the bird, pierce the leg with a skewer – if the juices run clear, the bird is cooked. Remove carefully from the oven and place on the serving dish or board. Cover the goose with foil, then a clean tea towel, tucking in the corners like a blanket to keep it warm. Leave it to rest for up to 1 hour.

10. Gently pour away all the fat from the tin – this can be kept for roasting potatoes and root vegetables to serve with the goose. Reserve the dark meat juices in the base of the tin for the gravy.

11. To serve the goose, remove the legs with a medium knife. Slice the breast meat from the leg end, moving towards the neck. Place the slices overlapping on a warm serving platter.

12. Slice the meat off the legs or, if easier, simply cut in between the drumsticks and thighs at the ball-and-socket joints and serve them alongside the breast meat. Serve the goose with the stuffing, bread sauce and hot gravy.

PECAN STUFFING

This recipe can be used with either turkey or goose and makes a delicious part of the meal. If your bird comes with its giblets, use the heart and liver in this recipe and keep the other parts for adding to the stock for your gravy.

....

SERVES 6–8

75g (2½oz) butter, softened
175g (6oz) fresh breadcrumbs (white, sourdough
 or wholemeal)
1 large onion, grated on large side of grater
1 large Bramley apple, grated on large side of grater
50g (1¾oz) pecans, walnuts or hazelnuts, roughly
 chopped
25g (1oz) dried cranberries, sour cherries or raisins
1 teaspoon chopped sage, rosemary or thyme
finely grated zest of 1 orange
1 egg, lightly beaten
chopped goose heart and liver (see page 291)
sea salt and freshly ground black pepper

1. Prepare a 20cm (8in) square ovenproof dish by smearing about 55g (2oz) of the softened butter over the base and sides. Set aside the remaining butter.
2. Mix the other stuffing ingredients together in a large bowl, adding the egg last with the reserved chopped goose liver. Season to taste with salt and pepper and press the mixture gently but firmly into the dish. Dot the remaining butter over the top and leave to one side. This may be prepared up to 2 days in advance and stored in the refrigerator.
3. Place the stuffing in the oven at 200°C (180°C fan), 400°F, Gas mark 6, while your roast potatoes and root vegetables are finishing roasting, and bake for up to 20 minutes until it is crisp on the outside and a little moist inside.
4. Serve the stuffing in the oven dish, to be scooped at the table. Alternatively, remove it from the dish using a palette knife and cut into 6–8 squares, to be served alongside the carved meat.

MINCEMEAT

Homemade mincemeat, a delicious mixture of apples, dried fruit, citrus and spices, is very easy to make and so much more satisfying than buying it from a shop.

Look beyond mince pies and you'll find it has a use in all sorts of other desserts – wrapped in marzipan cases (see page 296), for stuffing baked apples (see page 297) or as the filling for a strudel-type cake. It will become a useful fallback in the store cupboard when you're short of other ingredients.

RECIPES

Marzipan and mincemeat pasties
Homemade mincemeat
Baked apple with mincemeat

MARZIPAN AND
MINCEMEAT PASTIES

Sally Clarke's pretty little pasties taste rich but make
delicate mouthfuls, picked up in your fingers. They are
the perfect gluten-free alternative to mince pies.

MAKES ABOUT 12 PASTIES

250g (9oz) ground almonds
250g (9oz) icing sugar, plus extra for rolling
    and dusting
2 egg whites, beaten
2 teaspoons lemon juice
2 drops of bitter almond extract
200g (7oz) Homemade mincemeat (see opposite)

1. To make the marzipan, place the ground almonds
and icing sugar in a food processor or mixing bowl
and mix together until well blended. Add the egg
whites, lemon juice and almond extract, and mix
until a dry-ish ball is formed.

2. Remove the marzipan from the bowl and knead
gently until it forms a smooth ball, adding a little water
or icing sugar if it seems too dry or too wet. Wrap with
clingfilm and chill for a few hours.

3. Unwrap the ball of marzipan, cut it in half and
roll out one-half like pastry on a surface dusted with
icing sugar. If it is difficult to handle, simply gather the
pieces together and start rolling again.

4. Once it is around 5mm (¼in) thick, cut into
8cm (3¼in) discs. Repeat with the other half of the
marzipan. Preheat the oven to 180°C (160°C fan),
350°F, Gas mark 4.

5. On to each disc, place ½ teaspoon of mincemeat.
With your finger, brush the rim with cold water.

6. Gather the marzipan up into a Cornish pasty
shape, pressing it over the mincemeat. Press the edges
together and crimp them decoratively. Place on a
baking sheet lined with baking parchment. Repeat
with the remaining discs.

7. Using a small sieve, dust a little icing sugar over
the pasties. Bake for 8–10 minutes until golden.

8. Serve the pasties warm or at room temperature,
dusted with more icing sugar. They are best with
vanilla ice cream and Madeira, port or Champagne.

HOMEMADE MINCEMEAT

Making just a few jars of your own mincemeat is easy, and what's more, it never goes to waste (keep a tray of pastry cases in the freezer for last-minute baking). A jar tied with a ribbon makes a sweet gift too.

MAKES 3 × 350ML (12FL OZ) JARS

225g (8oz) Bramley apples, cored and finely chopped
110g (3¾oz) shredded suet
175g (6oz) raisins
110g (3¾oz) sultanas
110g (3¾oz) currants
110g (3¾oz) mixed candied peel, finely chopped
175g (6oz) dark soft brown sugar
zest and juice of 1 orange
zest and juice of 1 lemon
25g (1oz) blanched almonds, chopped
2 teaspoons ground mixed spice
1 teaspoon ground cinnamon
a few gratings of nutmeg
3 tablespoons brandy

1. In a bowl large enough for all the ingredients, stir everything together well. Cover and leave overnight.
2. The next day, put the mixture into a large pan and gently heat, stirring, until the fat has melted and the mixture is heated through. Remove from the heat and allow to cool before packing into sterilized jars. The mincemeat is best left for a week or so before use so that the flavours mingle. It keeps for up to a year in a cool place.

BAKED APPLE
WITH MINCEMEAT

Despite being partial to a mince pie, I am ready to move on by the time January arrives. To use up leftover jars of mincemeat (and our apples, stored since autumn), I created this simple pudding. It is easy to prepare and very comforting, and makes a gluten-free alternative to a pie.

SERVES 6

6 apples (I use dessert apples, which take longer to cook than cooking apples)
350ml (12fl oz) jar Homemade mincemeat (see left)
60g (2¼oz) unsalted butter

1. Preheat the oven to 150°C (130°C fan), 300°F, Gas mark 2. Slice a small disc off the base of each apple so that it sits upright. Remove the cores and create enough space inside to fit the mincemeat.
2. Score the skin around the equator.
3. Put the apples in a baking dish and fill the empty cores with mincemeat. Divide the butter into equal pieces to place on top of each apple.
4. Cover the baking dish with foil and bake for around 25 minutes, removing the foil and basting 5 minutes before the end. Test with a skewer to check that the apples are soft all the way through.
5. Serve with crème fraîche, cream or ice cream.

GLOSSARY OF UK/US TERMS

Aniseed .Anise

Aubergine . . . . .Eggplant

Barbecue . . . . .Grill

Beetroot . . . . .Beet

Bicarbonate of soda . . . . .Baking soda

Biscuits. . . . . .Cookies

Broad beans. . . . . .Fava beans

Butter beans . . . . .Lima beans

Caster sugar. . . . . .Superfine sugar

Celeriac . . . . .Celery root

Chickpeas . . . . .Garbanzo beans

Chicory. . . . . .Belgian Endive

Chilli. . . . . .Chili

Chopping board . . . . .Cutting board

Cider . . . . .Hard cider

Cider vinegar. . . . . .Apple cider vinegar

Clingfilm . . . . .Plastic wrap

Cooking apple . . . . .Baking apple

Coriander. . . . . .Cilantro

Cornflour . . . . .Cornstarch

Courgette. . . . . .Zucchini

Cutlery .Flatware

Demerara sugar . . . . .Light brown sugar

Digestive biscuits . . . . .Graham crackers

Double cream . . . . .Heavy cream

Flaked almonds . . . . .Slivered almonds

French beans. . . . . .Green beans

Frying pan . . . . .Skillet

Golden syrup. . . . . .Light corn syrup

Griddle pan . . . . .Grill pan

Groundnut oil . . . . .Peanut oil

Hob . . . . .Stovetop

Icing sugar . . . . .Confectioner's sugar

Jam . . . . .Jelly

Kitchen paper . . . . .Paper towels

Minced fatty lamb . . . . .Ground fatty lamb

Mixed spice . . . . .Apple pie spice

Pastry case. . . . . .Pastry shell

Pepper. .Bell pepper

Plain flour . . . . .All-purpose flour

Porridge oats . . . . .Rolled oats

Rapeseed oil . . . . .Canola oil

Roasting tin. . . . . .Roasting pan

Rocket .Arugula

Runner beans . . . . .String beans

Self-raising flour. . . . . .Self-rising flour

Single cream . . . . .Light cream

Soured cream . . . . .Sour cream

Spring onions . . . . .Scallions

Starter .Appetizer

Stock cube . . . . .Bouillon cube

Store cupboard . . . . .Pantry

Sultanas . . . . .Golden raisins

Swede . . . . .Rutabaga

Sweetcorn . . . . .Corn

Tea towel . . . . .Dish towel

Tomato purée . . . . .Tomato paste

Vanilla pod . . . . .Vanilla bean

Wholemeal flour. . . . . .Wholewheat flour

INDEX

·····································

ACKNOWLEDGEMENTS

Thank you to the inspiring cooks, chefs and food writers whose work has featured in *House & Garden*, especially the following, who have been kind enough to allow me to include some of their recipes in this book:

Annie Bell, Erchen Chang, Sam and Sam Clark, Sally Clarke, Helen Evans, Charlie Hibbert, Lucas Hollweg, Honey & Co., Phil Howard, Asma Khan, Merlin Labron-Johnson, Rowley Leigh, Lens & Larder, Giorgio Locatelli, James Lowe, Stevie Parle, Amy Poon and Claudia Roden.

Thank you to Albert Read, Condé Nast and all the team at *House & Garden*, especially the editor Hatta Byng, Creative Director Jennifer Lister, Photography Director Owen Gale and Art Director Joshua Monaghan.

To Features Assistant Christabel Chubb, who helped me organize everything, and her predecessor, now Features Editor Elizabeth Metcalfe, for helping me arrange and style some of the shoots.

To our brilliant and thorough subediting team, Caroline Bullough, Sue Gilkes and Rose Washbourn, who have read every recipe with laser eyes. Also Editorial Operations Manager Kate Shaw and Editorial Assistant Barbara Uzoigwe.

Thank you to Alison Starling at Octopus for commissioning the book and leading the project so admirably, to Jonathan Christie for his beautiful design and project manager Leanne Bryan.

To Cressida Connolly, Tilly Trivelli and Jessica Boncutter for taking the time to read through the text and share their valuable thoughts with me.

And to Julian Alexander from The Soho Agency for his professional and sage advice throughout the process.

Thank you to all the hugely talented photographers who have brought life and context into these beautiful pictures:

Lucas Allen, Simon Badaja, Susan Bell, Simon Brown, Sharyn Cairns, Helen Cathcart, Issy Croker, Laura Edwards, Mark Anthony Fox, Greg Funnell, Annaick Guitteny, Oivind Haug, Dean Hearne, Line Klein, Athina Kontos, John Laurie, Emma Lee, David Loftus, Davide Lovatti, Paul Massey, Andrew Montgomery, Kristen Perers, Nassima Rothacker, Matt Russell, Toby Scott, Michael Sinclair, Alicia Taylor

Thank you to the brilliant and creative food and prop stylists who work their magic on the food shoots:

Food Styling: Julia Azzarello, Rosie Birkett, Henrietta Clancy, Kitty Coles, Emily Ezekiel, Imen McDonnell, Aya Nishimura, Cliodhna Pendergast, Claire Ptak, Rosie Ramsden and Bridget Sargeson.

Prop Styling: Linda Berlin, Alexander Breeze, Tabitha Hawkins, Elfreda Pownall, Zoe Regoczy and Wei Tang.

Finally to my husband Hugo and my daughter Alba, my companions in the kitchen and at the table.

First published in Great Britain in 2023 by Mitchell Beazley, an imprint of Octopus Publishing Group Ltd
Carmelite House, 50 Victoria Embankment
London EC4Y 0DZ
www.octopusbooks.co.uk

An Hachette UK Company
www.hachette.co.uk

Distributed in the US by Hachette Book Group
1290 Avenue of the Americas, 4th and 5th Floors
New York, NY 10104

Distributed in Canada by Canadian Manda Group
664 Annette St, Toron to, Ontario, Canada M6S 2C8

ISBN 978-1-78472-895-3

A CIP catalogue record for this book is available from the British Library.

Printed and bound in China.

10 9 8 7 6 5 4 3 2 1

Illustrations by Alice Pattullo

Publisher: Alison Starling
Creative Director: Jonathan Christie
Senior Editor: Leanne Bryan
Copy Editor: Vicky Orchard
Production Controller: Emily Noto

BLANCHE VAUGHAN

Blanche Vaughan's first job was at renowned London restaurant Moro, where she worked her way up through the positions in the kitchen. Over seven years as a chef she cooked at The River Café on the banks of the River Thames, Chez Panisse in California, and finally St John back in London. She has written books under her own name, including *In One Pot* and *Egg*, and worked with brands that include Itsu and the Great British Food Revival. She has been Food Editor for *House & Garden* magazine for eight years.

blanchevaughan.com

HOUSE & GARDEN

House & Garden, published by Condé Nast, is the market-leading lifestyle magazine in the UK with a readership of more than 300,000 and a social media following of eight million across all platforms.

houseandgarden.co.uk